"Cherish your freedom



John Katsaros

# CODE BURGUNDY
## The Long Escape

**by John Katsaros**

ISBN 13 978-1-57256-108-3
ISBN 1-57256-108-4



Oakford Media LLC
617 Connecticut Avenue
Norwalk CT 06854-1614
(203) 899-1630
www.oakfordmedia.com

5th Printing

## DEDICATION

I dedicate this book in Honor of the WWII French Resistance, who saved my life during the spring of 1944 And To Mother, Father And Siblings, Sotiris "Sot", George, Ann, Madalene and S. Charles "Chuck".

From Left to right: Sot, Madalene, Mother, Father, Ann, George. Kneeling: John and Chuck. Photo taken 1931.

# Contents

# INTRODUCTION

By G. STEVE CHIRIGOTIS, COLONEL USAF, (RET.)

This is the story of John Katsaros, a twenty year old American airman who beat the odds and survived flying on dangerous air bombing raid out of England, as a gunner on a B-17 Super Flying Fortress Heavy Bomber of the 612th Squadron 401st Heavy Bombardment Group, 8th Air Force, during World War II; and on 20 March 1944, was shot down by ground 88mm guns, and .50 cal. machine-gun and 20 mm cannon fire from German Luftwaffe fighter aircraft, on a mission to disable an enemy aircraft factory at Frankfurt, Germany.

Severely wounded and unable to reach the "D" ring to release the parachute, he made his life-saving bailout in time, before he passed out, to see his aircraft exploding in a "Mountain of Flame". The rapid parachute descent incurred a rough bone-breaking earth landing, compounding the shrapnel wounded body of the young American aviator, setting him up for capture by the enemy; and then the miraculous rescue and escape from the Gestapo by the courageous men and women of the Free French Underground. The battle to save his severely injured arm, his survival at the hands of the enemy and his health are at risk as he works his way south, slipping through the battlefields and enemy lines of France, ever cognizant of military targets seen in his travels, to scale the Pyrenees Mountains to reach Spain.

As a battle hardened veteran at his early age, he is grateful for the generosity and is overwhelmed by the bravery of the Free French Underground who day and night fight to free their enemy-occupied France. Over sixty-three years have passed, yet the memory of the carnage of war remains a graphic nightmare.

**ACKNOWLEDGING EDITOR-MENTOR**
**G. STEVE CHIRIGOTIS, COLONEL USAF, (RET.)**

I would like to thank Steve Chirigotis, my editor; his help enabled me to complete this book that I began in 2008, as otherwise it would probably have taken several more years to complete. Besides being a great editor Steve was completely knowledgeable about all aspects of what a bomber crewman had to endure. He experienced combat flying as a radio operator/ gunner on a B-24 Liberator Bomber on 50 combat missions with the 15thAir Force out of Pantanella, Italy during WWII. Names, places, bombing missions, experiencing daily dangers, etc., were second nature to him.

The extensive research undertaken gave *Code Burgundy – The Long Escape*, integrity and completeness. Steve retired with over twenty year's service from the USAF as a Full Colonel. He also retired as an engineering systems writer from a major industrial corporation.

Any errors or omissions in fact, committed are the responsibility of the author. The reader is reminded that this story took place early in 1943 and 1944, before the D-Day Allied Invasion of France 6 June 1944. I relied on memory, information provided by my former crewmen and from personal interviews with the French Resistance who helped to identify people, names, dates and locations.

Finally, I wish to thank Col. Chirigotis for his knowledge, kindness, input, understanding, and especially, patience in collaboration with me while writing my story.

John Katsaros

G. Steve Chirigotis, Col. USAF, (Ret.) & John Katsaros

# CHAPTER 1
## Code Burgundy - The Long Escape
## Sworn To Secrecy for Sixty Years

This story is written for personal catharsis to reveal the inconceivable experiences and misfortunes of war to those individuals who clamored over the years for the whole story and to leave this narrative for posterity.

The facts, as written, are authentic and every effort has been made to tell the story as best recollected after these many years, as to events, times and places; and to insure honor to those individuals and groups of individuals without whom this story could not have been written. I am not a hero; the heroes, during World War II, are those killed or dead from wounds received engaging the enemy in mortal combat.

Sworn to secrecy by the United States Government on 15 June 1944, my experiences, and those of many airmen like me, have rarely been addressed. Because of the secrecy imposed by the government, my father, mother, a sister, and two brothers, now deceased, will never learn of my story. Now, with a sharp mind, I reflect on combat mission experiences, my aircraft being shot down by enemy fighter aircraft fire, being wounded, and suffering additional injuries on contact with Mother Earth. In my struggle to survive injuries and broken bones, I am captured by the enemy. A miraculous escape takes place but I am soon recaptured. In a second escape I confound the enemy and make my way through the battle lines and hostile territories of southern France, across the Pyrenees Mountains to the smell of fresh air and the feel of freedom in Spain.

Without the help of the French Resistance, this story could never have been told and my remains would be buried in France.

## CHAPTER 2
## Pearl Harbor, Sunday, 7 December 1941

It was spring of 1941; war was in full blossom in Europe. As a seventeen year old, a few months before my 18th birthday, I was working a shift at our grocery store, and during slow periods I looked through the latest issues of *Collier's* magazine dated 14 June 1941 and my favorite magazine *Life*. There on *Life's* front cover in amazing color was the assemblage of a total of eight or more of our Naval Battleships, birthed in pairs at Ford Island; with Heavy Cruisers, Light Cruisers, Destroyers, Mine craft, PT Boats and other auxiliary ships lined up at the docks, like ducks in a row. The caption at the top of the page, in large, bold print read: "Impregnable Pearl Harbor". Admiral Kimmel, as a precautionary measure, had removed the three aircraft carriers from Pearl Harbor and had taken them out to sea. The impregnability of Pearl Harbor was graphically laid out within the magazine pages in words and beautiful color, and black and white photographs. The whole magazine, showing the pictures of this great armada of ships was daunting to me then, and is today, as my memory recalls it vividly.

The entry of the United States into World War II began at Pearl Harbor with the surprise bombing of the harbor, minutes before 8 AM on Sunday morning, 7 December 1941, by fighter-bomber and torpedo bomber aircraft from the Imperial Empire of Japan.

I was a senior at the Haverhill High School and ambition burned in me, so my brother George and I opened the Katsaros Brothers, Emerson Street, Haverhill grocery store. It was my shift at the store that Sunday evening and like most people, in those days, I got my entertainment by listening to the radio shows. The radio, besides the movie theater, was the only source of entertainment and news. The interruptions to the radio program came at 7 PM and the announcer gave the news that Pearl Harbor, attacked at 8 AM their time, was bombed and strafed with cannon and machine-gun fire, and torpedo-bombed by aircraft identified as Japanese by the big red-painted sun-ball, the "Rising Sun", on their wings and on both sides of the aircraft fuselage. Damage to the harbor and ships were reported on the radio and in the newspapers in the days to follow. I was excited as heck and telephoned to inform the family, who were unaware of the news. "Where is Pearl Harbor?" they asked. "Hawaii", I screamed. On Monday, the next school day, the high school principal, Mr. Earl McLeod had a student assembly in the auditorium where we listened to the President of the United States, Franklin Delano Roosevelt, address the nation: "Japan, Germany and other axis nations have declared war on the United States of America. Sunday December 7, 1941 is a day that will live in infamy." All classes, activities and social functions were dismissed for the balance of the day.

This *Collier's* magazine article dated June 14, 1941, nearly six months prior to the Japanese air raid December 7, 1941 at Pearl Harbor, was obtained through the courtesy of the Public Libraries at Haverhill and Boston.

# CHAPTER 3
## Navy Air Cadet, 1942

Two days later, on Tuesday, 9 December 1941 several classmates and I decided to join the Navy Air Cadet program so we applied at the local recruiting office at the Haverhill, Massachusetts Post Office. After several days we were given a battery of intelligence tests and told to go home to await tests results.

In a few days we were notified, and told to report to the Navy building on Causeway Street, Boston. For two days we were subjected to additional intelligence tests, eye tests and physical examinations. I, with those that had favorably completed all the examinations, was sworn into the Navy Air Cadet program.

I now considered myself to be in the service of the U.S. Navy. However, due to the great numbers who joined the Air Cadet program, I was told to return to my home to await call-up.

My classmates and I while attending the senior year at the High School took advantage of our Trade School co-education, and went to work at a submarine building facility at the Portsmouth Navy Shipyards. George continued to run the grocery store until he joined the U.S. Army.

Several weeks later I was contacted by the Navy to report to a Navy Building at Boston. I was given another physical exam. An eye doctor gave me the Japanese *Ishihara* color test - a color perception test, consisting of many pages of colored dots on a page forming a number. I couldn't distinguish the numbers. So I failed the test, as did the six other applicants of the group. A high-ranking officer approached to tell us that all members of this group and I failed the admissions programming, and to return to civil life. The wind was knocked out of me as I was dumfounded.

I believed that I had been sworn into the Navy Cadet Program several weeks ago, so why was I not accepted for the regular officer training? "There is no second choice," the Navy said. "You did not pass the preliminary examinations."

I was very taken by James Bradley's book, *Fly Boys, A True Story oj Courage* and also by his number one best seller, *Flags of Our Fathers*

John Katsaros in front of Haverhill High School on graduation day May 1942.

and was certain that had I completed the U.S. Navy Air Cadet Program, won my Navy pilot wings and that I surely would have joined the fight against the Japanese Empire in the Pacific Theater of Operations.

Bradley wrote about the daring and courage of nine American flyers, Navy and Marine airmen sent to bomb, strafe and destroy the Japanese Communications Towers on the island of Chichi-Jima which had a large harbor, serving as the supply base for the Japanese forces on the Island of Iwo Jima. The nine American bombers and flyers were shot down by Japanese ground fire, and all but one, a Navy Lieutenant, were captured by Japanese soldiers. The Navy Lieutenant escaped capture by bailing out over the Pacific Ocean within sight of Chichi-Jima and was picked up by a U.S. submarine, minutes before Japanese in a small surface boat could reach him. The young Navy pilot who escaped capture, George H.W. Bush, was destined to become President of the United States.

The fate of the downed and captured flyers on that raid became known after WWII. The Japanese military had interrogated, tortured and beheaded all eight flyers. The Japanese officers ate the livers, the hearts and other body parts. I wondered what my fate would have been had I been selected for Navy Air Cadet training and followed the paths of these Navy Flyers.

(Gazette Staff Photo)

"REMEMBER PEARL HARBOR" GROUP—Sgt. George E. Gagnon, Army recruiting officer, sent 27 men to Boston this morning for their final examination and induction into the Army. The group will be known as Pearl Harbor Avengers.

Front row, left to right: Martin W. Sullivan, Jr. Martin H. Donovan, Manuel Valavanes, Joseph A. Plouf, Jr., Walter D. St. Armand, leader; Wilbert C. Hardy, Jr., assistant leader; Russell E. Hall and Elmer G. Bailey.

Second row, left to right: Nicholas Valoras, Robert J. Viens, Bernard Gaudreau, George E. Warner, Albert B. Sayers, Kenneth N. Glover, John A. Hutchins, Jr., and John W. Small.

Back row, left to right: John Katsaros, Richard D. Sweeney, Everett E. Pickering, Robert W. Girard, William C. Curry, William R. Hirsch, Robert Minchin, Pietro A. Romano, Paul W. Hinch, Jr., Joseph H. Stapleton and Alan H. Noyes.

"The Pearl Harbor Avengers" Photo taken by *The Haverhill Gazette* newspaper on 7 December 1942 irard. William C. Curry. William R. Hirsch,

# "PEARL HARBOR AVENGERS" LEAVE

## 27 Sent To Boston To Take Army Tests

Sgt. George E. Gagnon, of the Army recruiting station, postoffice building, today marked the first anniversary of Pearl Harbor by delivering 27 men to Boston Army authorities for final physical examinations and induction. The group, one of the largest sent from the station since war was declared, was also the last recruited before the executive order closing all voluntary enlistments.

The men leaving were: John W. Small, 25, 389 South Main street, regular army; Wilbert C. Hardy, Jr., 20, 539 Main street, regular army; John Katsaros, 19, 24 Forest avenue, air corps; Robert W. Girard, 19, 2 Benjamin street, air corps; Alan H. Noyes, 18, 40 Dalton avenue, air corps; Martin H. Donovan, 19, 62 Arlington street, air corps; Manuel Valavanes, 21, 32 Washington street, regular army; Martin W. Sullivan, Jr., 19, 99 Williams street, air corps; Joseph A. Plouf, Jr., 18, 14 Haseltine street, air corps; Robert J. Viens, 18, 63 Charles street, armored force; George E. Warner, 19, 15 Mechanic street, air corps; Everett E. Pickering, 19, 19 Welcome street, air corps; Albert B. Sayers, 20, 316 River street, regular army; Bernard Gaudreau, 18, 40 Ninth avenue, paratroops; William C. Curry, 19, 83 Kenoza street, armored force; Nicholas Valoras, 20, 69 Washington street, regular army; Richard D. Sweeney, 18, Merrimack street, Merrimac, air corps; Elmer G. Bailey, 20, Locust street, Merrimac, regular army; John A. Hutchins, Jr., 18, 2 East Main street, air corps; Russell E. Hall, 18, Highland street, Merrimac, air corps; Walter S. St. Armand, 19, Elm street, Salisbury, air corps; Kenneth N. Glover, 18, Elm street, Plaistow, N. H., air corps; William R. Hirsch, 21, Pleasant street, West Newbury, regular army; Ro[illegible] Minchin, 18, 398½ Main street, Amesbury, air corps; Paul W. Hinch, Jr., 19, 428 Lowell street, Methuen, air corps; Pietro A. Romano, 18, 83 Oak street, Lawrence, air corps; Joseph H. Stapleton, 18, 5 Stafford street, Lawrence, air corps.

# CHAPTER
# 4 Army Life

The episode with the Navy Air Cadet program behind me, I returned home to Haverhill. Several days later with patriotism jumping in my veins to join the U.S. Army Air Force, I went to the local Army Recruiting Station and enlisted. The flying section of the Army in May 1918 had grown from the Army Signal Corps to the Army Air Corps, and in June 1941, the flying branch of the Army, was incorporated into and became the United States Army Air Force (USAAF). In September 1947, The USAAF became a separate component of the military, the United States Air Force (USAF) and together as do the Army and the Navy, reports directly to the Secretary of War and the President.

After graduation from high school, I still had my job at the Portsmouth Navy Shipyard and received mail to report on 7 December 1942 to the Army Recruiting Station so; I obtained a leave of absence from my job. *The Haverhill Gazette*, the local newspaper, took a photograph of the group of enlistees which was printed in the paper the following day with the caption: "The Pearl Harbor Avengers." We were eighteen and nineteen year old kids, "green" recruits who had no idea how to handle a gun or to fight a war.

As part of a group, I was transported by Army truck from the local Recruiting Station directly to Fort Devens, Massachusetts, where we all were given comprehensive physical exams and intelligence tests, called the Army General Classification Tests (AGCT), having successfully completed the exams, we received eye exams, consisting of identifying the solid colors in strips of yarn. Successfully completing the exams, we were assigned to the flying branch of the Army (USAAF). Those individuals not selected for flying duty were inducted into the regular Army (USA).

Forty-eight hours later as part of a group, I was loaded aboard a passenger train at Fort Devens with the destination to Basic Training Center #9 at Miami Beach, Florida. Security routed the train from Devens through Albany, New York, south to Miami, taking a circuitous route and several days to arrive at the final destination.

There were so many inductees that the Air Force had two Basic Training Centers in Florida: (BTC) #1 and #9. My brother Sot was attending Officer Candidate School (OCS) at Miami. Other training centers on the east coast were located at Atlantic City, New Jersey.

At Basic Training Center #9, I bunked with Alan Noyes and Martin H. Donovan, two Haverhill friends, at the Seascape Apartments. We bedded down on mattresses placed on the kitchen floor, in a duplex home, confiscated by the government for the duration of the war, and that homey atmosphere helped to make Army life more endurable. The Army had a name for servicemen such as Alan who could not follow orders. They called them "screw-ups". For example, he never made roll-call, the "line-up" outdoors for body count each morning scheduled at 0500 hours. When a flight officer called Alan's name, Alan would be in bed lying on his backside, and since it was still dark at this hour in the morning, the group would answer for him by yelling "here." One morning the officer in-charge warned the recruits of punishment if this practice continued, as he was aware that they were covering for Alan. From then on, when Alan's name was called, no one would answer. The game was over - each man had to take care of himself. Finally, Alan got the message but continued with his errant ways. His name was being called at the formation and Alan responded, "Here," from the bedroom window.

Alan's action did not fly with the flight officer and, as a result of Alan's misbehavior, the complete flight of about fifty men was restricted for the weekend. Alan was ordered to scrub the sidewalk with a G.I. brush. Instead, smart-ass that he was, he decided to use a toothbrush and personally extended the cleaning detail to the adjacent Group Headquarters building. When the Group General saw Alan, he asked, "What are you doing?" Alan told the General, "Sir, I was ordered to wash the sidewalk for missing roll call."

All hell broke loose, and the General placed the flight under restriction, no weekend passes. We were all pissed at Alan, he was in the "dog house" with many of us in the flight and it took some convincing to persuade the avengers not to physically harm him. Joseph Azzarito, another hometown friend, also had joined the Army Air Force and was stationed at Boca Raton, Florida, about an hour up the dusty Military Trail from Miami. The Military Trail, built several miles inland, west of US Route 1 by the Army engineers during World War II, was a dirt highway used for military transportation and exists today as a paved eight-lane highway.

Joe Azzarito, Alan Noyes and I went through high school together, and, after the war, we were graduated from Boston University. After college we three worked at the Haverhill radio station (WHAV); Joe in sales, and Allan and I broadcasted football games for several years.

The saga of Alan Noyes endures. Upon separation from the U. S. Army Air Force, he continued his career in the Air Force Reserves, working his way to become a Commissioned Officer and was eventually promoted to Brigadier General and Assistant Adjutant General for Air, Vermont National Guard. Great going, Alan! Presently, he is Executive Director of Vermont Association of Broadcasters. Allan's son is the Deputy Adjutant General for Air, Vermont National Guard.

Whenever possible, I visited brother, Sot, at OCS, a few miles south at Miami Beach. Bernard "Barney" Gallagher, another friend from home, was also stationed at Miami Beach.

One day Barney was walking along the beach with us in a windstorm and was hit on the head by a falling coconut. Sot retrieved the coconut, put it away for safekeeping, and in 1995, some sixty years later, I presented it to Barney as a souvenir at their Haverhill Kiwanis meeting. Barney's career in the Air Force ended in the Pacific Theater of Operation at Okinawa, 7th AF Communications, and the first American Air Force to occupy the island. He was the official photographer and took the pictures of the B-29 bomber, *Enola Gay*, the 27 year old pilot Major Paul W. Tibbets Jr. of Miami that dropped the first atomic bomb 6 August 1945 on Hiroshima, Japan.

On one of my visits I told Sot how BTC #9 performed guard duty on the beach with a broomstick as a weapon. Sot was taken by surprise and asked, "Doesn't the military at BTC #9 realize that German U-boats are torpedoing U.S. merchant ships and oil tankers every night off the coast of Florida?" That weekend an oil tanker was seen to explode a few miles offshore. Upon returning to BTC #9, I complained about standing guard duty unarmed and gave the obvious reason for our request. The Commanding Officer immediately requisitioned a .45 caliber pistol and a carbine rifle for each airman on guard duty.

After WWII the *Palm Beach Post* wrote an article stating that twenty-seven American ships were sunk during WWII between Jupiter and Fort Lauderdale, Florida. Each sunken ship and the Captain was named with the number of crew members lost and the identity of the German Commander with the name and number of the U-boat credited was also given for the ship sunk. Research of the ships that were sunk continues to this date, and records reveal that the German submarines were supplied with fuel from a mother ship operating out of Brazil. It was also reported that English speaking, German sailors would come ashore by rubber dinghies at nighttime from the U-boats to purchase food and other sundries.

Private John Katsaros at Basic Training Center #9 Miami Beach, Florida
December 1942

## CHAPTER 5
## Air Crew Training

Upon graduation from basic training, a choice was given to each trainee for selection in the Army Air Force. I chose flying duty, said goodbye to BTC #9, and was shipped to Buckingham Army Air Field, Fort Meyers, Florida for aerial gunnery training.

The army barracks at Fort Meyers each housed from 40 to 50 trainees and did not present the luxury and comfort of the confiscated sleeping quarters of three men to a room that were left at Miami Beach. The single level building was approximately 60 feet by 20 feet to accommodate all the single cots with rod space for each recruit to hang clothing, and a footlocker for personal belongings on the aisle side end of each cot. The Sergeant who stayed with a class night and day had a private room at the front of the building and at the rear of the building were the enclosed shower room with ten showerheads and the adjacent lavatory with ten hoppers and a urinal trough with constant running water. The "head" light shone night and day. Discipline was always at a high point when meted out by the Sergeant. He put us to bed with "lights out" and got us up for "roll call", whatever the hour, and it was always on the double! Nobody ever wanted a run-in with the Sergeant because he had the power and the ability to discipline and destroy. He was not a mean guy - just firm and he was all business. That was his job and he was good at it.

My class consisted of about fifteen or twenty men. One day the group was assembled along the tarmac of the airport runway. An officer asked, who wants to be first to take a ride on a two-seater airplane the AT-6, called *The Texan*? I, the "brave-hearted one," raised my hand and took my first ride in an airplane. The pilot was a Native American whose rank was Buck Sergeant. The pilot asked, "Do you want the works, John?" I said, "Yeah," and was strapped in the back seat before takeoff. The Sergeant flew the AT-6 over the airfield and did thirteen consecutive barrel rolls and since I was enjoying myself, the pilot performed several trick maneuvers including diving and stalls.

When the plane landed, there were a number of green faces on the group of the future gunners while I enjoyed my first airplane ride and told them so. Some of the guys could not believe this was the future they chose.

The classes were marched to chow, back to the barracks, everywhere- to study classrooms, and to the shooting ranges for trap, skeet, mobile base, B-B gun, and familiarization of a .30 caliber machine-gun. Trap shooting involved the shooting of a clay pigeon, using a 12 gauge double-barreled shotgun, ejected from a single trap house, on command, always away from the shooter. Skeet shooting provided the same shooting experience as that of trap shooting, with the exception that two trap houses, one high (10-12 feet) and one low (about 3 feet) on opposite sides of the shooter, ejected the clay pigeon on command. Mobile base skeet shooting was performed on a special circular oval track range where the shooter shot at clay pigeons released automatically by the 100 equally spaced trap houses as he approached on the flatbed of a 6 X 6 truck. The BB gun shooting range was housed in an especially equipped building, somewhat like an arcade, with metal rabbits and ducks and ships as targets.

The .30 caliber machine-gun familiarization training with live ammunition was the last step prior to testing a student's shooting ability in the air at a moving target, but not before learning the nomenclature of the .30 caliber and the .50 caliber machine guns and to strip down and re-assemble them blindfolded.

All these shooting ranges were not only good shooting training experiences but also a hell of a lot of fun. Scores were kept at each range for each student and as far as was learned, no one flunked out because of the shooting training. It was great preliminary buildup to the airborne firing of .30 caliber ammunition from the back end of the AT-6 at a target sleeve drawn at a distance by another AT-6 to test the individual's shooting ability in the air at a moving target.

We were schooled in the use of Morse Code, learned the alphabet in code and practiced receiving messages from a mechanical sender, as well as learned to send and receive hand operated messages on the wireless, to include S.O.S. and weather reports. The radio operator, who was to excel in this form of communication, went through intensive training at a military radio operator school.

For aerial gunnery training, a parachute with harness was strapped on me, enabling me to stand in the open cockpit to fire the .30 caliber machine-gun using live rounds. Three AT-6 Texans flew in formation, two airplanes consisted of a pilot and one gunner, and the third airplane, the target plane, dragged a long white sock at some distance from the plane allowing the gunners a clear target. Different colored .30 caliber shells were fired by each gunner, which identified the number of hits to be credited to him. Safety practices strictly enforced, there was no danger to the target plane or to the training gunner.

On the way to the target area over the Gulf of Mexico or over the Florida Everglades, the pilots would enjoy themselves, each taking a turn trying to tip the other airplane by placing the wing of one plane under the wing of the opposing plane, and with a violent flip try to upend the other plane.

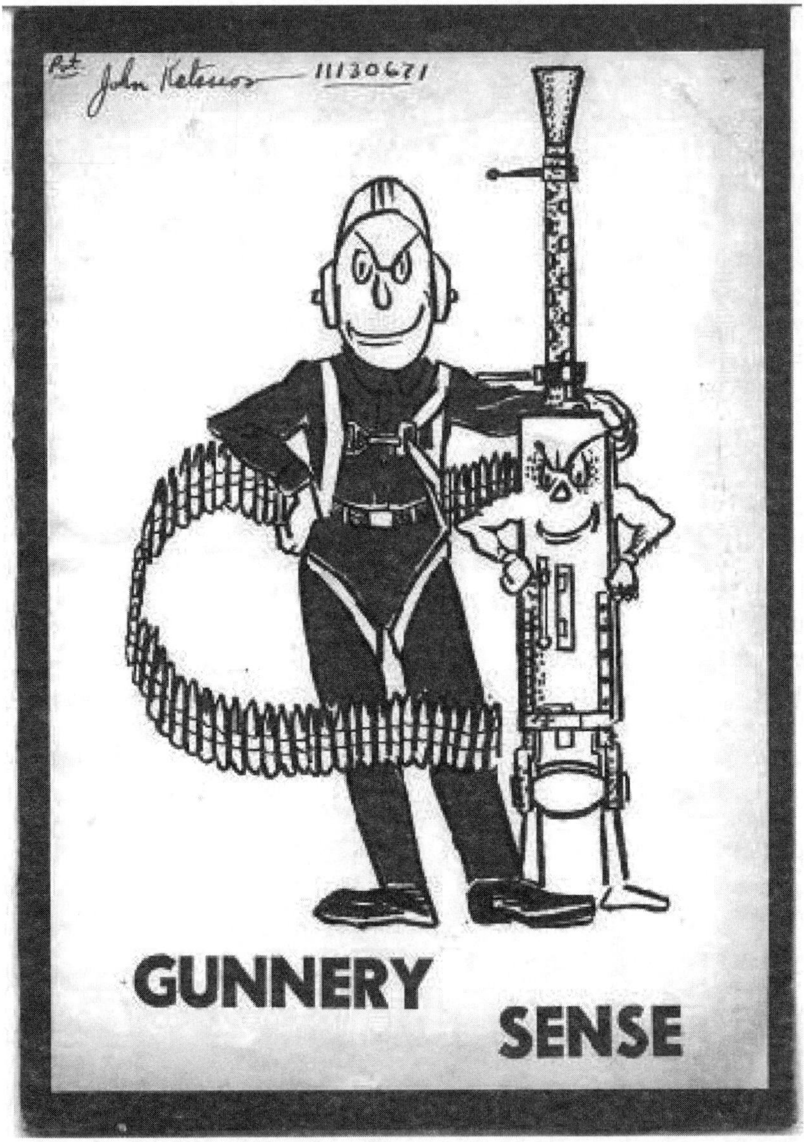


Manual cover drawn by Theodor Seuss Geisel, better known to the world as the beloved Dr. Seuss, was born in 1904 on Howard Street in Springfield, Massachusetts.

As soon as the AT-6's reached the target area, the gunners fired at their intended targets and a split second after the last round of ammunition was expended, the pilot would turn the airplane upside down so that all bodies hung upside down in the plane, held only by a strap attached from the parachute harness to the floor of the plane. On the first such mission, I asked the pilot, "What would the consequences be if the strap did not hold and I was tossed from the plane into the Gulf waters, or the Everglades?" His answer was, "That is why you are provided with a parachute, and a Mae West if you land in water." Through my experience with flyers and their behavior, I learned to believe that antics such as this was one of the reasons all pilots were not officer material, and some were assigned to this duty instead of being sent overseas into combat. "I must give them credit for being exceptional pilots and I always enjoyed flying with them," ("Oh, to be that young again!") The gunnery training successfully completed, now these new aerial gunners knew they were destined to be flyers. Wow! Was I proud! Graduation day was 6 March 1943. As one of the graduating students, I was presented with Gunner's wings, sunglasses and an A2 leather flight-jacket; and was promoted to Sergeant with PCS orders (Permanent Change of Station) for shipment to a technical training school. Sergeant John Katsaros, that's me, was selected to go to aircraft mechanic school at Goldsboro, North Carolina. I liked that, all of it.

THE BOSTON GLOBE • WEDNESDAY, JULY 3, 1991

**AERIAL ANTIQUES** – *A pair of World War II-vintage T-6 trainers take a practice run above Route 128 yesterday near Bedford's Hanscom Field, where they will be taking part in the annual air show this weekend.*

Air gunners practiced with a .30 caliber machine-gun standing-up on the rear of this AT-6 Texan training plane.

HEADQUARTERS
ARMY AIR FORCES FLEXIBLE GUNNERY SCHOOL
BUCKINGHAM ARMY AIR FIELD
Fort Myers, Florida

March 6, 1943

SPECIAL ORDERS)
:
NUMBER 65 )

**E X T R A C T**

1. Pursuant to authority contained in AR 615-5 and letter from Headquarters, Army Air Forces, Washington, D.C., dated August 10, 1942, Subject: Flexible Gunnery Training for Enlisted Men, file 352.9, the following named Enlisted Men, AAFU, having successfully completed the prescribed course of instruction in Aerial Gunnery at this Post, are promoted to the grades indicated.

TO BE STAFF SERGEANT (TEMPORARY)
Graduates of Army Technical School

Pvt. ADAIR, UHLAND S., 14150043
Pvt. ALBONESI, HENRY F., 31128423
Pvt. AUCOIN, JOHN J., 31080084
Pvt. BAUER, HERBERT P., 33187531
Pvt. BEHRENS, AUGUST H., 38113414
Pvt. BENSINGER, Jr.,NOLAN, 35366560
Pvt. BLALOCK, JOHN P., 34357580
Pvt. BOHN, JAMES W., 17060293
Pvt. BROSNAN, CHARLES A., 31168777
Pvt. BROWN, JAMES H., 35366441
Pvt. BURGESS, GEORGE C., 33222700
Pvt. BURNS, HUGH R., 32446765
Pvt. CAMPBELL, ZANCEL Y., 34337705
Pvt. CANNON, JAMES E., 34333892
Pvt. CASSABAUM, DAVID W., 37428173
Pvt. CIFELLI, GEORGE B., 32459370
Pvt. COLAMONICO, MICHAEL (NMI)32429421
Pvt. COON, EBEN B., 11088169
Pvt. COPELAND, WILLIAM J., 34337788
Pvt. CRABTREE, RAYMOND A., 35436017
Pvt. CROSS, Jr.,VASSIL W., 15331000
Pvt. DECKER, GILBERT R., 33331307
Pvt. DILLON, JAMES A., 33329319
Pvt. DOANE, DONALD D., 32394312
Pvt. ENGLERT, ROBERT T., 35336302
Pvt. FARLEY, JACK W., 38131074
Pvt. FERGUSON, ALAN H., 31082061
Pvt. ADAMS, ROBERT F., 35318775
Pvt. ALEXANDER, ROBERT B., 14150049
Pvt. BASWELL, Jr.,HENRY T., 37217681
Pvt. BEAMS, HAROLD G., 11071294
Pvt. BELKO, Jr.,JOHN A., 33247762
Pvt. BLACKBURN, LYNWOOD E., 34357924
Pvt. BOGACKI, EARLE F., 35316394
Pvt. BRIGGS, RAYMOND O., 34036067
Pvt. BROWN, Jr.,GROVER C., 34037706
Pvt. BUGANSKI, SIGMUND J., 35389312
Pvt. BURGESS, JAMES E., 34357100
Pvt. BURTIS, CHARLES F., 32427593
Pvt. CANNON, CECIL A., 15330929
Pvt. CARTER, HENRY A., 32459662
Pvt. CHAPMAN, DAVID L., 31168534
Pvt. CLARK, Jr.,WILLIAM J., 32405696
Pvt. COLGAN, FLOYD C., 31155548
Pvt. COOMES, JOHN H., 31168570
Pvt. CORBIN, RICHARD W., 35387868
Pvt. CROFT, ARTHUR F.,31081018
Pvt. DABBS, OTTIS J., 34284142
Pvt. DEMETRIUS, NICHOLAS P,32429752
Pvt. DISHONGH,Jr,JEFFERSON B,34367792
Pvt. DRAKE, EUEL T., 14108227
Pvt. ENGLISH, CHARLES L., 34209905
Pvt. FAWCETT, EDWIN (NMI) 12135328
Pvt. FLOWERS, CHARLIE H., 34311576

Special Order 1

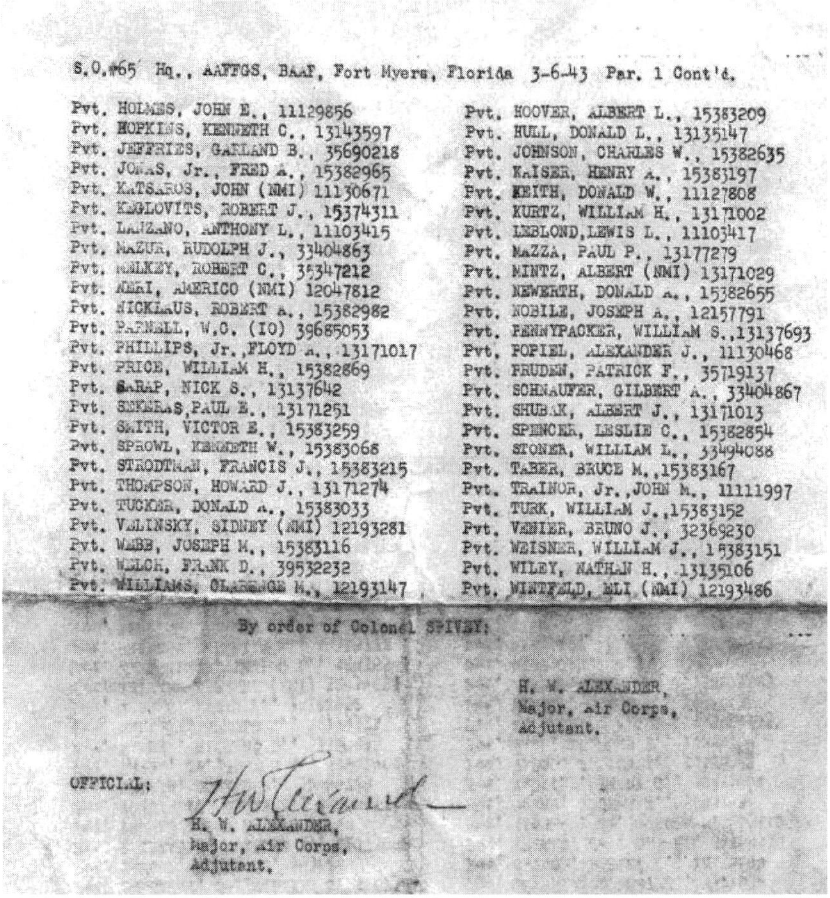

S.O.#65 Hq., AAFFGS, BAAF, Fort Myers, Florida 3-6-43 Par. 1 Cont'd.

Pvt. HOLMES, JOHN E., 11129856
Pvt. HOPKINS, KENNETH C., 13143597
Pvt. JEFFRIES, GARLAND B., 35690218
Pvt. JONAS, Jr., FRED A., 15382965
Pvt. KATSAROS, JOHN (NMI) 11130671
Pvt. KEGLOVITS, ROBERT J., 15374311
Pvt. LANZANO, ANTHONY L., 11103415
Pvt. MAZUR, RUDOLPH J., 33404863
Pvt. MULKEY, ROBERT C., 35347212
Pvt. NERI, AMERICO (NMI) 12047812
Pvt. NICKLAUS, ROBERT A., 15382982
Pvt. PARNELL, W.O. (IO) 39685053
Pvt. PHILLIPS, Jr., FLOYD A., 13171017
Pvt. PRICE, WILLIAM H., 15382869
Pvt. SARAP, NICK S., 13137642
Pvt. SEKERAS, PAUL E., 13171251
Pvt. SMITH, VICTOR E., 15383259
Pvt. SPROWL, KENNETH W., 15383068
Pvt. STRODTMAN, FRANCIS J., 15383215
Pvt. THOMPSON, HOWARD J., 13171274
Pvt. TUCKER, DONALD A., 15383033
Pvt. VALINSKY, SIDNEY (NMI) 12193281
Pvt. WEBB, JOSEPH M., 15383116
Pvt. WELCH, FRANK D., 39532232
Pvt. WILLIAMS, CLARENCE M., 12193147
Pvt. HOOVER, ALBERT L., 15383209
Pvt. HULL, DONALD L., 13135147
Pvt. JOHNSON, CHARLES W., 15382635
Pvt. KAISER, HENRY A., 15383197
Pvt. KEITH, DONALD W., 11127808
Pvt. KURTZ, WILLIAM H., 13171002
Pvt. LEBLOND, LEWIS L., 11103417
Pvt. MAZZA, PAUL P., 13177279
Pvt. MINTZ, ALBERT (NMI) 13171029
Pvt. NEWERTH, DONALD A., 15382655
Pvt. NOBILE, JOSEPH A., 12157791
Pvt. PENNYPACKER, WILLIAM S., 13137693
Pvt. POPIEL, ALEXANDER J., 11130468
Pvt. PRUDEN, PATRICK F., 35719137
Pvt. SCHNAUFER, GILBERT A., 33404867
Pvt. SHUBAK, ALBERT J., 13171013
Pvt. SPENCER, LESLIE C., 15382854
Pvt. STONER, WILLIAM L., 33494088
Pvt. TABER, BRUCE M., 15383167
Pvt. TRAINOR, Jr., JOHN M., 11111997
Pvt. TURK, WILLIAM J., 15383152
Pvt. VENIER, BRUNO J., 32369230
Pvt. WEISNER, WILLIAM J., 15383151
Pvt. WILEY, NATHAN H., 13135106
Pvt. WINTFELD, ELI (NMI) 12193486

By order of Colonel SPIVEY:

H. W. ALEXANDER,
Major, Air Corps,
Adjutant.

OFFICIAL:

H. W. ALEXANDER,
Major, Air Corps,
Adjutant.

Special Orders 2 - It reads: "Pvt. Katsaros, John (NMI) 11130671"

Sgt. John Katsaros received his wings at the Headquarters Army Air Forces Flexible Gunnery School, Buckingham Air Base, Fort Myers, Florida, on March 6, 1943.

# CHAPTER 6
## Aircraft Engineer Training

Many of the new gunners were transferred to Seymour Johnson Field at Goldsboro, North Carolina to attend the airplane mechanic course and as luck would have it, the summer was very hot with temperatures for a period of thirty days and nights remaining at over 90 degrees. There was no air conditioning in those days, nor were there screens in the windows and the flies bit incessantly. Sleeping hours were from 1700 to 2300 hours (5 PM to 11 PM). On weekends at a technical school, students were allowed 24 hour passes for a change of pace. As a result of this freedom, "short-arm" inspection, in the barracks by a medical doctor, was given in the middle of the night to insure the health of the students by keeping them "VD" free. Regular classroom hours were 1200 hours (midnight) to 0800 hours taken in a standing position to keep the students awake but they sometimes fell asleep on their feet. Breakfast was at 2300 hours. As a member of a student squad, I was marched for miles everywhere, at all times, always in formation, even to go to the dining room at the mess hall across the street from the barracks (sleeping quarters).

On Sunday morning, the Drill Sergeant would holler, "Church Call" and all those who had a mind for prayer fell out to be marched to church by the Sergeant's assistant. Dinner (chow) was at 0600 hours after which the students are called out of the barracks to be lined up in formation for a march by a Drill Sergeant. Discipline was strict to get people to learn to follow orders, so it was march, march, march to the cadence of the Sergeant's booming, sing-song voice -"Hup, two, three, four." "Get in line; this is not a stroll in the afternoon sunshine. You are soldiers in the United States Army. Show some backbone. Ok, now, let's pick it up - hup, two, three, and four! That's better, you're looking good." When the Sergeant spoke, we all listened. If one man was singled out -man, he was in trouble. This strict discipline not only taught the new soldiers to follow orders by which we managed to learn in the classroom in order to pass the tests and to graduate, but in the making of men of them to prepare the students for the tough times to be faced in combat. Many of the students believed that the technical education and military training, the use of firearms and military discipline was to prepare them for combat against the Japanese in the Pacific Theater of Operations. They later learned that their destination was the European Theater of Operations (ETO).

After eight grueling weeks of discipline and being "zombie" students, classes in aircraft mechanics were successfully completed. While waiting for assignment orders to ship us newly trained airmen to duty stations across the country for combat crew training, I and my new friends were issued weekend passes to give us a break from the military regimen. We visited tobacco plantations in Wilson, North Carolina and had a pleasant stay at the YMCA in Rocky Mount, N.C. where we were treated warmly to Southern hospitality. Military life does have its moments.

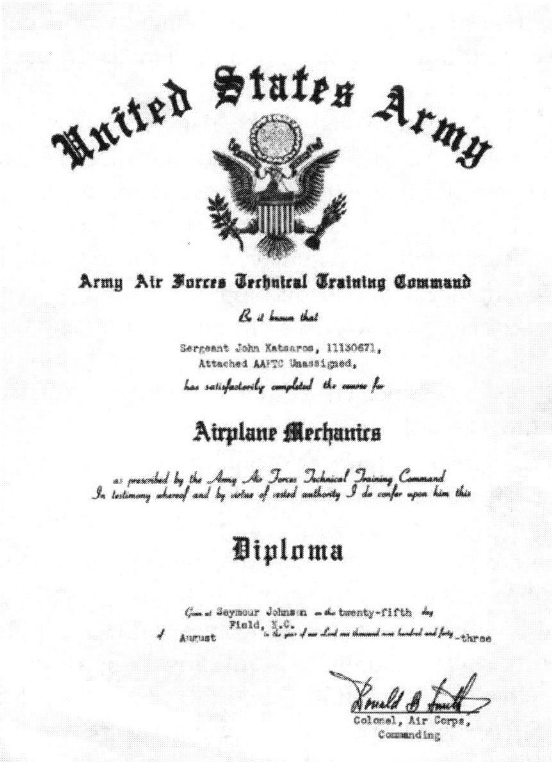

United States Army

Army Air Forces Technical Training Command

Be it known that

Sergeant John Katsaros, 11130671,
Attached AAFTC Unassigned,

has satisfactorily completed the course for

Airplane Mechanics

as prescribed by the Army Air Forces Technical Training Command
In testimony whereof and by virtue of vested authority I do confer upon him this

Diploma

Given at Seymour Johnson Field, N.C. on the twenty-fifth day of August in the year of our Lord one thousand nine hundred and forty-three

Colonel, Air Corps,
Commanding

## CHAPTER 7
## Combat Crew Training

After graduation, the Air Force arranged a PCS cross-country train trip from North Carolina through Chicago, Kansas City, Denver and points west that took the new trainees to Salt Lake City where individual assignments were made. I was assigned to B-17 crew training at Peyote Air Base, Texas right in the middle of cattle country at the King Ranch, one of the largest cattle ranches in the country.

That night, I thought about the chow here at Peyote, "I had the best steak and eggs dinner that I ever had in my lifetime. The steak could be cut with a spoon, it was so great. I spent one month in Peyote and had steak and eggs at the mess hall every day. Food I had on the air base was the best I had of any mess hall while in the service".

The next day I was assigned to the Air Force Bombardment Group stationed at Peyote, Texas, where I was introduced to my new B-17 crew: pilot, Jack Dunaway; co-pilot, Henry Kane; bombardier, Ted Krol; navigator, William Mock; radio operator, Frank Mastronardi; ball-turret gunner, Walter Rusch; left waist gunner, Jack Crowley; tail-gunner, Marvin Benz; and the engineer, J. Nichols, top-turret gunner, (who was later replaced by Harry Horst). I was assigned as assistant engineer, right waist gunner and photographer.

Intelligent men are expected to train individually for their respective positions in the USAAF as aircraft engineers, radio operators, radio mechanics, armorers, hydraulics specialists. All are trained as aerial gunners before being brought together with men of a different training specialty than themselves, to form into combat crews for the purpose of training together as crews for the heavy bombers. Here the non-commissioned officers also met and trained with a pilot, co-pilot navigator and bombardier. As newly formed crews, they are expected to train together for several months to learn to work as a team in order to be transformed into a cohesive unit. I met all the members assigned to my crew at Peyote, Texas and learned that we are to train as a crew through three phases of air combat crew training. The first phase of this training at Peyote lasts three weeks; then we are shipped to

Dalhart, Texas for training phases two and three.

For experience purposes, during crew training, the gunners alternated stations to familiarize themselves with the aircraft. I became familiar with the ball-turret, tail position, the top-turret and was also responsible as the photographer. On simulated bomb runs, in turn, I used a K-20 and a K-24 camera; one camera took a picture every few seconds as the bombs dropped, and the other camera took pictures of the actual target and the bomb damage. A moving picture camera was issued and used extensively during combat missions over Europe, and especially over Germany.

Of course, these were only practice missions over cities in the USA. For example, if the simulated mission for the day was Albuquerque, New Mexico, no "dummy" bombs were actually dropped. However, attempts were made to take pictures of the target. Many times curiosity arose as to what the people in our cities would think if they knew that the bombers above were using their city as simulated targets.

On several occasions I would ask the pilot, Jack Dunaway, for permission, much to the dismay of co-pilot Lt. Kane, to fly the big B-17 once the airplane was taken up to the scheduled cruising altitude. I was enthusiastic about flying and wanted to be certain that I could handle the aircraft in the event of an emergency, to keep the B-17 flying while the crew bailed out. I had no prior flying lessons or experience, not even in a single-engine plane and here I was asking to fly the B-17 Flying Fortress with four powerful engines. Lt. Dunaway began to give me some instructions and one day, he called me up to the cockpit where I was allowed to sit in the left seat, the pilot's seat, to fly the plane most of the way to Albuquerque, New Mexico. Fortunately, that emergency never arose, not even in combat, to require me to take control of the plane.

The pilot with the crew aboard and an instructor pilot went through instrument flying, flying blind with a hood covering the windshield and practiced landing on instruments. It was not uncommon to see or hear of a crew that "cracked up", with all members lost as a result of this intensive training. On the ground the crew went through "ditching" procedures by releasing the water dingy and going through time schedules to evacuate the aircraft after sounding of the alarm bell. The men learned, as second nature, by practice in flight, to handle their weapons, parachutes, use of the oxygen system and intercommunications system. The radioman, on other special flights operated the radio equipment sending and receiving messages by Morse code, to include the weather, with central communications in the control tower.

All crew members attended lectures and demonstrations presented by group headquarters operations and intelligence dealing with plane safety procedures on the ground and in the air. One such demonstration by a British RAF member with combat experience, how gunners should "lead" the enemy aircraft in firing of the .50 cal. machine-gun. The gunners were also given the opportunity to shoot their .50 cal. machine-gun at ground targets.

Upon completion of Phase 1, we, as a crew, were transferred PCS to Dalhart, Texas for advanced bomber crew training. Here, we were to complete Phases two and three which was to include more of the same intensive training as Phase 1 and heavy concentration in formation flying. As a result of heavy losses to the U.S. 8th Air Force in England, training phase number three was cut from the scheduled program. These training crews were destined to become replacement crews for bomber groups with shortages in combat crews and planes as a result of combat losses.

Training at Dalhart was arduous for all crew members, but Lt. Dunaway's confidence and skills in handling of the B-17 were noticeably elevated. He was put through a series of flight tests under the watchful eye of an instructor pilot. When the plane reached altitude, Lt. Dunaway was instructed to put the airplane into a vertical climb until the plane would shudder and almost stall. This test was first attempted with the four engines running, then with a series of two engines running after shutting down two alternate engines, causing a near stall-out and aircraft drop in altitude. On each occasion the engines recovered rapidly and the B-17 returned directly to horizontal flight. These exercises were excellent pilot training preparing the pilots for utilization of these skills, as needed on combat missions. The skeleton flight crew on this test mission consisted solely of four members: Pilot Lt. Dunaway, Co-Pilot Lt. Kane, the instructor pilot and Sgt. Katsaros, engineer. All crew members wore parachutes on this training exercise, and seat belts were always engaged.

Before leaving Dalhart, Texas our good friend and wing mate, Pilot Bid Fichette and his crew, decided to fly their B-17 under a bridge near San

Antonio, Texas. Bid tried this with the 100% approval of his crew. On his approach he realized too late, that they might hit the bridge. He pulled the plane up to avoid hitting the bridge, but one propeller blade hit a guy cable. Luckily they survived.

When all planes had returned to Dalhart, Lt. Dunaway was ordered to line up his B-17 along the edge of the runway next to several others. A line-up inspection of each aircraft, called by the General of the 2nd Bomber Group, revealed the damaged propeller blade on Lt. Bid Fichett's B-17. Lt. Fichett and his crew faced a Special Courts Martial and Lt. Fichett's crew taken from him. Other crews in attendance at the Courts Martial provided moral support, objected to the findings of the Court and threatened to refuse to fly unless command of his crew was returned to Lt. Fichett. The Court acquiesced with the provision that Lt. Fichett never be promoted beyond 2nd Lieutenant.

Lt. Jack A. Dunaway, Crew #56, U.S. Army Air Base, Peyote, Texas, 22 November 1943. From left to right: John H. Crowley, Walter R. Rusch, John Katsaros, Henry Kane - Co-pilot, Jack Dunaway – Pilot, Ted J. Krol – Bombardier, William G. Mock – Navigator, Marvin H. Benz, J. Nichols, Francis J. Mastronardi

# CHAPTER 8
## Emergency Orders

Rumors abounded concerning the tremendous losses the 8th Air Force had sustained during the daylight combat missions in the year 1943. An example of the losses reported by the 8th Air Force during the month of July 1943: eighty-eight Fortresses lost, nine hundred men killed, MIA or POW's on the air raid at Oscherslaben about eighty miles southwest of Berlin, Germany; the 100th Group (called the Bloody One Hundred) on one mission, lost all twelve airplanes. Waiting for the return of their airmen and planes, officers and ground crews were devastated when it became evident that none would return. Could anyone imagine how excruciating it had been to those on the ground, waiting and praying for return of their friends, hoping for the sight of returning B-17's, and not to be seen again. It was horrible! During October 1943, one hundred planes were lost in three days. The date 14 October 1943 became known to the 8th Air Force as "Black Thursday", as sixty-five B-17's were lost on a combat mission to Schweinfurt, Germany; five hundred and ninety-four airmen missing, wounded, taken prisoner or dead, seventeen returning Fortresses suffered category E battle damage, never to fly again. In these bombers fifty were dead and thirty-three airmen were wounded, 10 critically.

Major General Delmar T. Spivey, our Commander at Fort Meyers Gunnery School was shot down in the lead B-17 over Schweinfurt on "Black Thursday". He was the USAAF expert on aerial gunnery and was on this mission evaluating on how to improve gun turrets. He became the highest ranking Air Force officer as a German POW. It was a great loss.

From October 10 through October 14 in the year 1943, the 8th Air Force licked its wounds from the hammering it took in losses to aircraft and airmen, and rested the tired combat crews and ground personnel. It was more than the hardiest staff officers or generals could stand. The men who flew the missions were numb with fatigue and mental strain from facing death in one form or another - from hundreds of thousands of shrapnel fragments, cannon projectiles, bursting bombs, bullets, fire, oxygen starvation, or a fall from five miles up to a sudden total destruction on the ground.

According to Martin Caidin, author of *Flying Forts*, *"The 8th's planners worried their hair grey trying to resolve the complex and interwoven factors of the formidable German anti-aircraft defenses, the depth and efficiency of their radar and fighter-control operations, and the known skill and courage of the men who flew the German fighters."*

The 8th A.F. had been accustomed to shorter mission flights in the area of France, and targets close enough for gasoline reach, but the mission to Schweinfurt was special, and suspicion prevailed that German Intelligence, fore-warned of this chosen deep penetrating target into Germany, had alerted the Luftwaffe. The British, opposed the 8th A.F. decision to bomb by daylight, preferred to bombing under the stars, as the belief was that the darkness cloaked the RAF with a mantel of protection.

Yet there would come a night when a swarm of the huge four engine Lancasters would strike deep into Germany and lose ninety-six of the finest bomber design to take wing.

The daylight bombing campaign by the 8th A.F. continued in high precision raids on industrial targets to cut short the enemies resources, while the RAF destroyed cities in saturated raids.

The 8th Air Force led by General Ira C. Eaker believed that daylight bombing would be successful because he had information that the bombers had firepower to go alone without fighter escort. Experimentation with daylight bombing in night raids took place on the mission to Schweinfurt Germany, much to the chagrin of the British Air Marshal, Hugh Traichard and Prime Minister Churchill who wanted the 8th Air force to be disbanded to join the RAF. Immediately, a clamor arose in the A.F. High Command to breach a gap in losses of aircraft and trained airmen to continue the air-fight against the enemy as preparation for the continent invasion. General Eaker was determined to keep the 8th A.F. intact and not be integrated with the RAF. He convinced Churchill at Casablanca January 1944 that with the British bombing at night and the 8th A.F. bombing in daylight, he would have "Round the Clock" bombing. General Eaker's argument was a reprieve to continue with daylight bombing. This saved the day temporarily from 8th A.F. disbandment.

This kind of war had no foxholes or dugouts, no hedgerows or earthworks, no place to hide, no place to run. It was a far different kind of conflict than man had ever faced before.

Since the third phase of our training was cut from the schedule, the Lt. Jack Dunaway crew was transferred to the air base at Kearney, Nebraska to pick up a brand new B-17. Lt. Dunaway signed for the aircraft. The handwriting was on the wall.

Brother, Sot, was stationed at Lincoln, Nebraska Air Base not far from Kearney. He had graduated from OCS in Florida and was now a 2nd Lieutenant. I phoned Sot and made a quick trip for an overnight visit. The Red Cross recorded our voices on a plastic disk and mailed it to our folks in Haverhill.

We spent two days at Kearney, and I flew with the crew to Detroit in our new B17 where the crew was disbanded. Each crew member was assigned to an Air Transport Command (ATC) carrier for shipment to England as individual B-17 crew member replacements. Now it hit us why our training was cut short at Dalhart - the Air Force needed B-17 aircraft replacements and crew members immediately.

## CHAPTER 9
## Transition to the ETO

Lt. Ted Krol, Walter Rusch and I were to fly to Presque Isle, Maine and to Gander, Newfoundland with final destination, Scotland. On the way to Maine, I requested the ATC pilot to land at Grenier Air Base in Manchester, New Hampshire, so I could visit my home in Haverhill, Massachusetts, about thirty-five miles south.

The excuse given for landing at Grenier Air Base was a possible oil leak. As one could imagine, the ATC pilot and co-pilot were very accommodating. Upon landing, much to the pilot's surprise, one of the engines was actually leaking oil. It would take at least a day to make the repairs.

The ATC pilot requested an overnight pass for me to visit with my family, but the Base Commander refused, basing his decision on security reasons. Yet, everyone involved, including the ground crews knew that we were to participate in combat in the ETO. Since the crew was going into aerial combat with little chance of survival, all had prepared for the worst; hence, I told the C.O. that I would go AWOL (absent without leave) overnight without a pass. The C.O. threatened imprisonment if I went AWOL.

That night, I phoned brother, George, who was on the verge of enlisting, and George drove his car up to Manchester, NH, to pick me up. I spent the night with my family, and the next morning George brought me back to Grenier Air Base. Without an overnight pass, I was not allowed re-entry on base by the MP's. Fortune smiled on me as Lt. Ted Krol was spotted heading for his morning shower in the latrine building. He quickly smoothed the situation, and the MP's allowed me entry on base. With the oil leak repaired, and the C.O., much to his consternation, satisfied to reprimand me orally, the ATC Pilot and co-pilot were free to put the B-17 into the air.

On take-off I requested another favor of the pilot: "How about buzzing my home town in Haverhill?" The pilot honored my second request, making me very happy. He buzzed Haverhill, and my parents later told me that they saw the big B-17 with four distinctive sounding engines. Most inhabitants in this city of 50,000 had never seen a plane as big as this before. The excitement lasted several days.

The fun part over, the pilot pointed the ship's nose toward Presque Isle, Maine, where we RON-ed (Remained Overnight) and the next morning headed for Gander, Newfoundland. We landed at Gander on an ice-cold day, well below zero, and as soon as the engines were shut down, the heater trucks arrived to keep the engines and fluids from freezing overnight. A truck took us to the mess hall for a hot meal. While standing in the mess line, I felt a tap on my shoulder, and turned to see Arthur Mitchitson, a friend from Haverhill who was a permanent party at Gander and remained there for the war.

At mess, we met a Military Band, which had unknowingly been transported from Miami to Gander, still in summer khakis and without a change in clothing. They were highly "pissed."

The next day was not as cold but cold enough for ice-skating. Arthur and I borrowed a couple pair of ice skates and gave a try at a local lake.

We met two nice looking Newfoundland gals who were also on skates, but once they smiled us guys were taken aback as the gals had no teeth. The U.S. Army Air Force employed the girls, who were subject to employee physical examination. Apparently water in Newfoundland lacked the needed calcium, the ingredient necessary for maintaining strong teeth, and in order to be employed on the base they had to have their teeth extracted and replaced with issued dentures. This condition was prevalent with the majority of the local workers.

We stayed at Gander two days and guarded the aircraft day and night. Ready to fly, the next evening our plane lined up with a number of planes to take off for the flight across the Atlantic Ocean, with destination Prestwick, Scotland. The first plane taxied out to the runway and lifted for takeoff - an explosion and a huge ball of fire erupted. The B-17 blew up. All passengers and crew perished. The remainder of the flights were then cancelled for immediate stand-down inspection of all departing aircraft.

A British subject, a traitor, Lord Haw Haw, had a daily news program on German radio, and he announced that a German spy had infiltrated American defenses at Gander and successfully stored a bomb on that B-17 airplane; and all planes leaving Gander would fall to the same fate. The information that he broadcast was astounding, giving the name of each pilot and the number of aircraft for transport that day.

The stand-down inspection completed, heartbeats ran rapidly as again the planes lined up for take-off. This time all planes took to the air without mishap.

I was the only flyer in the plane's waist section, while Lt. Ted Krol flew up front with the pilot and co-pilot, on the upper deck just behind the cockpit. All machine-guns and ammunition had been removed from the aircraft, to allow for extra fuel to be brought on board for the long flight across the Atlantic Ocean. Walter Rusch was transferred to another plane for the flight.

It was a beautiful night. The moon and stars were out in their glory. Since I had no responsibility during the early stages of the trip, I read a *Reader's Digest* condensed version of Charles Lindbergh's first successful solo flight from New York to Paris nonstop. The name of the book was *We*. Actually he named the book *We* because there was another passenger, a mosquito. Rather than swat the mosquito that kept buzzing around his head, Lindy decided to have it keep him company. He credited the mosquito for keeping him awake during the long, lonely flight.

On nearing the completion of the flight, the pilot called me on the intercom, advising to keep a sharp eye for enemy planes. I was still alone and decided that the best vantage point for observation was in the tail section of the plane.

All went well and every B-17 flying out of Gander 19 December 1943 arrived at Prestwick, Scotland without incident. It was an uneventful and enjoyable trip for me to cross the Atlantic Ocean.

After short visits to Valley, Wales and to Stone, England, Lt. Dunaway and our crew were re-united and were assigned to the 612th Squadron, 401st Bomb Group, 94th Bomb Wing, 1st Division of the 8th Air Force headquartered at Deenethorpe, England, Station 128. I thought we were split-up forever. Deenethorpe, the most northerly Heavy Bomber Station of the 1st Division, was located east of Corby on high ground, south of Deenethorpe Village. The base had the standard AMDGW layout for a Class "A" heavy bomber airfield, with the usual 2000 and 1400 yard concrete runways with tarmac and wood chip surfacing. The USAAF standard for bomber stations was adhered to - two T2-type aircraft hangers and fifty hard stands for B-17 parking, spread around on the adjoining perimeter track.

The majority of the hard stands were in the shape of a frying pan. The main runway had been installed with Mark II airfield lighting equipment, and the campsite housing temporary buildings was located south of the airfield.

The 401st Bomb Group had moved onto the base at Deenethorpe in early November and began combat operations on 26 November 1943.

John Katsaros in Combat Gear, December 1943

General Henry H. "Hap" Arnold
Commanding General, U. S. Army Air Forces

General Henry H. "Hap" Arnold

Lt. General Ira C. Eaker
Former Commanding General, Eighth Air Force

General Ira C. Eaker.

Colonel Harold W. "Hal" Bowman, 401st Bombardment Group (H) Commander, Deenethorpe, England 1943-44

MAJOR GENERAL ROBERT B. WILLIAMS
*Former Commanding General, 1st Air Division*

Lt. General Robert B. Williams, Commander of the 1st Air Division, Eight Air Force, England 1943-44.

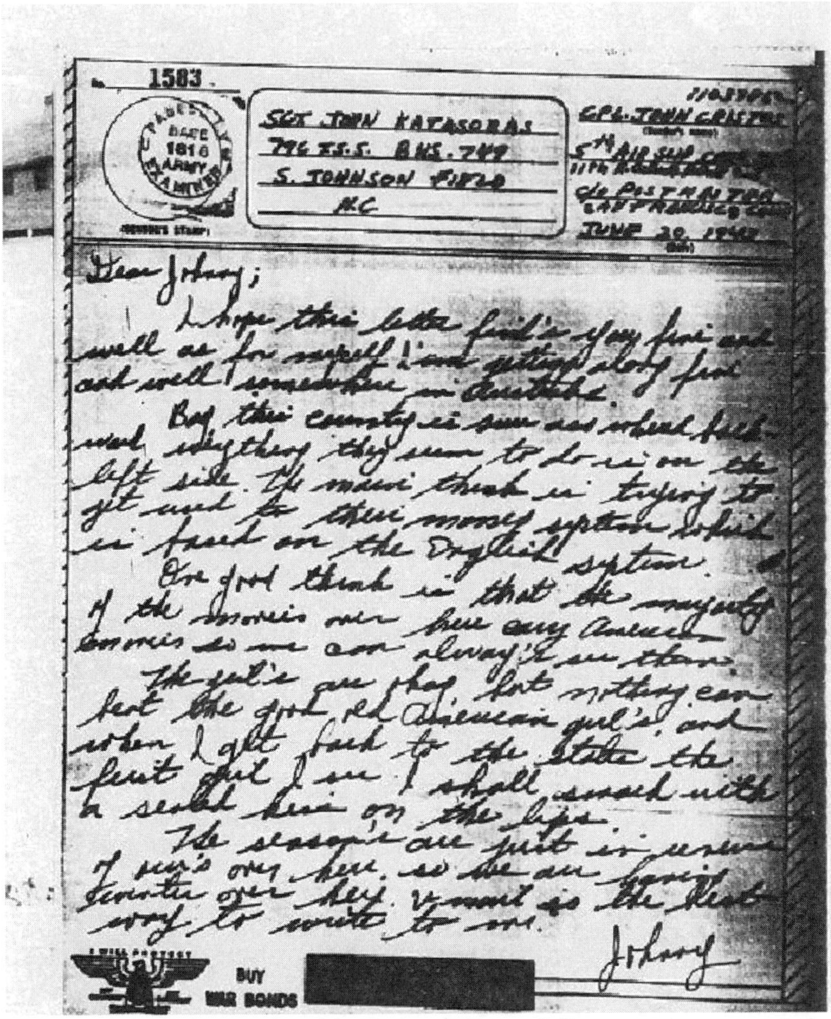

1583

PASSED BY ARMY EXAMINER 1816

SGT. JOHN KATASORAS
796 T.S.S. BKS. 749
S. JOHNSON FIELD
NC

CPL. JOHN CRISTOS
5th AIR SUP
c/o POSTMASTER
SAN FRANCISCO
JUNE 30, 1943

Dear Johny;

I hope this letter find's you fine and well as for myself I'm getting along fine and well somewhere in Australia.

Boy this country is sure ass wheel backward, why they they seem to do is on the left side. The main think is trying to get used to their money system which is based on the English system.

One good think is that the majority of the movies over here are American movies so we can always see them.

The girl's are okay but nothing can beat the good old American girl's, and when I get back to the States the first girl I see I shall smack with a sealed kiss on the lips.

The season's are just in reverse of our's over here, so we are having winter over here. V-mail is the best way to write to me.

Johny

BUY WAR BONDS [redacted]

A typical V-Mail letter reduced in size to conserve delivery storage space, during World War II. Note my cousin Cpl. John Cristos sent this V-Mail to me from an unnamed overseas location June 30, 1943, and it followed me to dozens of military installations before it reached my final station in Deenethorpe, England, December 1943, six months later.

The worst accident occurred in December 1943 when a Fortress, failing to lift off the ground, careened over the farmland and came to rest after crashing into a cottage on the edge of Deenethorpe village. The aircrew just had time to evacuate the wreckage and warn the villagers of the imminent explosion of the bomb load before it detonated, damaging many houses in the village. The blast was heard in Kettering, twelve miles away. None of the villagers was hurt.

ENTERTAINING PRIZE PUZZLE for Young Folks Page 3

Kettering Leader & Guardian

AND NORTHAMPTONSHIRE ADVERTISER

CZECHOSLOVAKS' PARTY TO LOCAL CHILDREN —Page 10

FOUNDED 1861. FRIDAY, DECEMBER 10, 1943 PRICE 2d.

# CRASHED U.S. AIRMEN SAVE VILLAGERS

## Deenethorpe Got Ten Minutes Warning Before Mighty Explosion

### MANY HOMES SHATTERED: ONLY ONE CASUALTY

The lovely Northamptonshire village of Deenethorpe, with its less than 100 inhabitants, escaped obliteration on Sunday morning by nothing short of a miracle.

**An American Flying Fortress, with its heavy bomb load of 6,000 lbs., crashed into the village, where ten minutes meant the difference between life and death for the inhabitants.**

The bomber had caught a tree and crashed full tilt into a cottage on the edge of the village of Deenethorpe. This fortunately was unoccupied, and the crash reduced it to a mass of rubble all in a moment.

Old Lady Saved

One Almighty Bang

Calf Halved

Firemen Injured

Saved Comrades

VETERINARY COD LIVER OIL MIXTURE

DEENETHORPE DISASTER (Continued from Page 1)

Prompt U.S. Aid

Ernest Woodcock Ltd of Kettering

CHRISTMAS GIFTS

— COUPON FREE

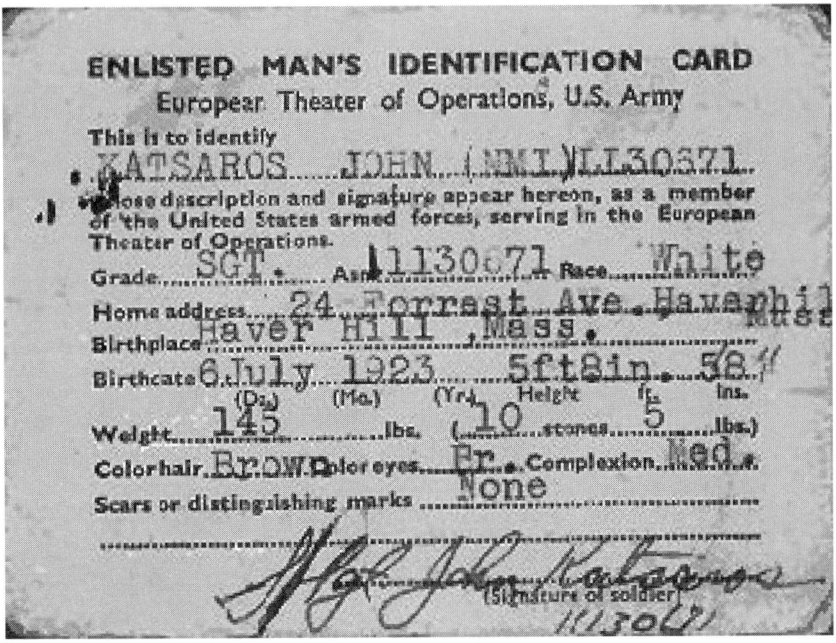

ENLISTED MAN'S IDENTIFICATION CARD

European Theater of Operations, U.S. Army

This is to identify

KATSAROS JOHN (NMI) 11130671

whose description and signature appear hereon, as a member of the United States armed forces, serving in the European Theater of Operations.

Grade SGT. ASN 11130671 Race White

Home address 24 Forrest Ave. Haverhill Mass

Birthplace Haver Hill, Mass.

Birthdate 6 July 1923 5ft8in. 58"
(Da.) (Mo.) (Yr.) Height ft. ins.

Weight 145 lbs. (10 stones 5 lbs.)

Color hair Brown Color eyes Br. Complexion Med.

Scars or distinguishing marks None

S/Sgt. John Katsaros
(Signature of soldier)
11130671

# CHAPTER 10
## Mission Briefing

At Deenethorpe, formation flying was practiced as required for bomber safety, strength in defensive machine-gun protection, and superior bomb pattern on target. The C.O., satisfied with the B-17 formation flying, gave the gunners opportunity to get in some air-to-ground firing with the .50 caliber machine-guns down at the "Wash", a summer beach resort. The crews were now combat ready.

The four officers on the Lt. Jack Dunaway crew, pilot, co-pilot, navigator and bombardier were housed in a Nissen hut, that had a concrete foundation and a round steel roof. The non-commissioned officers, the G.I.'s, had their own Nissen hut, housing eighteen aircrew men. A potbelly stove with a few pieces of coal provided the heat. Extra blankets were needed to keep warm. Coal was in short supply and was considered a luxury item but the English, a hardy people, kept a stiff upper lip, evoking great admiration and respect for the English from the American G.I.

A typical day of a usually tough combat mission was similar to our crew's first of three combat missions to Frankfurt, Germany. It began around 0400 hours, when a whistle was blown by the CQ (Charge of Quarters) who awakened the crew calling out names to report for duty. A truck ride to the mess hall for breakfast of real eggs and milk was always scheduled before every mission. On non-mission days it was powdered eggs and powdered milk. Not a tasty meal.

After breakfast the crew was trucked to a large Nissen hut with all the aircrews scheduled to fly that day for mission briefing. The 401st Bomb Group consisted of four Squadrons: The 612th , 613th , 614th and 615th. Each squadron scheduled nine or ten air worthy B-17's for the mission of the day, and when all assembled as a group totaled between thirty-six and forty aircraft.

Between three-hundred and sixty and four hundred officers and enlisted men were seated until the Commanding Officer of the group, usually Colonel Harold Bowman, entered the hut. The combat crews were called to attention and briefing for the day's mission began with a "Good morning, men."

Behind the C.O. was a map of Europe with a drawn shade cover. The mission route and target were visibly exposed when the C.O. raised the shade cover. A red ribbon indicated the flight path to target, and a red arrow pointed to the city of the selected target. Today, the target was an aircraft factory in Frankfurt, Germany. The intelligence officer briefed the group on enemy fighter expectations and the kind of strength of the ground anti-aircraft fire from .88 mm guns. The weather officer gave a briefing on the weather at take-off, the route weather, and the weather to expect at the target. Lastly, the C.O. revealed the type of installations to be attacked - a munitions factory, ball bearing plant, an aircraft factory, supply depot, an aerodrome or railroad yard. The targets were plentiful and are passed down to Division Headquarters from the 8th Air Force.

Each mission was flown to bomb military targets of war resources and not specifically to bomb German cities or the people. Of course, there was always the accidental collateral damage.

After the group briefing each crew member was issued a parachute, wired underwear for heat, a flak vest, and a "Mae West". A "Mae West" was a yellow inflatable floatation device to keep a water-ditched airman afloat for rescue. Each flyer had his own oxygen mask, heavy fleece-lined jacket, pants and boots. I snagged an English type chute, for which, later I was thankful to be wearing.

My faith is Greek Orthodox Christian and, during WWII, the Army gave recognition only to Catholic, Protestant and Judaism religions. My dog tags were stamped Catholic, so I decided to receive absolution before every mission from the Catholic chaplain, Major Joseph H. Burke, a Catholic priest in civilian life, from Haverhill, Massachusetts (as I was to learn some sixty years later, in a book *Guardian Angel* by Captain Paul Campbell, a pilot with the 615th Squadron.) Together with his junior partner, Captain Ward J. Fellows, the Protestant chaplain, they arose at 0300 hours each morning the group scheduled a mission, and rode their bicycles a mile to the briefing room. After the briefing, they witnessed the take-off and at the appropriate time, the return of the aircraft from their life-threatening mission.

Catholic Chaplain Major Joseph H. Burke and Protestant chaplain Captain Ward J. Fellows.

Catholic Chaplain, Major Joseph H. Burke, of Haverhill, MA

After picking up their flight gear, the airmen are trucked, as a crew, to their assigned aircraft for this mission, for as a replacement crew, they do not have a B-17 to call their own. My job, as assistant engineer, was to pre-flight the aircraft; check all visible parts and inspect to insure that the fuel tanks are filled. Each crew member was given a specific pre-flight job to accomplish and lastly the pilot and co-pilot followed through with a double check of the total aircraft.

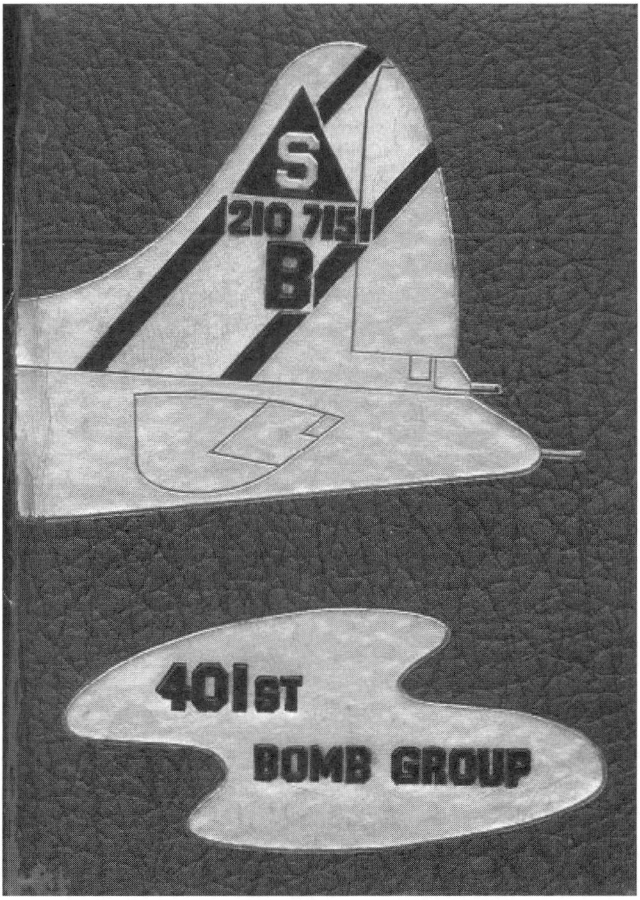


Triangle "S" Tail Insignia

612th BOMBARDMENT SQUADRON

A formation of B-17s, a bomb and the official Air Corps wings form the background for this insignia. This is the second insignia adopted by the 612th. The first contained a replica of "Mangler", squadron mascot.

612th BOMBARDMENT SQUADRON
A formation of B-17s, a bomb and the official Air Corps wings form the background for this insignia. This is the second insignia adopted by the 612th. The first contained a replica of "Mangler", squadron mascot.

613th BOMBARDMENT SQUADRON
Drawn by the famed cartoonist, Walt Disney, this "punching bomb" is symbolic of a squadron which was "always right in there, punching!"

614th BOMBARDMENT SQUADRON
"Lucky Devil's" head design originated with Mrs. J. J. Casagrande, wife of the squadron's first navigator, later a Prisoner of War in Germany.
All insignia officially approved.

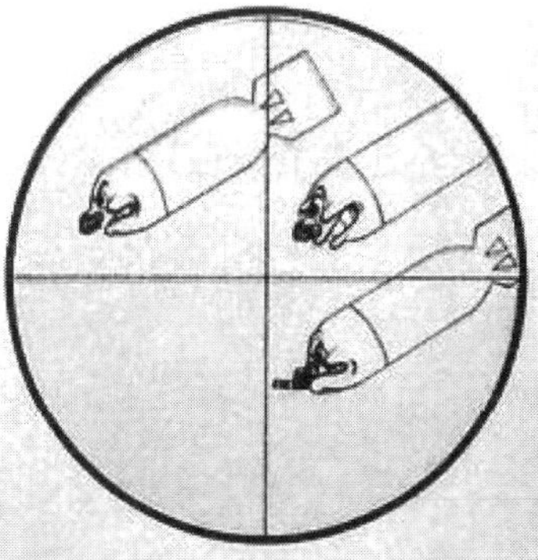

615th BOMBARDMENT SQUADRON
These angry bombs come from the pen of Milt Caniff, author of "Terry and the Pirates" and "Male Call". Faces represent Roosevelt, Churchill, Stalin.

Other Squadron Insignias - These were officially approved.

A-2 leather jackets with air-crew art.

Bottom R. "Lt. "Bid" Fitchett wearing his A-2

CREW MEMBERS CHECKING OUT EQUIPMENT

SGT. CHARLES R. WARELE helps Lt. J
Evans, navigator, don his parachute, flak s
Mae West, etc.

## Equipment Room

CPL. Wm. J. BARLOW stores flak suits in the fliers individual bins.

CPL. FRED W. GRESCHENZ hangs electr
heated flying suits on the racks to dry
locker room.

## CHAPTER 11
## Mission to Frankfurt, Germany

On the early morning of 11 February 1944, Pilot Jack Dunaway and the crew of *Man O' War* sat through mission profiling as we prepared ourselves mentally for our first combat experiences - to carry destruction to an aircraft factory at Frankfurt, Germany.

The aircrew and I performed the pre-flight checkout procedures and boarded the aircraft, then the pilot and co-pilot went through the pilot check-list, started the engines and warmed them up to check their operation. Engines running smoothly, the aircraft was taxied to the runway and lined up as to pre-arranged instructions, prepared to take-off. The engines were revved up and the aircraft waited for the "go" signal from the tower. One behind the other, in thirty second intervals, the planes took to the runway, lifted into the air and assembled, like a flock of geese into the "V" flying formation at the predetermined low level. Once the formation organized, the lead plane took the formation up to flying en-route altitude.

The group, in formation, flew to 2900 feet over the English Channel, and when halfway across the Channel, the pilot gave his OK to test-fire the .50 caliber machine-guns, weighing sixty-five pounds and expelling 15 rounds per second. The knowledge of this information became very evident. The .50 caliber was mounted in the waist window on a gun mount, using a gun mount adapter. Apparently, I did not properly check out the gun mounting, and when the weapon was test-fired, the recoil hit me in the chest, knocking me on my ass. What a shock! The gun also fell back onto the floor and was pointed directly at Marvin Benz, the tail gunner. Instinctively, I recovered from my knockdown and flipped on the gun safety button, stopping a possible runaway machine-gun. This action averted killing the tail gunner, or destroying the plane and other planes in the formation. Faulty installation of the gun adapter by the armorer could have caused an irreparable catastrophe. The fright tapered down, I secured the gun properly to the gun mount using the gun adapter. The coast of France came into view. Whew! That was a scare! In retrospect, there was failure to inspect for proper gun mount installation.

*Gamoto* (Damn) "*Mea culpa*," say I to myself.

Now, my concentration was put on the mission, the enemy guns and the warplanes. Soon enough reality awakened the crew as 88mm guns began pounding the sky, putting up black plumes of smoke as the anti-aircraft timer shells began exploding all around the ship. Sometimes, the flak cloud was so thick; it resembled a carpet to walk on. The German artillery units included female gunners who were also excellent at their jobs.

The flak stops. Within minutes, the German fighter aircraft, line abreast in formation, for maximum firepower, attacked the formation of heavy bombers. This was their first pass, as they came back, in single file to select and take down individual bombers. On one such occasion, an FW-190 on a pass by my window lined up for a straight short burst from my .50 caliber, hitting the tail section. The tail exploded. I saw smoke and the tail gunner saw smoke. The fighter suffered some damage and did not return to re-engage our guns. No credit for shooting a fighter down was given unless someone saw his plane crash or the pilot bail-out.

The I.P. (Initial Point) was the turning point of the flight path to the target because the bomb run was never directly to the target; this kept the enemy off guard as to direction of the final bomb run. The I.P. came up and from this turning point onto the bomb run the ack-ack guns gave us a welcome with a barrage of flak. No serious damage to the aircraft and no crew members were hurt, but the flak was high, accurate and intense, fracturing nerves.

*Man O' War*'s combat experience was initiated on this bombing mission. Heavy enemy anti-air 88mm batteries trained their sights to shoot the bombers down over the target area with as many as 1500 guns sighted in box formation to the altitude of 20,000 to 27,000 feet, as radioed by their fighters. The bombers, empty of their bombs, assembled in a staggered formation, enabling the gunners to train their .50 caliber machine-guns at the attacking German fighter planes.

I spot a bomber in a spin down below off my right side and tell the pilot. "Any chutes?" "Yes sir, I count six." "Keep your eye on them for more." When all crewmen were on oxygen, my job, at altitudes over 10,000 feet was to periodically check by intercom with each crew member on his oxygen supply function. Minutes before the I.P. I checked with the tail gunner but got no answer. I looked to the tail section and saw Marvin Benz slumped over. I sensed an emergency situation with Benz and called on the intercom to the pilot who agreed that I should crawl back to the tail section with a 10 minute oxygen bottle to assess the situation.

19 February 1944 Commendation reads:

*1. While flying on the operational mission to Frankfurt, Germany, on 11 February 1944, Sgt. John (NMI) Katsaros, left waist gunner, was called on the interphone and asked to check the tail gunner, who had not answered. The A/C, #9979, Was then at 27,000 feet and about 20 minutes before the I.P. Sgt. Katsaros carrying a walk-around bottle, found the tail gunner unconscious and with his mask off. Sgt. Katsaros gave him emergency oxygen and attempted artificial respiration. While making these attempts, the oxygen supply in the walk-around bottle gave out, since it had previously been used by the other waist gunner who was not sure of his main oxygen system. Sgt. Katsaros had to go to the waist to secure another bottle. When the tail gunner, suffering from anoxia, was partially revived, he became temporarily crazed and resisted efforts of Sgt Katsaros to assist him. Sgt. Katsaros was forced to wrestle with him for from (5) to ten (10) minutes. The pilot then ordered the navigator, Lt. William G. Mock, to go back to the tail to help. Lt. Mock and Sgt. Katsaros finally fully revived the tail gunner. By this time, however, the aircraft's oxygen supply had been dangerously depleted, and the supply in the tail was exhausted. Not being sure that the interphone system functioned properly, Sgt. Katsaros made his way forward without oxygen to inform the pilot. It became necessary to pass bottles to the rear from the forward part of the ship. In this action the radio operator and other members of the crew took part.*

1. *In spite of the above mentioned difficulties, Lt. Dunaway and his crew bombed the target and returned safely from enemy territory. This was the first combat mission for Lt. Dunaway's crew.*
2. *The devotion to duty and the determination to do their assigned job by these crew members is exemplary. It is desired that this commendation be included in the permanent records.*

*A True Copy -John M. Weidner, Captain, MAC Registrar*
*Jere W. Maupin, Capt. Air Corps, Commanding*

The emergency is further developed in the following citation awarded to John Katsaros. This is a copy of the original document.

612TH BOMB SQUADRON (H)
401ST BOMB GROUP (H)
AAF STATION 128

19 February 1944.

SUBJECT: Commendation of Crew Members.

TO : Commanding Officer, 401st Bomb Group (H), APO 634, U. S. Army.

1. While flying on the operational mission to Frankfurt, Germany, on 11 February 1944, Sgt. John (nmi) Katsaros, left waist gunner, was called on the interphone and asked to check the tail gunner, who had not answered. The A/C, #9979, was then at 27,000 feet and about 20 minutes before the I.P. Sgt. Katsaros carrying a walk-around bottle, found the tail gunner unconscious and with his mask off. Sgt. Katsaros gave him emergency oxygen and attempted artificial respiration. While making these attempts, the oxygen supply in the walk-around bottle gave out, since it had previously been used by the other waist gunner who was not sure of his main oxygen system. Sgt. Katsaros had to go to the waist to secure another bottle. When the tail gunner, suffering from anoxia, was partially revived, he became temporarily crazed and resisted the efforts of Sgt. Katsaros to assist him. Sgt. Katsaros was forced to wrestle with him for from five (5) to ten (10) minutes. The pilot then ordered the navigator, Lt. William G. Mock, to go back to the tail to help. Lt. Mock and Sgt. Katsaros finally fully revived the tail gunner. By this time, however, the aircraft's oxygen supply had been dangerously depleted, and the supply in the tail was exhausted. Not being sure that the interphone system functioned properly, Sgt. Katsaros made his way forward without oxygen to inform the pilot. It became necessary to pass bottles to the rear from the forward part of the ship. In this action the radio operator and other members of the crew took part.

2. In spite of the above mentioned difficulties, Lt. Dunaway and his crew bombed the target and returned safely from enemy territory. This was the first combat mission for Lt. Dunaway's crew.

3. The devotion to duty and the determination to do their assigned job by these crew members is exemplary. It is desired that this commendation be included in their permanent records.

JERRY W. MAUPIN,
Capt., Air Corps,
Commanding.

A TRUE COPY:

JOHN M. WEIDNER
Captain, MAC
Registrar

## CHAPTER 12
## Combat De-Briefing and Interrogation

The mission over and crews returned to base, we were all trucked to the briefing room for debriefing and, as individual crews, were interrogated by an intelligence officer. A double shot of scotch, set up by Captain Charles C. Henrie, medical officer, was offered to each crew member, for medical purposes, as a nerve settler, and to put feet back on terra firma.

The purpose of the interrogation was to learn about the experiences of the crew coming in contact with the enemy, i.e. the make and number of fighter aircraft, the attack procedures used, the observed competence of the enemy fighter pilots, and the location and the intensity of the flak. Observations were given of the condition of the group formation under fire, aircraft hit and falling out of formation, parachutes and ground location seen in the air, and a multitude of incidents seen with the naked eye, as radio silence was maintained over enemy territory. The K-20, K-24 and movie cameras containing the exposed film were turned over to an intelligence officer.

Exhausted, we returned to our Nissen hut for a much needed rest. Suddenly and without warning one of the gunners in our hut started rambling and waving his .45 cal. pistol around. We had no idea of what his intentions were when suddenly the weapon fires and the bullet penetrated the metal roof of the hut. I pulled my .45 from under my pillow, pointed my weapon at him and ordered him to drop the gun. He began to sob and cry and put the gun down on the bed. We notified the Military Police (MP's) who came and escorted him to the base hospital for observation. It appeared that the hazard of flying bombing missions had got to him, and he would not fly again, permanently grounded. I never saw this airman again.

In the event that the primary target could be reached or was not visible due to cloud cover, a secondary target was always given. The crew's first mission to Berlin as the primary target was deviated to the secondary targets at Kiel and Wilhelmshaven, Germany because of low oxygen supply.

The second mission to Berlin as the primary target was deviated to the secondary target, an aircraft factory at Augsburg, Germany, makers of the ME-109 fighter.

The temperature at altitudes of 25,000 to 30,000 feet reached between -60 and -70 degrees Fahrenheit (below zero). The so called waist windows on each side of the aircraft fuselage were uncovered openings where the .50 caliber machine-guns were mounted, and there was no shelter from the weather at those altitudes and without wind deflectors on the windows, the gunner was at mercy of the winds. Many times the gunners in the waist section of the aircraft wound up in the hospital with frozen limbs, hands, toes, feet, and exposed body parts.

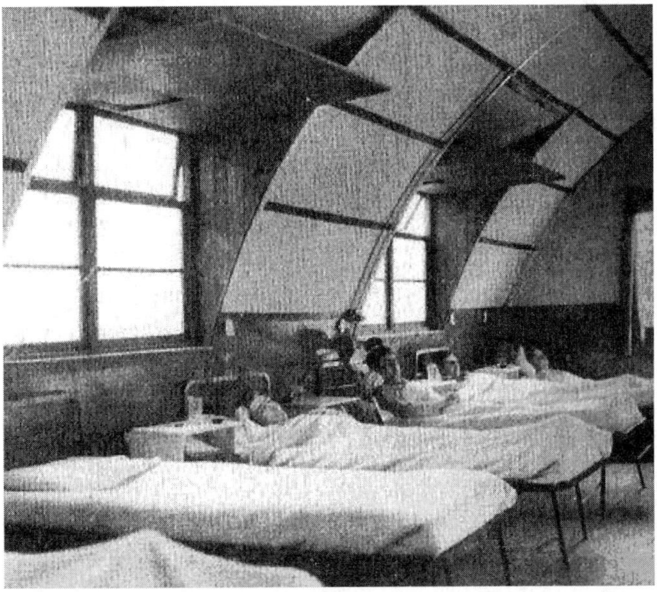

Walter Rusch and I were treated for frozen hands and feet, after a Feb 1944 bombing mission to Germany, at this 401stBomb Group Hospital.

401st Bomb Group, 612th Squadron, release bombs on target.

John at Right Waist Gun window.

Walking over the narrow B-17 bomb bay catwalk, circa 2007.

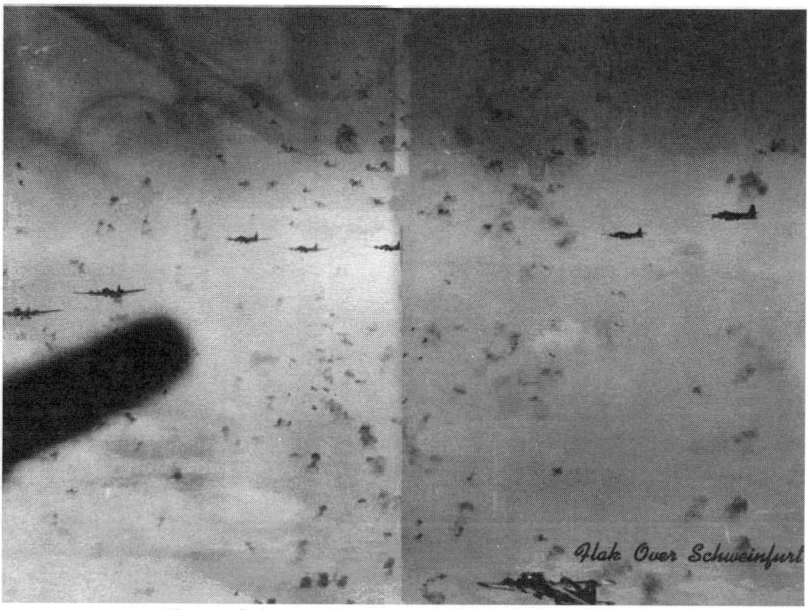


Heavy flak over the target at Schweinfurt, Germany.

FW-190 similar to the one I damaged on my first mission to Frankfurt, Germany.

How did we ever fly in the B-17 ball turret?

K-24 Camera Gunners/photographers take still pictures on combat missions.

# NISSEN HUT "ART" GALLERIES

Nissen Hut "Art" Galleries.

BOMBERS BACK TO BLIGHTY AFTER BLIGHTING BOCHE—These flyers have just returned from a successful bombing operation over Germany. They are awaiting a jeep which will take them to the interrogation where they will enjoy "java and sinkers" while being questioned.

Bombers Back To Blighty After Blighting Boche -These flyers have just returned from a successful bombing operation over Germany. They are awaiting a jeep which will take them to the interrogation where they will enjoy “java and sinkers” while being questioned.

## BOMBER CREWS CONCERNS
**By Martin Caidin**

*Excerpt from the book, "Flying Forts", by Martin Caidin, will give you an insight into the life experiences of B-17 airmen on a mission to "Hell".*

*"The Flying Fortress was a big airplane. But, it was not one in which its crew could find comfort. It was a machine for making war; comfort took last place in the requirements for the combat mission. It was a noisy airplane, insulated only in a limited area in the forward section. It was bitterly cold inside, not only from the ambient cold at high altitude but because of the knife-like winds that stabbed through every narrow opening. Guns jutted from the open hatches. Bomb bay doors leaked and were often open. It's bad enough to be exposed to cold that would drop as far as 75 and 80 below zero; its worse when the wind shrieks demon-like and turns the cold to cruel pain.*

*Filled with the implements for waging war, the Fortress presented the crew with a maze of sharp projections and nasty objects against which one often stumbled and brushed. Even with the four big propellers synchronized perfectly there was so much equipment, from machine-guns to radio and oxygen bottles that it couldn't help but rattle and vibrate within. After a while the crews never felt it; it was the sound of flight and it became second nature. At high altitude, even without combat, every man was remote from his airplane despite his being linked through umbilical cords to its very fiber. A man didn't touch a part of that plane with his naked skin. That isn't wise with the temperature down to forty - eighty degrees below zero. In that cold simply exposing the hands to the ambient air can be disastrous. Placing raw skin against metal at that sub-zero temperature can mean leaving a patch of skin on the metal and drawing back bloody flesh. The crews were bundled in cumbersome, bulky flight garments, electrically heated, (Quite often the heated suits did not work subjecting the crews to frostbite); heavy fleece trousers with leather on the outside; jackets, boots, gloves, helmets; goggles to hold off the screaming wind, to keep a man's eyes from tearing when he most needs his vision.*

*A man in his flight attire was a clumsy, bear-like creature. His parachute strapped over and around his body, heavy, binding and often distressingly uncomfortable, didn't make matters any better. And then there were the leads to connect oxygen masks on the face, strapped tightly, cutting against the skin to prevent the precious oxygen from escaping when a man needed it most. The mask plugged through a hose into the airplane, electrical leads to the heated flying suit, leads for radio and intercom to be plugged in. Symbiosis of ten men and one machine.*

*Those leads were life itself. Strange then that these men should be unable to secure themselves tightly to the machine to prevent stumbling, falling or being hurtled about. A bomber in combat can be a wild and flailing creature. There are air currents to begin with. Bursts of flak mean concussion, sharp blows of air rammed to the strength of steel. In formation flying, there is turbulence from all those propellers ahead, flailing the air with thousands of horsepower.*

*There are ten men in a Flying Fortress. In combat only two of them are seated, the pilot and the co-pilot to his right. That's all, just those two. Strapped in a seat belt and shoulder harness, they are snuggled tightly to the machine. But only they, who must be certain that they are not blown away by explosion or other disaster from the controls.*

*Ten men crewed the B-17E and its successors. In the nose, during battle, the bombardier and the navigator crouched like animals at bay, each grasping a heavy machine gun. Directly behind and slightly above them were the pilots. Immediately behind the pilots was the flight engineer top-turret gunner, standing in his complicated nest of steel and Plexiglas and machine-guns. Behind this man, past the bomb bays, stood the radio operator, leaning back awkward in his stance, swinging a heavy machine-gun through an aperture in the fuselage, trying to sight on fighters high above and slightly aft. And immediately behind and beneath him, the ball-turret gunner, bent into a half-ball of human stuffed into his round world of a power turret, his feet on level with his ears, his bottom the lowest part of the airplane. Still further back within the fuselage were the two waist gunners, two men who lived and fought from within a tubular world, with the walls, floor and ceiling made of thin metal skin and it's supporting heavy ribs that completely encircled them. Finally, the tail gunner kneeling and sighting enemy fighters behind twin .50 caliber machine guns.*

*After an encounter with the enemy fighters, the waist floor would be littered with the rain of empty machine gun shell casings, making the floor a hazardous walking place. Back at the tail section, the tail gunner neither stands nor sits, but crouches, like a roll-up, as he rests on his knees to see to the outside and fire his twin .50 caliber guns.*

*The Fortress was the most rugged bomber ever built, but with an easy push a man could jab a screwdriver right through the thin metal that made up the skin of the airplane. Strength in the B-17 came from outstanding design.*

*Ten men in a machine five miles above the earth - sitting, standing, crouching, curled-up, and kneeling - that's how they fought the war, with winds up to 300 MPH in open gun positions.*

*The B-17's two waist guns each had 300 rounds of .50 caliber ammunition and the chin had 365 rounds. When the B-17 G arrived, the waist carried 900 rounds and the chin, 964 rounds. The B-17 G had a total fire power of 5770 rounds of .50 caliber ammunition and the B-17 G, when fully loaded, had a service ceiling of 35,000 feet with a much heavier bomb load than its predecessors along with many other improvements. Most of our combat missions were flown at around 200 M.P.H. with the open waist windows.*

*The B-17-F is tight on space, designed only for workstations and under conditions of stress when body maneuverability is necessary, care must be taken to prevent personal injury.*

*Bomber fighter protection by the 8th Air Force included the P-47 Thunderbolt that became operational in mid-October 1943 but its radius of action, 340 miles, limited its usefulness for long range, deep penetrating B-17 bombers. The P-38 Lightning, with its identifiable twin fuselage, a very effective fighter, capable of an extended range of 520 miles from home base, was greatly respected by the German Luftwaffe; the P-51 Mustang became the most favored escort because of its long range, 800 miles from base, and its great speed, maneuverability and climbing power."*

## MARTIN CAIDEN'S *FLYING FORTS*

In his book, *Flying Forts*, Martin Caiden wrote as follows:

*"The break in the weather came on the 19th February 1944, and air planners hurried to put into effect their long-delayed Project ARGUMENT, "a series of coordinated precision attacks by the Eighth and Fifteenth Air*

*Forces against the highest-priority objectives, most of which by February 1944 were situated in central and southern Germany. The RAF agreed to make its night area attacks coincide with the daylight missions both in time and place." The first assault was scheduled for the 20th February 1944.*

*That morning sixteen combat wings of heavy bombers rose like gigantic locusts over England and assembled into strike formations. More than one thousand heavy bombers took off of which 941 arrived over their targets. The RAF provided short-range escort with sixteen squadrons of Spitfires and Mustangs, while seventeen groups of American fighters -thirteen P-47's Thunderbolts, two P-38's Lightning's, and two P-51's Mustangs - flew with the bombers. Fighter escort for maximum range went to the bombers that would strike targets in central Germany, normally those most heavily defended. In all, the heavy bombers blasted no less than twelve targets critical to the aircraft industry of the Reich. The preparations were carried out with exhaustive care. The night before the big raid the British slammed Leipzig with a roaring assault, not only tearing up great parts oj the city but also wearing out much of the night fighter force that would have been available to hit the Fortresses and Liberators. The routes were carefully chosen, the fighter escort assigned studiously, so that those fighters of shortest range were able to return to England, refuel, and take off at once to provide withdrawal escort for the returning bombers.*

*The mission proved to be an outstanding success. On 14th October 1943, against Schweinfurt, sixty bombers out of 257 were shot down. On 11th January 1944, out of 651 bombers carrying out sorties against multiple targets, another sixty bombers went down. Now, on the 20th of February, attacking many of the same targets, a force of almost one thousand bombers suffered losses of twenty-one heavies, barely two percent of the attackers. Even more cheering was the confirmation that a staggering blow, accomplished through excellent and accurate bombing, had been dealt the production capabilities of Germany's aircraft industry.*

*For the 23rd, the Eighth was assigned six major cities, as targets, while the Fifteenth would go after Regensburg. One major part of the B-17 force from England ran into trouble immediately. So severe was the weather over their fields that rendezvous and assembly of formations became impossible, and when several bombers collided in the air the bombers were ordered back to the fields. Many Fortress formations on that day were decreased from their planned sizes because of weather. The Liberators were strung out badly. The Fortresses from Italy found themselves facing German fighter forces much stronger than had been expected - mainly because the planned heavy strikes to the north had been so weak. The fighter escort had its own devil of a time trying to provide cover to bombers that had made a mockery of assembly points and of timetables.*

*This was the opening blow of a massive strategic operation that gained fame as the "Big Week". The Eighth had been prepared to accept losses as high as two hundred bombers for the first mission of the 20th February - and lost but a tenth of that number in return for spectacularly effective results of the bombings.*

*The next day another mighty force rose from England. Hopes for multiple blows, with the Fifteenth and Ninth Air Forces adding their weight to that of the Eighth, were thwarted by weather. On the night of 20/21 February the British came through with a terrifying strike by six hundred heavies against Stuttgart. The morning of the 22nd, despite the severe weather, the Eighth went out again in strength of nearly a thousand bombers. The weather frustrated the hopes for another decisive blow against the Reich; crews took solace by plastering secondary targets with high bomb concentrations.*

*The result was bitter fighting. In a long running battle the German fighters shot down forty-one bombers out of the 430 heavies of the Eighth that were credited with combat sorties. The Fifteenth lost another fourteen bombers, bringing the German score for the day to fifty-five. But the*

*American fighters, for their part, "had a field day." For a loss of eleven American fighters, they shot down at least sixty of the enemy.*

*On the 24th excellent fighter protection showed its worth in quality but lacking in quantity. Mustering all its available strength ("The Luftwaffe had all their planes up but their trainers," a gunner reported afterward.) The German Air Force struck with furious intensity against the many formations hitting widely dispersed targets throughout Germany. The task force of eighty-seven Fortresses that hit Steyr lost eleven. Sixty-one bombers had gone down in battle. The fighters, often outnumbered by the enemy, lost ten of their own and shot down thirty-seven German fighters; bomber gunners had claimed 108 kills. And, once again, there was no way of knowing how many fighters had been shot down by the bombers that were lost. On the 25th the Eighth and Fifteenth put up some 1,300 bombers, plus fighters sent out with the Eighth from England. Making the longest penetrations of the Big Week, they ran into heavy opposition despite strong fighter escort. The Fifteenth sent out 400 bombers, of which 176 made the deep penetrations to the Regensburg area. This force took a beating with thirty-three bombers- nearly twenty percent of the strike force - shot down. The Eighth had 738 bombers credited with sorties and lost thirty-one oj their number, a percentage more to the liking of those who flew the mission.*

*The 25th February was the end of the Big Week. The next day the weather closed in over most of the bomber bases. It would remain bad for another month. In the meantime the crews rested and the strategic forces built up their strength.*

*A study of the Big Week produced impressive and satisfying figures. Most of these have been derived from German as well as American sources. First, the 8th Air Force, flying out of England on these five missions sent up more than 3,300 bombers, and the 15thAir Force, flying out of Italy, put another 500 heavy bombers into the air for a combined tonnage of bombs dropped on assigned targets.*

*The 3,800 bombers had hit their main targets dropped a tonnage roughly equal to the total bomb tonnage dropped by the Eighth Air Force in its entire year of operations - approximately 10,000 tons of bombs. Planners had expected losses to be heavy; they were considerably less than anticipated. The Eighth AF lost 137 bombers and the Fifteenth AF another eighty-nine, producing an overall loss ratio of about six percent of the strike armadas. Fighters from the Eighth, Ninth and Fifteenth Air Force flew, respectively, 2,548, 712 and 413 escort missions.*

*Twenty-eight fighters were shot down. Approximately 2,600 men were lost -taking into account killed, missing and seriously wounded. Added to the totals produced by these five heavy raids, the British during this same period sortied 2,351 of the giant RAF night bombers and dropped 9,198 (US) tons of bombs. Their losses were 157 bombers -about 6.6 percent oj the attack forces. "This figure", notes the AAF, "Slightly higher than that of American losses, is most interesting in the light of earlier estimates of the relative costs of day verses night bombings."*

The U.S. Strategic Bombing Survey, after ransacking German sources, estimates that the 4,000-odd tons of bombs dropped on targets in the aircraft industrial system alone damaged or destroyed 75 percent of the buildings in plants that at the time accounted for 90 percent of the total German production of aircraft. The immediate reaction in the industry was one of consternation as they looked for better protection by the Luftwaffe. The German authorities, whose plans had hitherto rested on unduly optimistic foundations, now apparently for the first time showed signs of desperation, As a result of the bombing, the aircraft industry in late February received a formal order to disperse its plants...also bombings helped to precipitate a crisis in the overall organization of aircraft production which culminated in the shifting of responsibility from German General Hermann Goering's Air Ministry to a special agency operating within the Ministry of Armaments and Munitions headed by Albert Speer. The February campaign would have paid off even if it's only effect had been to force the enemy into an intensive program of dispersal. For that program not only accounted indirectly for much wasted effort and production loss, it also left the industry vulnerable to any serious disruption in transportation. The dispersal policy did, in fact, defeat itself when Allied bombers subsequently turned to an intensive attack on transportation. There is reason to believe that the large and fiercely fought battles of those six days, 20-25 February 1944, had more effect in establishing the air superiority on which Allied plans so largely depended than did the bombing of industrial plants. Claims of enemy aircraft destroyed amounted to a tremendous total, with more than a third of these victories credited to then fighter escort and roughly another third to the bombers of the Fifteenth Air Force, which enjoyed no long-range escort.

The simultaneous raids to Regensburg to take out the aircraft factory and to Schweinfurt to take out the ball bearing plant on 20 October 1943 cost the 8th Air Force 60 bombers and 600 airmen that day and became known as "Black Thursday". During "Big Week" 20-25 February 1944, the 15th Air Force lost 90 aircraft and over 900 airmen. The summer of 1944, the 8th Air force sent up 2100 bombers and lost 900 aircraft with 9000 airmen, totaling 42.9% loss. During the same period, the 15thAir Force's losses totaled 1100 bombers and 11,000 airmen a figure higher than the 8th AF. In July alone, targeting the oil refineries at Ploesti, the 15thAF dropped 13,469 tons of bombs, denying the Reich of 1.8 million tons of crude oil at a cost of 350 bombers and over 3500 airmen. Between June and October 1944 with the new P-51 pursuit plane providing escort to the B-17 and B-24's, the Luftwaffe lost 70% of their fighters to the P-51 and the bomber gunners. It was a bloody air war not only for air superiority but for survival of the invasion.

The movie, *12 O'clock High*, depicted the heavy losses in bomber aircraft in the 8th AF and collapse of discipline due to the loss of morale. Yes, discipline was not "gung ho", spit and polish, but morale is in the character of the men and they are aware that the lives of hundreds of thousands of men in the Army who are preparing for the mighty invasion of the European Continent depends on their recapture of air supremacy. When an air crew went out to the flight line and boarded their aircraft, they knew that they had a job to do. They received a chaplain's absolution and prayer, for this flight was their last. The commanders aware of the "final mission theory", allowed harmless liberties to be taken by the airmen. So was born aircraft art, hut (sleeping quarters) art, and A-2 leather jacket art, which in no small way provided spiritual uplift and union among all the flyers and ground personnel. After all nothing like a pretty girl to lift their spirits and boost their morale.

The chaplain and ground personnel, the aircraft mechanics who checked out the airplane, the ordinance and armament personnel who loaded the bombs and cleaned and armed the .50 caliber machine-guns, the medics, the staff from personnel, operations, intelligence and supply - they were all there out on the flight line to see and to send their sons and brothers and friends off for the last time to do combat with the enemy; and they waited, eyes searching the skies over England for return of aircraft with their sons and brothers and friends, no matter what their condition, only to return. No, these Air Force personnel did not fly on combat missions, yet they waited in anxiety and suffered the pain in loss for those airmen who failed to return and never to be seen again. "God, why do we have WAR?" It is a nasty gut-wrenching business. But we had our jobs to do. These men had great morale for men who took to the air on their "final mission." "God Speed."

Tears were common when a returning bomber shot up a red flare indicating wounded aboard or a ship lumbered to the air base with part of a wing or tail missing, only one landing gear visibly down or engines feathered and knocked out, coming in on a wing and a prayer. Hearts watched and prayed for the miracle landing.

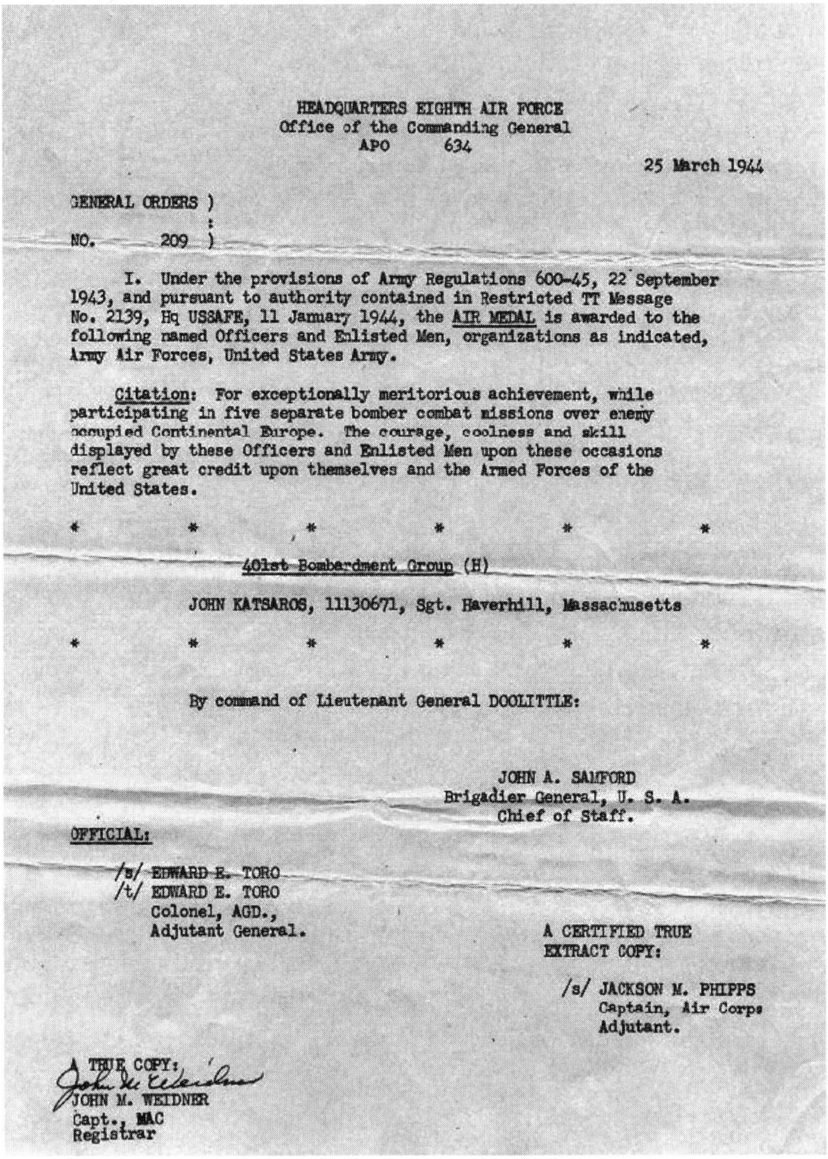

HEADQUARTERS EIGHTH AIR FORCE
Office of the Commanding General
APO 634

25 March 1944

GENERAL ORDERS )
:
NO. 209 )

I. Under the provisions of Army Regulations 600-45, 22 September 1943, and pursuant to authority contained in Restricted TT Message No. 2139, Hq USSAFE, 11 January 1944, the AIR MEDAL is awarded to the following named Officers and Enlisted Men, organizations as indicated, Army Air Forces, United States Army.

Citation: For exceptionally meritorious achievement, while participating in five separate bomber combat missions over enemy occupied Continental Europe. The courage, coolness and skill displayed by these Officers and Enlisted Men upon these occasions reflect great credit upon themselves and the Armed Forces of the United States.

* * * * * *

401st Bombardment Group (H)

JOHN KATSAROS, 11130671, Sgt. Haverhill, Massachusetts

* * * * * *

By command of Lieutenant General DOOLITTLE:

JOHN A. SAMFORD
Brigadier General, U. S. A.
Chief of Staff.

OFFICIAL:

/s/ EDWARD E. TORO
/t/ EDWARD E. TORO
Colonel, AGD.,
Adjutant General.

A CERTIFIED TRUE
EXTRACT COPY:

/s/ JACKSON M. PHIPPS
Captain, Air Corps
Adjutant.

A TRUE COPY:
JOHN M. WEIDNER
Capt., MAC
Registrar

Air Medal Award.

## CHAPTER 13
## Mission to Leipzig

The bombing mission on 20 February 1944, to take out the Erla factories, makers of the dreaded ME-109 fighter aircraft at Leipzig, Germany, was the beginning of a dramatic series of strategic operations called "Big Week." Colonel Harold "Hal" Bowman, Commanding Officer of the 401st Bomb Group, was selected by Major General Robert Williams, C.O. of the 1st Air Division, to lead the 8th Air Force on the first mission consisting of 1,000 B-17 bombers carrying 10,000 airmen and 2,500 tons of demolition bombs.

It was a great day for "daylight" bombing and the 8th Air Force in delivering destruction to the German war machine. Colonel Bowman, as leader of the first of a series of missions for "BIG WEEK", asked by General Williams, to speak at a critique held by General Williams, stated, "The mission was run as briefed; I have nothing unusual to report." "Nothing unusual?" cracked General Williams, "Except that it was the largest and most successful mission ever run." General Williams proceeded to award Colonel Bowman the Silver Star, and the 401st Bomb Group received the Presidential Unit Citation.

It was a great day for the 8th Air Force, General Bowman, later wrote in a book entitled, *Birds of a Feather*, from which excerpts of the bombing mission to Leipzig are listed below:

*"Due to the nip and tuck weather forecast, each group was provided with two Pathfinders, radar bombing crews and planes in case visual sighting was an impossible bombing mission. Weather in England and en route was overcast, and we had grave doubts about the possibility of seeing our targets. Flak and fighters met us in considerable force, but thanks to weather and to enemy misinterpretation of our destination - and of course to our effective escort - our losses were not as severe as might have been expected on such a deep penetration into enemy territory. Just before we reached the IP (initial point) for our bomb run, breaks appeared in the clouds below. As we turned toward the release point, Leipzig and the entire*

*area opened up for a clear run. The only factor reducing visibility was the smoke rising from the city - a reminder of the British raid the night before. Even that factor was minimal; the wind carried the smoke away from our objective. Although our fighters were doing a beautiful job fending off the enemy, some German fighters still got through. The flak was heavy, and we had to fly right through it to reach our target. Evasive action during the bomb run was impossible, as it would have significantly reduced the bombardier's accuracy. After spine-tingling moments we released our bombs on target and made a diving turn back toward England. Soon we were joined by other formations as we assembled for the long trek homeward."*

COLONEL BOWMAN . . . . . . . . . . . . . . . . . . led the mission

Colonel Harold Bowman, Commander of the 401st Bombardment Group, led the 8 Air Force 20th February 1944 on the highly successful mission to Leipzig, Germany. The *Man O' War* crew with all flyers of the 401st Bomb Group was awarded the Presidential Unit Citation.

**The William R. Lawley Jr. Took Place on That Day**

*"The "Big Week" had also produced a name written in the archives of the VIII Bomber Command. "William R. Lawley, Jr.", flew a Fortress on the 20th February in the strike against Leipzig. The mission had gone uneventfully until the moment of bomb drop - then bombardier Harry G. Mason gave the pilot distressing news that their bombs had hung up. The timing was, to say the least, unfortunate. No sooner had Mason made his report when a swarm of German fighters hit their formation, concentrating fire on their bomber. Almost at once the fortress was battered from nose to tail. A cannon shell exploding in the cockpit killed the copilot instantly and sent steel fragments tearing through Lawley's body. At the same moment an engine exploded in flames. The body of the dead co-pilot slumped forward against the control yoke. Still stunned by the blast from the exploding shell, Lawley regained his senses slowly - to discover that one engine was on fire, the B-17 was in a howling dive, and he couldn't see outside the airplane. The cannon shell in killing the co-pilot had splashed blood all across the windshield, blotting out the outside world. Lawley snapped his eyes to the instruments. To his dismay, these were also splattered with blood and could not be read. Mason, during this time, was struggling to salvo the bombs. Without their heavy weight, control of the Fortress would be easier. No one in the crew was aware of the dead copilot or the struggle that was going on in the cockpit, where the wounded Lawley was straining with ebbing strength to regain control. Desperate, convinced they were finished, he shouted on the intercom for the crew to bail out. The replies that came back were not reassuring. Eight men of the crew of ten, including himself, were wounded. Two men were in serious condition. Bailing out was unthinkable; they would never survive the jump.*

*There was no other way, Lawley fought with renewed determination to save the ship. He punched the extinguisher system to kill the burning engine - only to have another wave of attacking fighters set another engine ablaze. Despite their wounds, most of the gunners fought back. Lawley smothered the second fire. Abruptly he felt some of the pressure easing;*

*Mason had salvoed their bombs. Elated at their success, Mason climbed upward to the cockpit where he faced the gory scene of the dead copilot, the wounded and bleeding Lawley, and the blood-sprayed windshield and instrument panel. Lawley took one look at Mason, accepted that help was there, and passed out. The bombardier, although not a pilot, had flying training behind him. The crew helped in removing the body of the dead co-pilot and Mason climbed into the right seat, from where he held course for England. There were no further attacks, and Mason started a long descent. The moment he sighted an airfield the bombardier managed to revive Lawley. Despite his terrible pain, Lawley took over the controls and started the landing approach.*

*An engine sputtered, out of fuel. The ground came up to them. Another engine exploded into flames. The gear refused to budge. Lawley knew he couldn't hang on much longer. He bellied in the bomber, sending sparks back for hundreds of feet. It was spectacular but, after what they had been through, harmless.*

When we returned from Leipzig, at briefing we were informed of the misery our friends on Bill Lawley's crew went through. Gunners on our crew questioned me if the training by our pilot, Jack Dunaway, to fly the B-17, "Could you fly the plane back to the base and land?" My answer was, "If I was not severely wounded and with the help of our navigator Lt. Mock giving me a reading back to England and help from bombardier, Lt. Ted Krol to remove the wounded Pilot and co-Pilot, yes. I could keep the B-17 on course back, but had no ability to land. We would all be required to bail out over England, provided the plane remained aloft."

The raid on Leipzig had taken a toll on the 401st Bomb Group. 60 of the Fortresses in the Division were knocked down with a loss of 600 airmen. Aircraft stand-down was called by the group and liberty was permitted. Our Squadron issued three day passes to the airmen. Jack Crowley was anxious to get laid, so he and I caught a bus to Kettering RR Station, 90 miles northwest of London, boarded the train to London where we took in the sights and engaged in the pedestrian traffic in Piccadilly Square. Crowley immediately got hooked up with a street-walking, good looking prostitute. There were hoards of them, at all prices, looking to tie up with the horny free-spending G.I's. There were girls and prices to suit every pocket book. I enjoyed the sights this evening. We spent the night at the local Red-Cross Shelter right there in Piccadilly.

The next day we took in the sights. We visited the British Parliament, saw and heard Big Ben, and took in a movie and in the presence of the Queen viewed the motion picture *Mrs. Miniver*, with Greer Garson. At dusk Jack and I hit one of the many pubs in Piccadilly to put on the feed bag at a restaurant owned by a Greek I had befriended. He offered us "steak" that was rationed and extremely hard to get. We quietly ate it, thanked him and left. It was awful and tasted like "shoe-leather"! Hitting another pub for drinks, low and behold, we were fortunate to be under cover as London suffered another Blitz by German bombers.

We met a couple of nice looking heads at the bar and they invited us back to their home where we met the mother of one of the gals, a young, willing, thirties looking woman. She served us tea in bed the next morning. We spent a lot of time in bed as that was the only way to keep warm. Coal was in short supply and naked body heat was a wonderful way to keep the chill off our backsides.

About noon, we bid adieus, told them that we would look them up the next time we were in town, if we survived our missions on the continent. Little did we know a month later that we would be shot down on a raid to Frankfurt?

We spent the day hanging around Piccadilly where there were faces and nationalities of every description. So we returned back into the pubs where the beer was warm but tasty and as the Luftwaffe bombed us again, we huddled in the pub, downing the beer in a friendly atmosphere and sang patriotic songs popular for the wartime.

Crowley and I had our fill of beers, gals and visiting for this trip and after a night's lodging at the Red Cross shelter, we caught the train for the two hour trip back to Kettering and the bus ride back to Deenethorpe.

By 14th October 1943, "Black Thursday", few leaders of the Eighth Air Force doubted but that the Germans had seized a firm grip on air superiority. When the Big Week ended late in February 1944, it was becoming just as evident that the Germans had lost what they had struggled so tenaciously to attain. That became evident when the Luftwaffe switched its old tactics and adopted a new plan that had *caution* stamped all over it. The Germans could, when they made the effort, put up an intense and effective defense. They could batter a bombing force with deadly results. But they could not do, not any longer, whenever they so wanted. They could not do so as a matter of policy.

The Germans, in effect, were defending their homeland on a partial basis, defending the most important war plants, abandoning other cities and industries to destruction by the massed Fortresses and Liberators. There were, and there would be, occasions when they would concentrate every plane available against a major raid. Other times the thousands of men in the bombers, and their escorting fighter pilots, would see only token defenders in the sky. Gunners one day might be forced to fight savagely for their lives - then for several missions they enjoyed the increasingly frequent milk runs. No one could predict when the Germans would explode in furious defense. But it was evident that the occasions were becoming increasingly rare."In short," noted AAF, "the policy was one of conservation of strength and it conceded to the Allies the vital point of air superiority."

## CHAPTER 14
## Second Mission to Frankfurt

My second mission to Frankfurt took place on 2 March 1944, the week following "Big Week" which ended on 25 February. The 612th Squadron put eight B-17's into the air for this mission, fortunate to have that many aircraft ready to fly, even with the ground maintenance crews working 'round the clock', as the aircraft and crew member casualties were climbing, and there was a loud "howl" for replacements. Crews and aircraft were being scheduled as often as feasible, weather permitting. At 0600 hours, the 401st Group traversed the English Channel as part of the 1st Air Division, to pass over the coastline of France, and within minutes, flak was encountered in black puffs of smoke, which by the time they zeroed-in the altitude, the formation was out of range of those big 88mm guns. Now, a group of General Hermann Goering's, yellow nose FW-190's fighters entertained the formation of B-17's with aerial ballet at a distance from our fighter escort. The friendly fighter escort departed for lack of fuel, and instantly the yellow noses attacked our formation. This was my first contact with the elite FW's with the yellow painted cowlings and propeller hubs (spinners).

The yellow noses came at the formation directly from one o'clock high, in tandem, searching out the stragglers and any aircraft lagging the formation. Fortune was with the 401st Bomb Group as it was flying in tight formation ready to repel any intruder, so it was not on the enemy charts for attack this day. A straggler was spotted and hit with machine-gun and cannon fire. He didn't stand a chance as the following FW's, one after the other, pounced on the wounded, like tigers on a kill, seeking appetite satisfaction. Fire broke out on a busted engine and the wing. Soon white puffs of smoke punctuated and laced the sky as parachutes burst open: one, two, three, four - where were the rest? The I.P. is coming up; the flak had increased in intensity, waiting to greet us on our bomb run. The FW-190 yellow nose, having done their damage, knew how many bombers they took down, headed for home. Explosions, fire, and white and black smoke appeared on the earth below from the lead plane having dropped its bombs on target. The flak was rough as *Man O' War* deposited its load of bombs to wing away with the squadron from the exploding aircraft factory. Not much to see with all the smoke cover, but the hits looked good. Soon the squadron left the flak area and the heart pumping eased off a bit, as the airmen caught a breather, before heading for the north coast of France, to run, again, the gauntlet of the enemy fighters and the coastal flak. The friendly withdrawal escort of British Spitfires came up to meet the formation on the Normandy coastline giving comfort for a safe return from enemy fighters. It felt great to get back to the quiet of the barracks and the sacks. It was a long day.

British "Spitfire" Fighter Escort, flown by USAAF fighter pilots.

## 401st BOMBARDMENT GROUP

*Constituted* as 401st Bombardment Group (Heavy) on 20 Mar 1943. *Activated* on 1 Apr 1943. Prepared for combat with B-17's. Moved to England, Oct-Nov 1943, and served in combat with Eighth AF, Nov 1943-Apr 1945. Operated chiefly against strategic targets, bombing industries, submarine facilities, shipyards, missile sites, marshalling yards, and airfields; beginning in Oct 1944, concentrated on oil reserves. Received a DUC for striking telling blows against German aircraft production on 11 Jan and 20 Feb 1944. In addition to strategic missions, operations included attacks on transportation, airfields, and fortifications prior to the Normandy invasion and on D-Day, Jun 1944; support for ground operations during the breakthrough at St Lo in Jul, the siege of Brest in Aug, and the airborne attack on Holland in Sep 1944; participation in the Battle of the Bulge, Dec 1944-Jan 1945, by assaulting transportation targets and communications centers in the battle area; and support for the airborne attack across the Rhine in Mar 1945. Returned to the US after V-E Day. *Inactivated* on 28 Aug 1945.

*Redesignated* 401st Bombardment Group (Very Heavy). Allotted to the reserve. *Activated* on 26 Jun 1947. *Redesignated* 401st Bombardment Group (Medium) in Jun 1949. Called to active service on 1 May 1951. Assigned to Strategic Air Command. *Inactivated* on 25 Jun 1951.

*Redesignated* 401st Fighter-Bomber Group. *Activated* on 8 Feb 1954. Assigned to Tactical Air Command and equipped with F-86's.

SQUADRONS. *612th:* 1943-1945; 1947-1951; 1954-. *613th:* 1943-1945; 1947-1949; 1954-. *614th:* 1943-1945; 1947-1949; 1954-. *615th:* 1943-1945; 1947-1949.

STATIONS. Ephrata AAB, Wash, 1 Apr 1943; Geiger Field, Wash, Jun 1943; Great Falls AAB, Mont, Jul-Oct 1943; Deenethorpe, England, c. 1 Nov 1943-May 1945; Sioux Falls AAFld, SD, c. 1-28 Aug 1945. Brooks Field, Tex, 26 Jun 1947; Biggs AFB, Tex, 27 Jun 1949-25 Jun 1951. Alexandria AFB, La, 8 Feb 1954-.

COMMANDERS. Col Neil B Harding, c. 1 Apr 1943; Col Harold W Bowman, Jun 1943; Col William T Seawell, Dec 1944-1945. Unkn, 1 May-25 Jun 1951. Col Walter G Benz Jr, 8 Feb 1954-.

CAMPAIGNS. Air Offensive, Europe; Normandy; Northern France; Rhineland; Ardennes-Alsace; Central Europe.

DECORATIONS. Distinguished Unit Citations: Germany, 11 Jan 1944; Germany, 20 Feb 1944.

DISTINCTIVE INSIGNIA: Unit Adopted World War II Class-C design.

On a silver shield divided bend sinister gold edged black a black triangle in dexter chief and edged white and bearing a silver letter "S".

Insignia design courtesy of:
Mr. Ralph W. (Rainbow) Trout, the Secretary/Treasurer of the 401st Bombardment Group (H) Association.

401st Bomb Group Presidential Distinguished Unit Citation for raids against German aircraft production on 11 January and 20 February 1944.

**612th BOMBARDMENT**

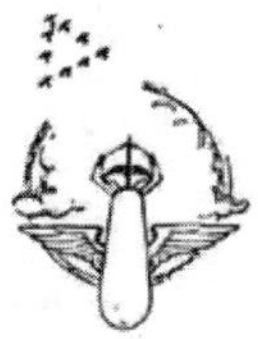

LINEAGE. Constituted 612th Bombardment Squadron (Heavy) on 20 Mar 1943. Activated on 1 Apr 1943. Inactivated on 28 Aug 1945. Redesignated 612th Bombardment Squadron (Very Heavy) on 27 May 1947. Activated in the reserve on 26 Jun 1947. Redesignated 612th Bombardment Squadron (Medium) on 27 Jun 1949. Ordered to active service on 1 May 1951. Inactivated on 25 Jun 1951. Redesignated 612th Fighter-Bomber Squadron on 24 Nov 1953. Activated on 8 Feb 1954. Redesignated 612th Tactical Fighter Squadron on 1 Jul 1958.

ASSIGNMENTS. 401st Bombardment Group, 1 Apr 1943–28 Aug 1945. 401st Bombardment Group, 26 Jun 1947–25 Jun 1951. 401st Fighter-Bomber Group, 8 Feb 1954; 401st Fighter-Bomber (later Tactical Fighter) Wing, 25 Sep 1957–.

STATIONS. Ephrata AAB, Wash, 1 Apr 1943; Geiger Field, Wash, 4 Jun 1943; Great Falls AAB, Mont, 8 Jul–19 Oct 1943; Deenethorpe, England, 3 Nov 1943–20 Jun 1945; Sioux Falls AAFld, SD, c. 1–28 Aug 1945. Brooks Field, Tex, 26 Jun 1947; Biggs AFB, Tex, 27 Jun 1949–25 Jun 1951. Alexandria AFB, La, 8 Feb 1954–.

AIRCRAFT. B-17, 1943–1945. F-86, 1954–1955; F-84, 1954–1957; F-100, 1957–.

OPERATIONS. Combat in ETO, 26 Nov 1943–20 Apr 1945.

SERVICE STREAMERS. None.

CAMPAIGNS. Air Offensive, Europe; Normandy; Northern France; Rhineland; Ardennes-Alsace; Central Europe; Air Combat, EAME Theater.

DECORATIONS. Distinguished Unit Citations: Germany, 11 Jan 1944; Germany, 20 Feb 1944. Air Force Outstanding Unit Award: 1 Jan–31 Dec 1963.

EMBLEM: Courtesy of Mr. Ralph W. Trout, a combat veteran of the World War II era 401st Bombardment Group.

A formation of B-17s in black profile overall trailing contrails of light blue. On a disc yellow, edged red and supporting a blue cloud superimposed thereon a green drop bomb winged silver.

NOTE: This is proported to be the 2nd unit insignia design. First one contained a replica of "MANGLER", the squadron mascot. No insignia design of "MANGLER" is on hand and according to Mr. Trout, the inisgnia was never used. Mangler was a bear.

According to Mr. Trout (now Secretary/Treasurer of the 401st Bombardment Group Association), contary to Maurer Maurer, all of the squadron insignia of the 401st Bombardment Group was officially approved.

612th Bomb Squadron Decorations: Distinguished Unit Citations, Germany 11 January 1944 and 20 February 1944.

Col. Chirigotis' *Hell's Belle* flew with the 781st HB Sqdn. 15thAF, Pantanella AFB, Cerignola, Italy during WWII.

Lt. General James H. Doolittle
*Commanding General, Eighth Air Force*

Lt. General, James H. Doolittle Commander 8th AF.

Thursday, March 9, 1944

# Heavies Rain 360,000 Bombs on Berlin

*U.S. Bombs Strike a Berlin Factory District*

Did the American bombs hit their mark in Berlin? This photograph, taken during the Monday raid, gives the answer. The bomb bursts shown are right in the midst of one of the German capital's important factory districts.

## Over 850 Forts, Libs Set Capital Aflame In Great Fire Raid

### Smoke Visible 100 Miles After Second Major Day Attack; Fierce Air Battles Deepen Gash in the Luftwaffe

Berlin got its second major daylight bombing yesterday. A force of American Flying Fortresses and Liberators estimated at more than 850 strong dropped more than 350,000 incendiary bombs and 10,000 high-explosive bombs on the German capital, and returning airmen said the smoke billowing from the burning ruins could be seen 100 miles away.

Thirty-eight American bombers and 16 fighters were lost in the operations according to an announcement from U.S. Strategic Air Forces headquarter just before midnight. U.S. fighters claimed 83 enemy aircraft destroyed; bombers crews' claims have not tabulated.

The attack, third by American forces on Berlin in four days, was probably the biggest daylight incendiary raid in history, far surpassing the German attempt to set London afire on Sept. 15, 1940, at the start of the London blitz.

A preliminary report from headquarters shortly before midnight said that the ball bearing plant at Erkner, 15 miles southeast of the heart of the city, was heavily hit and that "other targets in the area also were bombed successfully."

The Erkner plant produces half the minimum requirements in ball bearings needed by the Luftwaffe. It is second in importance only to Schweinfurt and Stuttgart, both heavily damaged by the USSTAF and RAF.

Furious air battles, possibly matching those of the Monday raid on the capital, raged across Germany from the time the bombers passed Hanover, 150 miles from the capital, shortly after noon until they emerged on the homeward flight.

Mustang pilots returning early in the afternoon said that Berlin's defenses were just as fierce and determined as in the first major assault on the city. The Monday operation cost the American forces 68 bombers and 11 fighters and the Luftwaffe 176 fighters, according to official figures at U.S. headquarters.

THE STARS AND STRIPES Thursday,

## Flak Over Berlin Earns a Double Scotch—at Least

Flying Fortresses pass through the flak-filled sky over Berlin during their great raid on the city Monday. Flak and enemy fighters brought down 68 U.S. heavy bombers of an estimated force of 850. Forts and Liberators and their escorting fighters destroyed 176 Nazi planes.

A post-Berlin double scotch is being poured for S/Sgt. Donald G. Rusen, of Muskegon, Mich., Fortress turret gunner, after Monday's raid. Bartender is Sgt. Ray Pentkoff, of Huntington, W. Va.

## Heavies Rain 360,000 Bombs On Berlin in 2nd Big Day Raid

(Continued from page 1)

many enemy planes up there today that we were choosy about which ones we shot down."

Men in Gentile's group expressed the belief the Luftwaffe had been under orders to hold off until there was no doubt the target was Berlin. "They did not attack in force until the bombers were practically on their bomb runs, after which they swept into the formations in twos and threes all over the sky," one said.

By a several-pronged attack the bombers managed to slip through the heaviest flak defenses to attack many vital targets in the city. One group which was in the middle wave of bombers reported fires springing up along Berlin's industrial perimeter.

They said that bombs ...

engined rocket-firing fighters, around which the Germans put protecting single-engined destroyers on the flanks and above to cover them from our fighters.

"These formations came at our bombers stacked up just like that. They dived in and rolled right through our formation."

Lt. Col. George Bickell, of Nutley, N.J., who led the fighters on both Berlin raids, said: "We were with the bombers for 50 minutes and saw very little stuff and no more than half a dozen enemy aircraft. It was nowhere near as rough as the other time. For us today there wasn't anything to it."

Bickell said another important factor was that weather was clear all the way, and that from high up bombing results looked excellent.

Ninth Air Force Mustangs ...

## CHAPTER 15
## Target: Berlin, Germany

Jimmy Doolittle, the Commanding General of the 8th Air Force, was determined to succeed with this mission to Berlin in order to shorten the war by crippling the enemy at his resources. This was a full mission target for Berlin; that's right, four consecutive days of missions the 6th , 7th , 8th and 9th of March 1944, with the maximum number of bombers to insure demolition of the target. Not only was this a long, energy-sapping flight, and even if the aircraft avoided some of the flak areas by flying around them, the bomber formation could not avoid the enemy fighter aircraft and their blazing guns and cannon fire en route to target.

Having flown three consecutive days to Frankfurt, Wilhelmshaven and Cologne on the 2nd and 3rd , and 4th and to Berlin on the 6th , the crew of *Man O' War* were exhausted and not scheduled to fly on the 9th. So, we went out for a feed at the Wheatsheaf Restaurant at Benefield, England. After chow down, we spent the evening at a local pub where we let our hair down enjoying a few beers, and playing chug-a-lug. Happily relaxed, we headed for our "sacks". My happy mood came to an abrupt end when I was shocked out of my bed by the night CQ at 0400 hours to be informed that I was a replacement gunner on a new crew about to fly its first mission. At group briefing, the C.O. enlightened the warriors with news that the target destination is Berlin, and told us that General Doolittle selected a target route through the Ruhr Valley where there was a heavy concentration of 88mm *ack-ack* guns and enemy fighter aircraft to the target - the ball-bearing factory in the Erkner section of the city. No mention was made of potential heavy losses. It was a dream target and it would not fall cheap. A "green" pilot with no combat experience and not schooled in formation flying was always assigned as "Tail-end Charlie, Purple Heart Corner", the last box position in the group formation, a formidable position for the prop wash created by the big engines up front and especially by the B-17 ahead, and above, and being the last, the tag-along, he was easy prey for enemy fighters, so it took a well-seasoned combat pilot to fly the slot at the tail-end of the group formation.

Airborne, the group assembled like geese in "V" formation and crossed the

English Channel. I kept in mind that I was a combat veteran with seven missions under my belt and wanted to make it eight. I was concerned with our safety and called the pilot on the intercom from my right waist position to close up the formation. Instead of closing, our plane drifts further back from the group. I called the pilot a second time and asked if we had engine problems. His answer was, "No", so I asked to have the ship brought in closer with the formation. The formation reached France and knowing that we can anticipate trouble, I called the pilot a third time, "Better tighten up the formation, I can see enemy fighters climbing up fast from the airfields below." "Stop calling," he said, "or I will have your ass court-martialed when we get back." I was hot! Steam was coming out of my ears. I was concerned about the safety of my life and those of the other nine crew members aboard. I spew, "Damn it, get your ass in there, or I will come up and fly the plane for you." (The pilot has no idea of my flying ability). Within seconds of this brew-ha with the pilot, enemy fighters came out of the sun and made a pass at the nose of our ship. Bullets were spitting everywhere. Our aircraft took several hits. Luckily no crew member got hit.

The pilot now got the message. He quickly brought the B-17 in line with the formation and did not fall back again all the way to Berlin.

Filling in another crew's roster didn't make me happy, especially after a night of settling. The flak was heavy and the left waist gunner of the ship off our right wing gave me a wave. I waved back and as I was watching, his ship took direct flak hit and bits and pieces of his aircraft were all over the sky. The sight was unbelievable. Did that really happen? I had to settle down now because anything might happen on this bomb run and the fighters would be on us when we came off target.

The bombing of the ball bearing factory was successful, and the group reformed to a tight combat formation successfully warding off enemy fighter attacks. The plane was riddled with flak and bullet holes, but fortunately we made it without enemy pursuit back to Deenethorpe. No member of the air-crew was seriously wounded nor hospitalized.

When we land, I got down on my knees and kissed Mother Earth and gave thanks to God for our successful return. The pilot came over to me, apologized and thanked me. I responded, "Lt., today you became a B-17 combat pilot." I never met up with him again. The rest of my missions were flown with my regular crew except for one mission that I did fly as a replacement gunner in a B-24 Liberator. I didn't need to relive these experiences with a "green" pilot.

The 8th Air Force began experimentation with daylight bombing, much to the displeasure of the British High Command, and on "Black Thursday" 14 October 1943, on a bombing mission to wipe out the ball bearing factory at Schweinfurt, Germany, the U.S. Air Force lost sixty B-17 Flying Fortresses to enemy fighters and anti-aircraft guns - the greatest single loss to date of aircraft in WWII. Six hundred trained air combat veterans were lost by the 8th Air Force, putting up a clamor for replacement aircraft and aircrews. Additional losses were counted in the crewmen killed or wounded in returned aircraft. The 8th Air Force had been accustomed to shorter missions, in the area of France, and targets close enough for gasoline reach, but the mission to Schweinfurt was special, and suspicion had it that German Intelligence, forewarned of this chosen, deep-penetrating target, alerted the German High Command. The British, opposed to the 8th Air Force decision to bomb by daylight, preferred to bomb under the stars as they felt that the darkness cloaked the RAF with a mantle of protection.

Yet, as previously mentioned, there would come a night when a swarm of great British Lancaster's - huge, four engine raiders, one of the finest bomber designs ever to take wing, would strike into Germany. On that night, ninety-six of the Lancaster's would fail to return to England. Essentially the 8th Air Force Bomber Command's program in Europe called for a sustained daylight bombing campaign carried out with high precision which rather than attempting to destroy cities in saturated raids would wreck carefully chosen industrial objectives.

Intelligence informed headquarters that the aircraft factory at Oscherslaben, Germany, 80 miles south west of Berlin was rapidly turning out nearly half of the FW-190 fighter's production in the Reich. On 11 January 1944, the 1st Division was assigned the target escorted by a limited number of American Mustangs with mechanical problems, from a single group, to cover the lead formation. (The British fifteen-hundred horsepower Rolls Royce Merlin engine mounted in the P-51B Mustang with a top speed of 425 MPH was not available until months later). Fighters and bombers were scattered all over the heavy clouded sky, unable to maintain formation due to the poor visibility. Fighter escorts unable to locate the bombers were returning back to bases in England. General Doolittle, Commander of the 8th Air Force, recalled the 2nd and 3rd Division due to the inclement weather.

However, General Robert Travis, of the 1st Division decided to carry the fight to the target, "Since we are closing in on the target we will continue the mission." This decision was a disaster for three of the groups of the 1st Division that suffered attacks by over 400 hundred enemy fighters for over three hours, sustaining losses of 42 out of 170 bombers shot down, at a loss of 420 crew members.

Colonel Bowman, Commander of the 401st Bomb Group, mission leader to Oscherslaben, initiated a report to General Doolittle, 8th AF Commander through the 94th Combat Wing and the 1st Air Division Headquarters citing witness, and testimony to credit the gallantry of Major James H. Howard, CO of the 356th Fighter Squadron, 354th Fighter Group, and his prowess in the protection of 40 B-17 Bombers and over 400 airmen of the 401st Bomb Group in singularly engaging 30 to 40 enemy fighters and took down at least six in a 30 minute battle, without aircraft loss by the 401st BG.

After further investigation to locate the previously unidentified pilot and verification of the events of that mission with the many airmen of the 401st BG; and in collaboration with General Arnold, Army Air Chief; General Marshall, Chief of Staff; President Roosevelt, and Congress, General Doolittle presented Major Howard the award of The Congressional Medal of Honor. Major Howard, was the only American fighter pilot in the E.T.O. to receive this high award.

On the last week of January, 1944, General Quesada, Commander of the 6th Fighter Wing, promoted him to Lt. Colonel and appointed him Commander of the 354th Fighter Group. On 7 April 1944 he was promoted to Colonel.

In March 1948 Colonel Howard was promoted to Brigadier General in the Air Force Reserves and took command of the 67th Fighter Wing, comprised of five fighter groups and one fighter training group. In 1966 he retired from the USAF Reserves. March18, 1995 General James Howell Howard died and is buried in the Arlington National Cemetery.

# THE PILOT WHO FOUGHT THIRTY ENEMY PLANES

WHEN a wing of Flying Fortresses returned from the great raid over Central Germany last week their crews wanted to know the name of the Mustang pilot who single-handed had challenged 30 to 40 enemy fighters to protect the bombers.

Seated in the cockpit of his plane, giving the O.K. sign (the picture right), is the 6ft. 2in. pilot, Major James H. Howard, former "Flying Tiger," now C.O. of a squadron of the new long-range Mustangs.

★

His identity was revealed yesterday when his report was read out in the briefing room of a U.S. base to a full company of pilots of the new long - range fighter Mustangs.

Uneasily and in a small voice he told his story. He said:

"I scared some of the enemy away by 'stooging' up to them suddenly. Others I gave a 'squirt,' which caused them to break away.

"On the first encounter, which turned into a melee, my flight lost me. I regained bomber altitude and then discovered that I was alone. I spent half an hour chasing and scaring away attacking enemy aircraft from 21,000 to 15,000 feet. I had five combat encounters during this time.

"For the first two encounters and combat all four guns fired. On the third I had two guns, and on the fourth and fifth encounter only one gun."

This is the lone pilot's official record of his fight: Two enemy planes shot down, two probably destroyed, two damaged.

On account of his height he has to have the foot-rests of his Mustang, "Ding Hao," moved forward and the seat back.

*—From London News-Chronicle*
*19 January 1944*

Major James H. Howard

*General Spaatz congratulates fighter pilot Jim Howard, winner*
*Congressional Medal of Honor on Recommendation of the 401st*

General Spaatz congratulates fighter pilot Jim Howard, winner of the Congressional Medal of Honor on recommendation of the 401st Bomb Group.

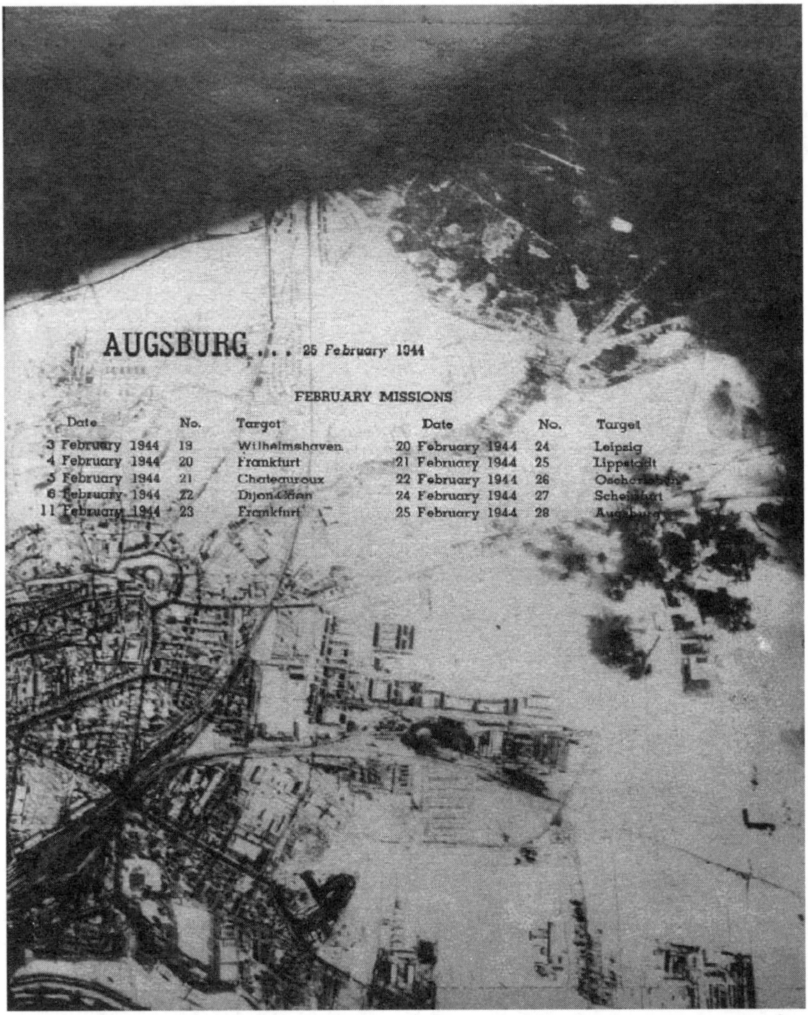
AUGSBURG . . . 25 February 1944
FEBRUARY MISSIONS
Date No. Target Date No. Target
3 February 1944 19 Wilhelmshaven 20 February 1944 24 Leipzig
4 February 1944 20 Frankfurt 21 February 1944 25 Lippstadt
5 February 1944 21 Chateauroux 22 February 1944 26
6 February 1944 22 Dijon 24 February 1944 27
11 February 1944 23 Frankfurt 25 February 1944 28

During "Big Week", the 8th Air Force, flying out of England, sent up more than 3,000 heavy bombers, and the 15thAir Force, flying out of Italy, put 500 heavy bombers into the air for a combined tonnage of 10,000 tons of bombs dropped on assigned strategic targets.

B-17 Flying Fortress nose art.

B-17 Flying Fortress nose art.

## CHAPTER 16
## The Luftwaffe Is Forced To Fight

By now the men who planned the air assault against Germany were more than primed to take every advantage of the sudden weakness in German defenses. Now they wanted the Germans to fight and they bent every opportunity to force the Luftwaffe into defending the Reich and its cities. The air strategists threw away their long-standing plans of protecting the bombers. Where they had planned missions to avoid the fighters, now they did their best to goad the Luftwaffe into battle. The AAF history notes, "Fighter escort, which hitherto had been held down to close support of the bombers, now was increasingly cut loose from strict defensive assignments with orders to seek out and destroy the foe. Whenever the role of the P-51 Mustang escort became a primarily defensive one, the extension of the P-51 fighter's range made it possible to send great fleets of escorted bombers all the way to Berlin."

This was the city that the Germans meant to defend. This was the target for which they would fight, in maximum number, with unbridled fury. Those who sent out the men in the Fortresses and Liberators knew that their policy of forcing the fight could produce severe casualties among the heavy bombers. They reckoned that the losses would be worth the damage inflicted on the enemy in the air. The invasion date was nearing and "it became correspondingly more important to force a higher rate of attrition on the German Air Force in being."

Intelligence informed headquarters that the aircraft factory at Oscherslaben, Germany, 80 miles south west of Berlin was rapidly turning out nearly half of the FW-190 fighter's production in the Reich. On 11 January 1944, the 1st Division was assigned the target, escorted by a limited number of American P-51 Mustangs with mechanical problems, from a single group, to cover our lead formation. (The British fifteen-hundred horse power Rolls Royce Merlin engine mounted in the P-51B Mustang with a top speed of 425 MPH was not available until months later.)

The first attack on "Big B" (Berlin) came on 4 March 1944. Severe weather limited results. Two days later the weather improved and Eighth

Air Force headquarters laid on the big strike. Six hundred and sixty heavies made it to Berlin to drop over 1,600 tons of bombs. The men who flew the mission knew it was going to be rough. More fighters than usual would be in the air to contest their presence. For several nights the RAF had failed to visit targets over central Germany.

The event justified their fears; the bombers "ran into exceedingly bitter and effective opposition." Intense anti-aircraft flak claimed its share - and before day ended no less than sixty-nine bombers went down, along with eleven escorting fighters. Those bombers that returned claimed ninety-seven kills. The fighters, with gun-camera records to back up their claims, racked up eighty-two German fighters shot down in battle. There was no way of knowing the kills scored by the sixty-nine bombers and eleven fighters that were lost. Was the mission overly costly? Sixty-nine bombers could not be shrugged off. Yet the loss ratio, for a mission of such importance and range from England, could be accepted. It was "just such air fights that the American commanders hoped to provoke, confident as they were in the ability of the airmen to impose a ruinous wastage upon the enemy." The moments when such fierce resistance could be offered would become even rarer than before.

Two days later four-hundred and sixty-two heavies again raided Berlin. A screen of one-hundred and seventy-four Mustang fighters escorted them to, over, and away from the target. The number of German fighters in the air was much less than on the 4th , while the heavy American escort which, included P-38s and P-47s, came to a record 1,015 sorties flown. During the day, five-hundred and ninety heavy bombers flew credit sorties. Flak and enemy fighters claimed thirty-seven of these. Once again, the Luftwaffe had suffered a battering. Losing seventeen of their own number, the escorts shot down nearly ninety German Fighters.

On the 22nd of March a force of six-hundred and sixty-nine heavy bombers returned to Berlin. Despite excellent weather for interception, few Luftwaffe fighters were up. Flak shot down ten bombers. One bomber went down from noncombatant causes. Total scored to German fighters: one bomber and that was over the capital of the Reich. At the close of March the Eighth Air Force noted that the Luftwaffe "could still hit, and hit hard; but it was no longer capable of that sustained counterattack which had at one time so nearly frustrated the entire Combined Bomber Offensive."

In respect to its original goals, the Combined Bomber Offensive "reached its legal end" on the 1st April 1944. Control of the strategic air forces of the AAF reverted from the British to the supreme Allied commander. The new phase of the air war was ready - the massed bomber fleets were now prepared to attempt to wreck the German petroleum industry and to paralyze the country's transportation system.

How best to judge the effect of the air assault program to destroy the ability of Germany to fight in the air? It is not the intention of this book to review the matter in all its complex detail but the conclusion is undeniably clear. After February the Luftwaffe could no longer properly defend the Reich. Their ability to fight in the air had been greatly reduced by their losses in fighter aircraft. The program to destroy Germany's fighting strength in the air had another goal – to gain air superiority to permit the invasion of Europe without molestation from the Luftwaffe.

On 6 June 1944, General Dwight D. Eisenhower made a statement to the invasion forces he was committing to the assault on German Europe "If you see fighting aircraft overhead, they will be ours!" He was right!

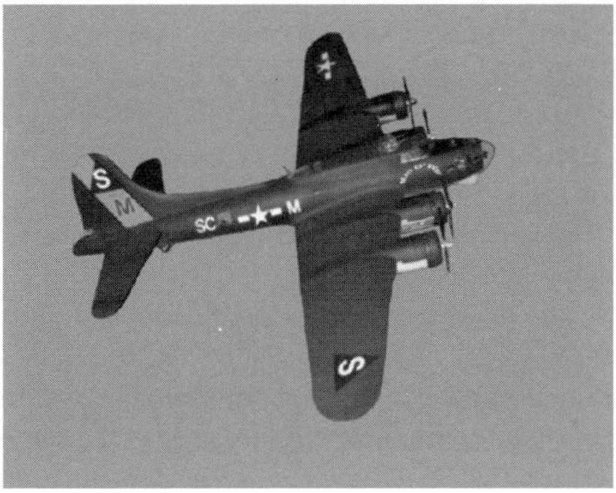


This is an exact model, two ft. wing span of the B-17 *Man O' War*, we were shot down in on March 20, 1944. Michael and Joseph Belmonte, Reading, MA. researched, built and presented it to me.

## CHAPTER 17
## Final Mission to Frankfurt, Germany

The mission began early on 20 March 1944 on a very cold, cloudy, windy day. Hundreds of bombers had tremendous problems attempting to complete their formations. Two bombers collided due to heavy cloud cover up to 27,000 feet. We continued over the English Channel into France then Germany - we had difficulty keeping formation. The 401st Bomb Group formation, flying over 27,000 feet altitude in a heavily overcast sky, was skimming through cloud cover and having considerable difficulty with the aircraft keeping in close formation.

Within minutes of the I.P. a bomb-loaded aircraft, out of control, fell from the formation above, almost wiping out *Man O' War*. Pilot, Lt. Jack Dunaway put our aircraft into a precipitous dive, to avert collision, with a pull to the left. Dunaway's quick thinking maneuver avoided an air crash and possible explosion of the two planes that would have caused many losses of planes and crews. The centrifugal force created by the planes dive and turns rendered the crew helpless, stuck to the fuselage, unable to move. The aircraft was now in a rough, turbulent downdraft as the plane dropped over several thousand feet before the pilot was able to bring the ship under control. The intercom buzzed, with crew members' concerns; "What the hell happened"?

Miraculously, once the pilot was able to straighten out the plane – breathing became easier! Now, the pilot had to regain the lost altitude to return to the group formation. The formation was nowhere to be found; the pilot decided to continue on to target with the expectation of meeting up with the group. At this time, while busy with lifesaving activity and observing radio silence, the pilot was unaware of the 8th Air Force recall due to bad weather conditions.

Navigator, William Mock, set the plane on course for the target at Frankfurt; the weather cleared giving a visible target. Bombardier, Ted Krol, sighted the factory through his Norden bomb sight, and set the plane on a steady run to drop the bombs for a direct hit on target. One B-17 bomber with 4,000 pounds of demolition bombs, all alone, was on a mission to hell!

Over the target the flak was heavy, accurate and intense, knocking out the two inboard engines, numbers two and three, and peppering the plane with a rain of steel fragments. The sight and sound of the exploding flak shells gave us cause to fear a direct hit. The Bombardier called out "bombs away" and saw a direct hit on the factory, makers of the dreaded FW-190. The pilot took control of the yoke and banked the aircraft away to the left from the target out of flak range only to be joined in the furor by attacking ME109 fighter planes. They pounced on our airship, and we were in a life and death firefight.

There were four or five of them, and their assault was vicious - guns and cannons blazing, determined and unrelenting. After one pass and doing considerable damage to the men and plane, they circled and returned for a second pass -this time hitting us on all sides timing their individual attacks. Thirteen .50 cal. machine guns trained on the attackers, poured out lead trying to ward off the chase. Bullets and 20mm cannon shrapnel fire was exploding all over the fuselage and ripping up the plane. Now, they attacked fast and at close range and caused grievous injury to the *Man O' War* and the crew members. We had no time to count the downed enemy fighters or assess our damage.

The weather cleared bright and German fighters continued their attacks from all directions, killing the tail-gunner and the top-turret gunner near Reims, France.

We were running low on ammunition and must fire only accurate, quick bursts. The fighters continued their onslaught. Shrapnel hit Crowley, left-waist gunner in the neck - severing a neck artery. Blood gushed from the wound.

Hot, rocketing debris and shrapnel pierced my body - penetrating my right arm, rendering it paralyzed and useless. Some of the fighters bull-dogged the stricken aircraft all the way back to Reims, France, chewing it up for target practice, wanting to knock it out of the sky. The right wing was ablaze with fire; the plane was teetering from damage and loss of two engines, and the pilot was having difficulty keeping the plane under control. I was aware of the injured and dead crew members. It was a miracle that more crewmen were not killed or wounded in this fire firefight, yet, the airplane was still able to fly. Now we knew these relentless, fierce and constant fighter attacks would continue and add to the number of the wounded and dead crew. We did not give up the fight but had accepted our fate!

Fearing an explosion, Dunaway gave the alarm to bail out. First there were dead and gravely injured men to care for. Crowley, the left waist gunner, was hit in his neck by flying shrapnel slicing an artery, and blood gushed from the neck wound, and even with the temperature 60 below zero, he was bleeding profusely. I received my wounds during the same onslaught and turned to see how Crowley was doing. At this time, I glanced back to the tail and saw Benz, the tail gunner, slumped on his back, spread-eagle, arms extended. I called Benz on the intercom, there was no answer. The plane got blitzed in the savage attacks, taking a pounding from the fighters, and with a direct hit in the tail section, Benz could not have survived. I turned my attention back to Crowley who without oxygen mask had dropped to the floor. Unmindful of the pain of my own wounds and my numb dangling right arm I had to look after Crowley who is bleeding like hell. So to hell with the spent shell casings and blood all over the deck, I baby stepped cautiously over to help Crowley, restored his lost oxygen mask to his face and made a bandage with my scarf and wrapped it around his neck. The blood flow ceased, and now the bleeding congealed quickly in the freezing cold, and he regained consciousness.

The intercom squawked, and the pilot announced that Sgt. Harry Horst, the top-turret gunner was killed during the last pass by the ME-109's. Horst received a direct hit by 20mm cannon fire and his severed head was blown into the bomb doors; his bloodied body lay on the forward deck.

The plane was on fire and the pilot, again gave the alarm to bail; and unaware that the crew was looking after the wounded and the gunner trapped in the ball-turret, set the plane with two feathered engines on automatic pilot and bailed out behind the navigator, bombardier and co-pilot.

Frank Mastronardi, the radio operator, rushed back to the waist section to see how the guys were doing and got hit by shrapnel; he gave me the OK sign. Frank and I ran out of ammunition, Crowley, severely wounded, could not fire. Walter Rusch, the ball-turret gunner, was now the only one firing his twin .50 cal machine guns. He couldn't have much ammo left.

Frank and I looked to the needs of Benz, the tail gunner, and to Crowley, the left waist gunner. I crawled back to the rear to assist Marvin Benz, replaced his oxygen mask and tried to revive him as he lagged unconscious. Hell, he was dead!

Two ME-109's continued their assault on the planes rear section, I mounted the two tail guns and expended whatever ammo remained; the fighters passed on.

In bad need of oxygen, I crawled back to the waist position, and clicked my airline to the rear supply. Walter Rusch was now out of ammunition and being wounded, complicated his ability to extricate himself from the ball-turret. Frank Mastronardi and I viewed the predicament of Walter Rusch, trapped in his damaged ball-turret unable to roll back the turret which was hung up by spent shell casings jammed in the gear track. Using my "good" left arm, I worked with Frank to remove the spent casings to free Rusch. Rusch rolled back the turret, opened the hatch and started to emerge. It was time to move. Meanwhile, Crowley remained slumped down, his back to the floor. The bail-out alarm had already sounded, the plane was on fire and in danger of exploding. Frank saw that I am badly wounded and yelled, "Get the hell out of here". I removed my heavy, shattered flak vest, which protected my body from flying shrapnel, and with Frank's help, I clipped the chest chute onto my body harness. I opened the right rear escape panel and tested the reach of my short left arm (32" sleeve) to the "D" ring, so I was slow to move. "Go", yelled Frank. As a man of faith, I said a fast prayer *Kyrie Eleison*, made the sign of the Cross over my body with my left arm and curled into a ball to avoid hitting the plane's rear horizontal stabilizers, and rolled out into space. Meanwhile, Frank had turned his attention back to Crowley who had regained consciousness, stood him up on his own two feet, snapped on the chest chute to his body harness and pushes him out the escape opening. As I twist and turn, waiting before attempting the "D" ring, I look back and saw the helpless plane turning slowly, in a sky of fire and fear for an explosion with the guys still in it. I murmured, "For god's sake, guys, get the hell out of there!"

Walter was not yet out of his ball-turret and Frank, seeing him half out of the turret removed a couple more spent casings blocking his exit. Walter managed to get out of the ball-turret and in his haste to get out of the plane; the "D" ring on his parachute got snagged, accidentally springing open his parachute and it blossomed all over the place. He busied himself with Frank to gather his parachute, then "Hit the silk". Frank, last to leave the plane, quickly followed Rusch, Crowley, and me out the escape opening. With seconds to spare I saw Walter and Frank bail out, the B-17 was engulfed in flames. Walter's chute unfortunately billowed - putting him into a head-long dive.

His descent was rapid, and the silk chute opened but hit a high tension wire. It skewed his ground approach and landed him on a picket fence, spearing him in the stomach. He was badly wounded, but miraculously, he was alive! A young French lad ran to assist Walter, put him in a wheelbarrow and to conceal him, took him 50 meters to a wood shed next to his home near Unchair, France. A trail of blood led the nearby German soldiers to his hide-out. The military transported him to a hospital in Reims for medical attention.

Jack Crowley, I later learned, landed near *La Bonne Maison* and Unchair, only to be captured by German soldiers and taken to a German hospital, because with warmer weather his neck bleeding started again. Jack's wounds proved fatal, and he died two days later.

Lt. William Mock, the navigator, bailed out and was killed by enemy aircraft machine-gun fire, as witnessed by a ten year old boy who saw Mock fall from the sky with a "candled" parachute. His body was recovered between the towns of Chery-Chartreueve and Courville.

Tail gunner, Marvin Benz, and top-turret gunner, Harry Horst, were killed at their stations by attacking ME-109's who were determined to take the plane down by hitting it from all sides, front, top, tail and waist with .50 caliber machine-gun and 20mm cannon fire.

Lts. Jack Dunaway pilot, and Henry Kane co-pilot, were captured near Breuell, France, held POW in Germany and liberated by the American Army. Dunaway died several years after WWII. Kane remained in the Air Force to fly as a pilot, attaining the rank of Lt. Colonel, and he died in an aircraft accident while flying the "Berlin Airlift" during the cold war of June 1948 to September 1949, transporting food, coal, clothing and medical supplies to the West Berliners.

I, John Katsaros, right waist gunner, was severely wounded, bailed out and incurred additional injuries and broken ribs as a result of my late parachute opening and hard landing. I was captured by the Gestapo, escaped from their hands twice, later held captive by a French Resistance cell and by the constabulary in Spain. My account of this horrifying adventure will be narrated later in this story.

Bombardier, Lt. Ted Krol, hit the silk and landed near Courville. Enduring the hurt of a painful leg injury, he stumbled and dragged his injured leg in a southerly direction to the town of Goussancourt, where he received help from the French Resistance.

Radio operator, Frank Mastronardi, the last to bail out, landed right in a German artillery camp, a few hundred yards from me, at *La Bonne Maison*. Several years later he was recommended for the Distinguished Flying Cross by Walter Rusch. He was written up by headquarters, and Frank was presented the DFC at the American Airbase at Alconbury, England. His crew mates, Ted Krol, Walter Rusch and I flew back to England from the states to view the honor bestowed on him.

A quick inventory of personnel damage revealed that the crew had taken a beating from the ME-109's: Horst, the top-turret gunner, and Benz, the tail gunner were killed at their stations by direct hits of exploding .20 mm cannon shells, from the ME-109's. Crowley, the left waist gunner, took a serious hit to a neck artery from flying shrapnel, causing spouting blood loss. I took shrapnel hits to my body and to my right arm breaking bones, rendering it useless. Lt. Mock, the navigator, was injured and helped by the bombardier to bail out when the alarm sounded. Lt. Krol, the bombardier, despite his injuries, bailed out safely. Lt. Dunaway, the pilot, and Lt. Kane, the co-pilot, bailed out safely - their injuries not known at this point. Mastronardi, the radio operator, although wounded, helped Jack Crowley and Walter Rusch to bail out. That accounts for the condition of the crew members at the time, but things did not go well after bailout and landing. Just about everyone received wounds during the attack.

ME-109

According to Jean Sirot, a French historian, John's parachute hard landing was fortunately on a recently plowed field in the approximate area indicated by the circle at *La Bonne Maison* farm. The flat land had been a WWI French Airbase. Frank Mastronardi and Walter Rusch landed near the areas marked by the arrows.

Crash of the Man-O-War and in the order of Bailouts: 1st to bail Lt Jack Dunaway and Lt Henry Kane, b. Lt. William Mock, c. Lt Ted Krol, d. Sgt John Katsaros, e. S/Sgt Frank Mastronardi, f. German Camp, g. Sgt Jack Crowley, h. Sgt Walter Rusch, a. Plane Crash with KIA's S/Sgt Harry Horst and Sgt Marvin Benz on board.

Approximate last route of your B.17.

A - Approximate landing place. When I've been to BREUIL, people could not show the exact place because it was too muddy.

B - The first to jump out of the plane fell there and was killed because his parachute did not open. I've met a witness who was 10 in 1944.

C - Ted landed somewhere in the area and then walked south (dotted line) to Goussancourt : about 10 miles !!

D - JOHN KATSAROS LANDED BY PARACHUTE AT "LA BONNE MAISON"

E - Frank landed here.

F - Approximate limits of the german camp.

G - There landed the 5th to jump; badly wounded, he fell in trees.

H - Walter landed in this village, exactly where I've put a red dot.

Crash of *Man O' War* and order of bailouts.

SGT. JOHN KATSAROS
. . . missing in action

# Katsaros Lost Over Germany

## Unheard From Since March 20 Raid

Sgt. John Katsaros, son of Mr. and Mrs. Speros Katsaros, 24 Forest ave., an aerial mechanic attached to the U. S. Army Air Forces based in England, today was reported missing over Germany since March 20 by the War department in a telegram to his parents.

The telegram, signed by Acting-Adjutant Dunlop read:

"The Secretary of War regrets to advise you that your son, Sgt. John Katsaros, is missing in action since March 20, following flight over Germany. Letter follows."

The telegram arrived at the Katsaros home almost simultaneously with three letters from the airman, the last dated March 18, two days before the raid from which he did not return.

The letters told of his participating in seven missions over enemy territory and of the recent visit to London.

Sergeant Katsaros enlisted Dec. 7, 1942, and from Fort Devens was sent to Miami Beach, Fla., where he received his basic training. He was later transferred to the Flexible Gunnery school at Fort Myers, Fla., and was stationed for brief periods at Amarillo, Tex., and Salt Lake City, Utah, before going overseas late last year. He spent the Christmas holidays at his home, flying to England soon after.

He is a graduate of Haverhill High school, class of 1942, and before his enlistment was employed at the Portsmouth Navy Yard.

He has a brother, Sotiris, in the Army Air Forces, now a cadet at Harvard university, following basic training at Miami Beach. The latter is a former member of the English department of Haverhill High school.

# 116 Enemy Planes Downed

## U. S. Air Attack Blasts Bucharest Rail Yards

By LYNN HEINZERLING

ALLIED HEADQUARTERS, Naples (AP)—Strong formations of U. S. Flying Fortresses and Liberators, in their first attack on Bucharest yesterday, caused considerable damage to the railway yards through which German supplies roll to the Russian front and left one third of the Rumanian capital covered with a heavy cloud of smoke, headquarters announced today.

First reports indicated that the gunners in the heavy bombers shot down 116 planes in a battle last-

Reims, February 6th 1989

Dear Ted, John, Frank and Walter

At last, I'm sending to each of you a letter about the end of your last flight and two maps with keys.

I've been a very lazy letter-writer since we met in october 1987 but, almost as zealously as Sherlok Holmes or Kojak, I've made inquiries (I even flew over the site of your landing and took some pictures, but you'll have to wait to get the pictures, the film-roll is not yet finished) and I'm now able to give you more informations.

I hope the three others won't mind but I'll start with a special message for Walter.

Walter, you landed in UNCHAIR, inside a farm. I've seen the metal stake on which you got hurt when landing. I did not see the shed under which you were laying because it was destroyed two or three years ago by a storm. I met the lady on which you almost fell (the owner of the farm). She told me that you were repeating the same sentence <u>in french</u> :"Ce lieu est-il dangereux" (Is this site dangerous"). Her daughter married a man who was 9 or 10 in 1944 and who saw the first member of the crew to leave the plane falling with his candled parachute. I also met the little boy to which you handed the small bag (MARK-II - F)containing three maps printed on a sort of silk, a tiny compass and money. The man still keeps these thing (I saw them) except the money which was given, after the war, to the Mayor of the village who used it to repair a class-room. Enclosed you'll find a picture he asked me to send to you. He wonders if you can recognize him (it was taken two years after your crash)

And now to the four of you. In BREUIL, I've met a man who was 24 at that time. He saw the plane flying very low (the right wing broke against poplars) and then crashing near the VESLE river. The german soldiers stationed in Breuil requisitioned him to search the wrecked plane: inside they found the bodies of the two pilots. On the following sunday, children discovered a third body at about 200 yards from the plane : the man was dead with a severe wound at the head. All the witnesses I've met think that the pilot was doing the most he could to land correctly.

About ten years ago, the bed of the Vesle river has been cleaned and they found some parts of the plane, especially an engine and a propeller. I've seen this propeller in Breuil (I also took pictures) and I can tell you that a bullet went through one of its blades

2/6/89 Sirot's Letter

## CHAPTER 18
## Bail Out and Capture

I bailed out at 25,000 feet and turned to take a last look at the plane, in a sky of fire turning lazily to the left. I took a long free-fall in the peace of a suspended air ride and felt great relief in removing myself from the stricken aircraft. I lost consciousness from lack of oxygen. Enemy fighters were not my concern now. When I opened my eyes, the ground was coming up fast. The free-fall was over.

Many bits and pieces of shrapnel had penetrated my body and my right arm putting it out of use. The ripcord of the parachute was on the right side, the same side as the useless right arm. With great strain, I managed with the short left arm to reach and pull the "D" ring, barely time for the parachute to blossom before mother earth came up to say "Hello". The descent was too swift and I took a hard fall as I landed on the farm, *La Bonne Maison*, near the towns of Courville, Breuell, Unchair and Fismes. Luckily, the farm had been recently plowed for the coming summer crops and the fall to earth was cushioned a bit. I did sustain injuries, however, and now had six broken ribs, as well as a fractured left ankle, a badly twisted and sprained right ankle, severe head, back and leg contusions in addition to the busted right arm and the many shrapnel wounds. I wondered if I could survive my injuries.

I lay on the ground, hurting and exhausted, and a ME-109 German Fighter buzzed by overhead. My concern was that I may get riddled with machine-gun fire, but when the pilot came around again, he saluted, so I returned the salute left-handed. He made several passes, marking my position for German forces in the area. On one of his passes, the pilot's face came into clear view, and I wondered if my ship had been his victim.

The English parachute harness with the quick release had been a fortunate choice for me. Twist the chest knob to the "red" marked position and punch the knob, "Bingo", the harness and the parachute fell off. The American parachute requires the release of three clamps to free one's self from the chute and harness. Surely being unable to do that with my mangled right arm, the winds would have dragged me across the farm, incurring additional injury.

The flat, elevated surface of *La Bonne Maison* farm had a perfect layout for the French Air Force, which occupied the farm during WWI where a monument on an entrance wall to the farm was erected, commemorating the Number 1 French Air Ace, Capitaine Georges Guynemer, with fifty-three kills.

Now, two Luftwaffe ME-109 fighters returned, gave my position away by flying over me three times. I actually saw the face of the nearest pilot as he saluted me. I again, gathered up enough energy to return his salute.

Henry, a farm worker, witnessed my parachute descent landing to earth, and another young man contacted the owners, Mr. and Mrs. Jean and Yvonne Chauvin. When the occupants of *La Bonne Maison* realized I had been wounded, I was placed in a wheel barrel by Henry, an employee and taken to the farmhouse. They managed to carefully carry me into the house and laid my painful body on the dining room floor to administer medical aid when the Gestapo arrived to take me prisoner. A pretty little girl entered the room and stood by quietly watching the goings-on. I was laid out on the living room floor of *La Bonne Maison*. The Gestapo questioned me for two days and a German doctor wanted to amputate my right arm. I refused both.

The Gestapo began the interrogation immediately and much to their surprise I gave only my name, rank and serial number, and refused to answer any other questions. They immediately recognized the futility of trying to get any information from a so seriously wounded airman, whose state of poor health and mind had no concern to answer any questions, so they decided to seek medical attention for me before continuing with the interrogation. The Gestapo posted two German soldiers, and a nurse to tend to my wounds. I fell asleep or passed out, to be awakened by a German doctor who told me that my arm was in bad condition and that he would have to amputate it. The thought of losing my arm horrified me, and I made it known that there would be no amputation. Then I remembered in my drowsiness that I saw the doctor sprinkle a white powder on my arm and all over my body. The doctor got my message, and after treating me he departed to return the next day to once again tell me that the arm was in danger getting of gangrene. "It should be amputated," he said. "NO!" I said. "Hell, No!" and the doctor understood that I was not to give in to his pleading.

I hurt all over and I wasn't going to give my arm…as a sacrifice for my life. I was now in critical condition and in severe pain and was not moved from the floor of the dining room. It seemed apparent to me that I was left in this condition to die. No other thought entered my mind, and I resigned myself to this fate by prayer and attempted to give myself last rites before passing out. My condition remained the same for a period of a few days. Was my mind playing tricks on me?

Mademoiselle Chauvin as a little girl witnessed the fracas at *La Bonne Maison*, March 1944.

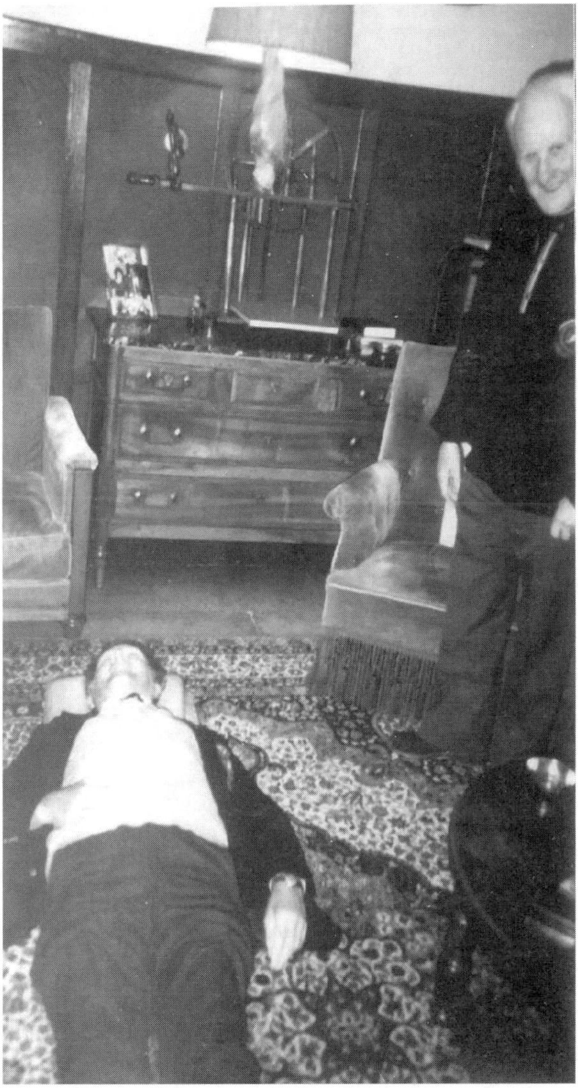

Pierre Demarchez, one of the three French Resistance Fighters who rescued me from the Gestapo, is pictured here, in the re-enactment of the March 1944 rescue.

Days went by without medical attention, and the Gestapo made several attempts to interrogate me without success. My condition continued to worsen. I felt lousy. Fever set in and my wounded body gave me excruciating pain. I imagined myself on a "death bed". The German guards paid little or no attention to me.

It is of interest to note that *La Bonne Maison*, on which I landed by parachute, is the location of a famous aerodrome of the WWI French Air Corps. At this particular base, the highly decorated French fighter pilot Capitaine Georges Guynemer was stationed and made his sorties against the German Luftwaffe. A plaque in his memory is attached to the outer wall at the entrance of this huge and beautiful farm.

## CHAPTER 19
## Firefight and Rescue by the French Resistance

Then, as if the Lord answered my prayers, I was awakened by gunfire. In a brief moment, I saw a man in civilian clothes enter with a pistol standing over me. Immediately, I thought that he was Gestapo and had come to threaten me, but the man winked and placed a finger to his mouth, making a silence gesture. The French Resistance, made aware of my capture, stormed the farmhouse to rescue me. They surprised and killed the guards, locked the nurse in the storage room, and carried me to their escape vehicle. On the get-away, a patrol of German soldiers blockaded our passage, and another firefight took place. The vehicle in flight sped by the patrol, shots blazing, and I took a hit in the back; none of my rescuers was hit in the skirmish. By pure luck, we got away. The patrol, on foot, did not pursue. I owe my life to the French Resistance rescuers, Jean Joly, head of the Reims Free French Underground, Pierre Demarchez, and Rene Felix. These men showed me, a boy, scared stiff, full of holes and too weak to stand, what courage was. Their actions, gave me strength, despite my wounded body, and they gave me hope for survival. The planned shock attack to rescue me was a surprise. I felt as though I was watching a movie - my rescuers were cold and calculating. They knew their job and had the courage to carry it out, willing to make the ultimate sacrifice. They feared not danger. They felt only love for France and Freedom. They hated *Les Boche*.

On the escape route, we ran into a second patrol. Several shots were fired on each side, and the German soldiers in their haste to take cover, gave the vehicle space to pass and the advantage of the time to accelerate away. No additional shots were fired, and no chase developed. Some distance from the patrol, I lost consciousness. In a daze, I recall being carried into a house. It was on the outskirts of Reims at the home of René Felix, one of the rescuers, and his wife, Madalene, 68 Rue de Bezannes. I had not received any medical attention for some time, perhaps five days now, not since the German doctor sprinkled the white powder on my wounds. My refusal to allow the doctor to remove the arm was vivid. My condition got worse, critical in fact, as I was continually falling into unconsciousness and emitting loud groaning noises.

This uncontrollable groaning in my sleep became a matter of concern to the rescuers who feared that I would give them away, and they considered turning me over to the Germans for medical treatment.

An English-speaking woman, Mademoiselle Ramoge, is contacted to come to the Felix house. When she arrived, she told me that medical treatment would be arranged for me in the morning. "You must stop the loud groaning", she advised. "Because the German soldiers are stationed next door and they will investigate the noise. Otherwise to protect themselves, your hosts will be forced to turn you over to the Germans. Would you rather have the Germans take over your medical treatment?" She asks. My immediate answer was, "Absolutely not! I'll stay with the Resistance". I asked her to place a muzzle over my mouth and to tie it around my head. The groaning was muffled all night as I bit down hard on the cloth. The muzzle worked, but it was a painful, sleepless night.

With the medical treatment arranged, the local taxi arrived in the morning consisting of a horse and buggy with driver, Polo. He drove me to a medical clinic located behind the Cathedral de Notre Dame in Reims. The taxi was a convenience to the local people, as autos or gasoline were not available due to war shortages. Polo with horse and buggy, easily recognized as the local taxi driver, was not stopped routinely by the German patrols.

René Felix and Jean Joly, are shown on the right of the picture; the French Resistance Heroes who stormed the farm house to rescue me from the Gestapo in March 1944. Pierre Demarchez (is not in the picture). René Felix is pictured at the bottom. Petitbon the butcher, (shown on left) supplied the resistance with the meager food he could spare.

Mr. and Mrs. Jean Joly, Head of the French Resistance Underground in Reims, France.

Madame Yvonne Chauvin and Henry, *La Bonne Maison* employee who saw my parachute landing and carried me to the farmhouse, with me and Pierre Dermachez, rescuer in my escape.

# CHAPTER 20
## Life Saving Surgery

At the clinic, I learned from the Underground that a French doctor from Paris was to perform the surgery on my shrapnel mangled right arm. This heightened my spirits and gave me hope that the wounded arm problems were going to be corrected, or I would lose the arm. Dr. Levy, in fact, a French Jew, married to a French nurse, owned the clinic. To avoid capture and shipment to a concentration camp, he concealed himself in the cellar of the clinic. Dr. Levy's identity and secret life was kept from me for many years, long after the war's end. As a French Jew, he was ever alert to the German military occupying France and the Gestapo rounding up Jews for deportation. The operation on my hurting, busted and useless arm, with minimum anesthesia, caused great pain, which rendered me unconscious at times and also kept waking me.

It was a horrifying night, the gnawing pain kept me half asleep, half awake; and I prayed for the morning to come with the prospect of receiving requisitioned anesthesia (which did not come). Dawn arrived after a torturous night. I was wheeled into the operating room where Dr. Levy operated on my arm a second time and applied stitches to my wounded scalp. Upon awakening, I felt joy to discover my arm still attached, but that happiness was short-lived as the awareness of the intolerable pain from my many wounds and broken bones sparked my consciousness. The surgery was incomplete and Dr. Levy advised that gangrene had set in and the poor condition of the arm warranted amputation. A definite "NO" by the French Resistance, emphasized by a pistol to his head, alarmed Dr. Levy. The doctor and I both needed rest, so a third operation was scheduled for the next morning. Without pain medication, I experienced another terrible night, hoping against hope that morning would arrive quickly so that I could be given whatever anesthesia was available.

Morning finally arrived; Dr. Levy, with his nurse assisting, performed the third operation to save my arm. He removed the metal fragments and reset the fractured bones while I clenched my teeth for lack of anesthesia. Then, he sanitized the wounded areas on my arm, applied surgical dressing and put a cast on the arm. My fractured left ankle and six cracked ribs were not considered life threatening or requiring immediate attention so were put off for another day. They wheeled me back to my room where sleep overtook me. Delirious with pain, a parched mouth and throat awakened me. It was early evening. I pressed the bell for the nurse and she came running with others and in her excitement told me that there was fear of discovery, as a night nurse, who had penetrated the French Resistance cell at Reims and a German collaborator, had tipped off the Gestapo. "*Allez, toute de suite*." Quickly, they helped me into my tattered flight fatigues and carried me out to the street, to abandon me on a curbside. I had become persona non grata. I forgot about my pain and dry mouth.

The receptionists and the entrance to the Reims, France Clinic as it appeared in 1997.

Dr. Levy performed the life saving operations on John's gangrenous arm here.

## CHAPTER 21
## Loyalty Questioned

It was Saturday night and in my drunken-like stupor, I slipped into the gutter where even German soldiers out on the town with their dates passed me by with little notice of the drunk in tattered fatigues lying in the gutter. From nowhere, a young man (later identified as Robert), with his female companion came over to check me out. They looked me over and stood me up. I sensed that they wanted to help. They half dragged my limp body to a former French Calvary Training Center, called "The Circus", where they hauled me up two flights of stairs to a room secured with iron barred windows. Roberts's last words were, "*Ne'fiez pas la fenetre et n'ouvrez pas la porte*". (Don't look out of the window and don't open the door). It was locked on the outside. One time I peeked out of the window from behind a curtain and saw German soldiers milling around in the courtyard with their dates. The room resembled a prison holding area, and any thoughts of escape in my poor physical condition were shattered. I was happy to be in out of the weather and off the streets where prying eyes would not stumble upon me.

The only guard was a Mr. Dumas, an elderly police officer, around seventy years old, who checked on me once every evening and occasionally spoke in French. I thought the old timer did not like the Germans because he kept repeating, "*Les Boche Kaput*", which to me meant in the German language, "Kill, destroy or finish the Germans." In fact, one evening he said, "*Moi kaput Les Boche soldier*." He led me to believe one evening he pushed a drunken soldier into the nearby river. I had no idea if this was truth, or whether he was bragging, so I just went along with his comments by shaking my head up and down.

It was at this time and this place that I learned upon my return to the States that my young brother, S. Charles 'Chuck' Katsaros was the first family member to learn that I was Missing In Action on 20 March 1944. He was handed the delivery of the Telegram, from the Secretary of War, dated 3 April 1944, that was addressed to my dad, Speros S. Katsaros, who was not at home from work. A great number of issues had evolved in my life at this time: my first capture by the Gestapo, the French Resistance's aid in my escape, three life-saving surgeries by Dr. Levy, becoming *persona non-grata* because of fear of exposure, picked up in the gutter by a different cell member, and threatened with execution at the "Circus' at my refusal to establish a qualified identity. My health and recovery from injuries were my top priorities. My concerns were with the ever present Gestapo and their determination to locate me. They offered a $10,000.00 reward for information on my location and re-capture. This information was verified by the French Resistance and by articles in the newspapers. I was removed from the "Circus" by Pierre Demarchez and taken to his home at Chaumuzy, where I became a danger to him and his wife Julienne. The booklet of French phrases in the escape packet tucked in the parachute, coupled with the senior high school year of French classes provided me with some communications capability with my rescuers. Also concealed in the packet were a small compass, a silk map of Europe, water purification capsules, hard chocolate, and some paper money in French francs . The Gestapo relieved me of the packet, returning only the phrase booklet.

Daily, around noon hour, an elderly woman came to my room to give me food and drink. One day, I understood her to say that she had a son who was being held prisoner of *Les Boche*. No doubt she was a frightened soul. The thought of getting caught aiding and feeding an American airman, and facing the consequences, put extreme pressure on her. Thankfully, she found comfort in tending to someone who was in similar circumstances as her own son!

Within this local group at "The Circus", the decision was made to avoid the risk of exposure by thoroughly interrogating me and learning my true identity. Several days later a French Calvary Colonel, dressed in jodhpurs and leather leggings, suitable for the Cavalry Training Center, appeared at my room and in a stern tone demanded that I tell him who I was and how I came to be in France. I felt to be a prisoner again, but of whom, the French or the Germans? I stuck to military code and gave only my name, rank and serial number. He insisted on more information of my activities, of which, I gave none. I didn't bend to his insistence. He became exasperated and stomped out of the room.

The interrogator returned the next day dressed in mufti and demanded, "If you will not answer my questions to you, then we have no choice but to stand you against the wall and shoot you." I did not trust this man and had decided that they would not actually kill me. So I gave the standard information: name, rank and serial number. This time he was thoroughly angry and stormed out of the room. Later, in the afternoon, Mademoiselle Ramoge, the English speaking woman who helped to muzzle my groaning at the home of René Felix, came to see me and said, "You must know that they are not playing games with you. They do not believe that you are telling the truth, and that you are hiding information from them. If you insist in not properly identifying yourself, tomorrow you will be shot". By telling me this I realized that my life was on the line, and trusting the words of Madame Ramoge, I gave them a full description of the location of the the 612th Squadron, 401st Bomb Group. "If you were to fly over my air base at Deenethorpe, England, the base looks like a pistol. At the end of the pistol are three little lakes, and it looks like they are bullets coming out of the pistol-shaped air base." Madame Ramoge said, "Now I have something of importance to tell them," and she let herself out of the room.

They seemed satisfied with this debriefing, and three days later Madame Ramoge told me that the information checked out. I can believe that my information to them was verified because the interrogator was not seen again, and I did not suffer additional inquiry. While they were acting on their own and deciding what to do with me, Pierre Demarchez, one of the rescuers from the Gestapo, learned of my maltreatment at the hands of his friends, stormed into my prison room and created a row, blasting anyone and everyone in sight. He calmed down somewhat and promised to take me to his home when it became workable.

I reflected on my behavior while under inquisition and realized that the military code of "name, rank and serial number" can get one killed. Self-sacrifice is martyrdom, and it is also death. At the "Circus" I had continued refusing to give up my identity to my new rescuers. Finally, in fear of being shot to death, gave up my identity. This action not only saved my life from the firing squad, but the French Underground acquired the code name "Burgundy" as an I.D. to track my location and movements in their exchange of intelligence with S.O.E. (Special Operations Executive). In my travels from cell to underground cell my only identity was "Burgundy". The French Resistance knew my code name through the S.O.E. network of intelligence, which reached back to headquarters in London. They were aware of the special requirements in observation and tracking of my whereabouts, for purposes of reporting. Once S.O.E. was contacted, they became involved in my every move and probably were responsible for the direction of my path to exit France.

Jean Joly & John in front of the “Circus” 1997

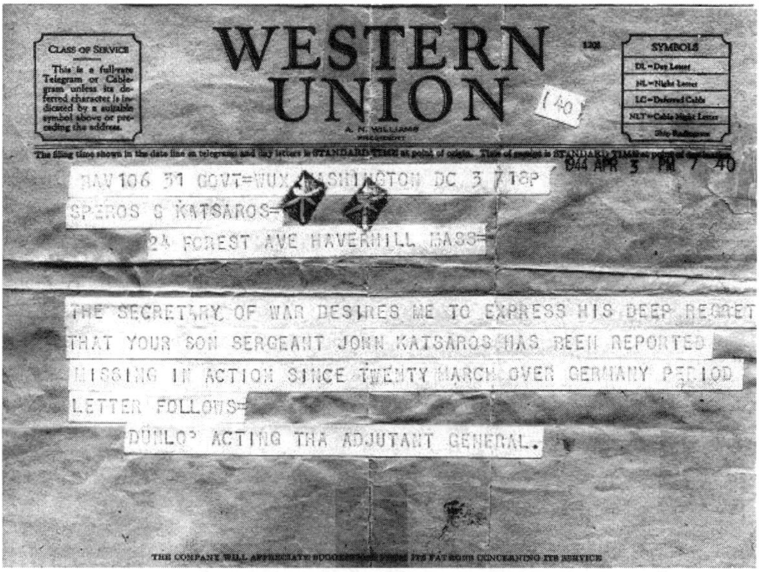

WESTERN UNION

CLASS OF SERVICE: This is a full-rate Telegram or Cablegram unless its deferred character is indicated by a suitable symbol above or preceding the address.

SYMBOLS: DL=Day Letter; NL=Night Letter; LC=Deferred Cable; NLT=Cable Night Letter; Ship Radiogram

A. N. WILLIAMS, PRESIDENT

1944 APR 3 PM 7 40

RAV106 31 GOVT=WUX WASHINGTON DC 3 718P

SPEROS S KATSAROS=

24 FOREST AVE HAVERHILL MASS=

THE SECRETARY OF WAR DESIRES ME TO EXPRESS HIS DEEP REGRET THAT YOUR SON SERGEANT JOHN KATSAROS HAS BEEN REPORTED MISSING IN ACTION SINCE TWENTY MARCH OVER GERMANY PERIOD LETTER FOLLOWS=

DUNLOP ACTING THA ADJUTANT GENERAL.

S Charles 'Chuck' Katsaros received delivery of this telegram to his family that, John Katsaros was reported Missing In Action. It reads: "THE SECRETARY OF WAR DESIRES TO EXPRESS HIS DEEP REGRET THAT YOUR SON SERGEANT JOHN KATSAROS HAS BEEN REPORTED MISSING IN ACTION SINCE TWENTY MARCH OVER GERMANY. LETTER FOLLOWS. DUNLOP ACTING THA ADJUTANT GENERAL."

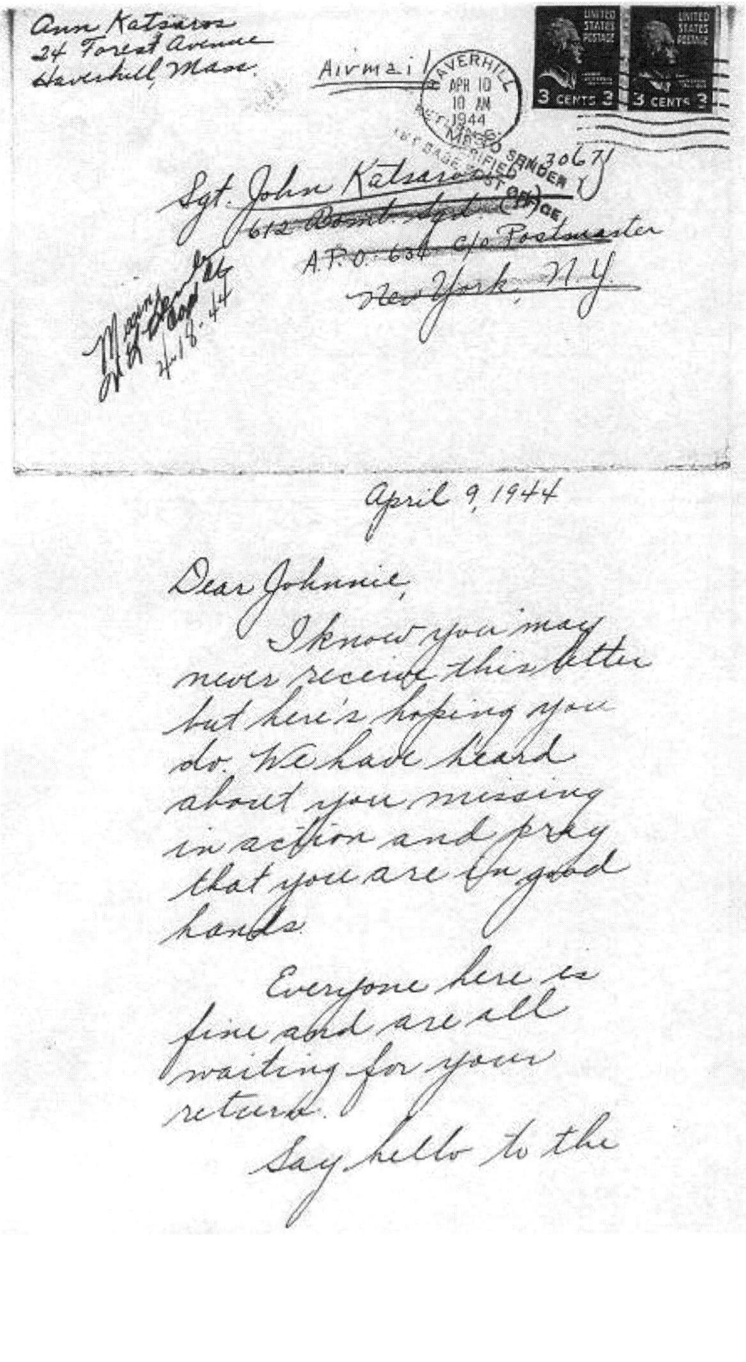

Ann Katsaros
24 Forest Avenue
Haverhill, Mass.

Airmail

HAVERHILL
APR 10
10 AM
1944
MASS.

Sgt. John Katsaros
612 Bomb. Sqd. (H)
A.P.O. 634 c/o Postmaster
New York, N.Y.

April 9, 1944

Dear Johnnie,

I know you may never receive this letter but here's hoping you do. We have heard about you missing in action and pray that you are in good hands.

Everyone here is fine and are all waiting for your return.

Say hello to the

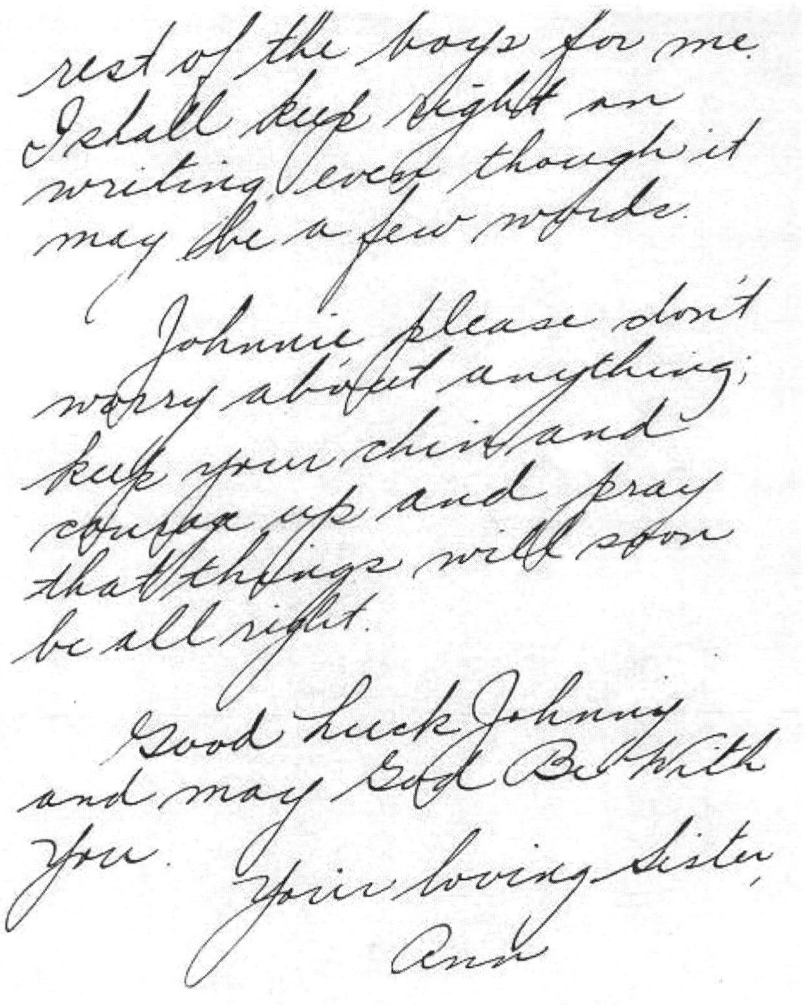

rest of the boys for me.
I shall keep right on
writing even though it
may be a few words.

Johnnie please don't
worry about anything;
keep your chin and
courage up and pray
that things will soon
be all right.

Good luck Johnny
and may God Be With
You. Your loving Sister,
Ann

Ann Katsaros Ziehl, John's sister, wrote this letter in 1944. It was returned to sender.

*L'église Saint-Jean-Baptiste reste fidèle aux messes du dimanche.*

I received holy communion at this church, L'Eglise Saint-Jean-Baptiste, April 9 1944. Easter Sunday.

## CHAPTER 22
## Easter Sunday, 9 April 1944

On Easter Sunday Pierre Demarchez returned to "The Circus", as promised, along with Jean Joly and René Felix, the other two members of the rescue team. This was like a reunion for me - I had not seen them all together for a fortnight. We climbed into Joly's auto and I am taken to Communion at Saint Jean Le Baptist where a large number of parishioners are seated, among whom are many German soldiers. The attendees had not been previously checked out, so our entrance exposed us in plain sight to the whole congregation. Fortunately, the soldiers gave no recognition to my presence, so I escaped detection and apprehension. Going to church invited us to unnecessary risk, and I did not like taking these kinds of chances. Members of the French Resistance were very gallant, but for me that was a very close call. After church services, we motored to meet a wrestler (name unknown) who promised to act as my body guard. We met Polo, Julienne Demarchez and Suzanne Joly at the farmhouse of René Felix where his wife, Madaleine, hosted Easter Sunday dinner. We sat down at the dining table and before supper had special prayers on this holy day, the Resurrection of our Lord, Jesus Christ. After prayer, I was asked to open a bottle of champagne about three feet in height. It was the largest bottle I had ever seen, and with my right arm in a cast, my left arm weak as a kitten; I failed to uncork the bottle. Someone else had to perform that chore. René asked us to keep our voices down because German soldiers were quartered nearby. My health condition did not warrant champagne, but I drank my fill and, as it affected me, I began to feel ill. It was time for me to return to "The Circus"; and Polo, the taxi man with the horse and buggy, drove me back to my lodging. But the ride was not without a scare as dusk had already turned to darkness and it was past curfew hour set by the German military.

British bombers targeted the marshaling yards at Reims that evening and Polo chose a roundabout way to return to the shelter at "The Circus", avoiding the strike area. A German patrol stopped Polo to ask questions of his comings and goings and why he was out after curfew. In my inebriated state, I was not too attentive to what they were talking about. I was just too sick to care. Polo, a familiar face on the streets, was given a "Bye" by the patrol. "Whew!"

The next day I was sick as a dog - my stomach and my throat parched from thirst. I drank a lot of water until the nurse came to give me a shot on my tail end. She told me to stop drinking water because after a "buzz" on champagne, water made one increasingly sick. Then she proceeded to stab a large hypodermic syringe into my buttocks. While I howled in pain, she filled the hypodermic with fluid from a second needle, after taking the time to fill the second needle with fluid. The day following, the nurse returned to administer another shot to my butt, but not before I insisted that she first prepare the second needle with fluid. It went much better this time; she mocked my complaining, and called me "Baby". So I told her, "Come over here and let me do that to you, see how you like it." "*Navaire*!", she said. Well, those shots to the buttocks, coupled with the restriction on fluids seemed to work, for in a couple of days, I was feeling better. I was especially thankful for the medication, mindful of its short supply. "*Merci*", "thank you" was my only way to show appreciation and gratitude for my nurse, all the kind, generous people, the Free French Patriots, the people of God who took risks, and made sacrifices to care for me. They gave me all they had, asked nothing in return, and only wanted me to be safe and well to continue on with my journey.

# CHAPTER 23
## At the Safe-House of Pierre and Julienne Demarchez

What went on in the hierarchy of the French Resistance or the communications between cells, I did not know, but Pierre Demarchez, through his negotiations with the Reims cell got me released to his custody and took me to his safe-house in Chaumuzy, several miles west of Reims, where I again met with his wife, Julienne. They had decided that, here, I should remain out of sight of the German military and Gestapo to enjoy a much needed rest period for recovery.

Pierre told me that the reason I was held prisoner by this Resistance cell, was that some of my statements contained the word "Yeah", that sounded too much like the German word, "*Ja*", (yes). This was a good lesson for me to be very careful in the future, as to the expressions and the words I use in conversation, even with my helpers. They could turn on you very quickly in order to protect themselves and the scores of other helpers in their Resistance cell. A flyer that was badly wounded and forced to parachute did not necessarily mean that he was an American or an Allied and not German. There was more than one occasion when a wounded German would volunteer to parachute into occupied German controlled France or Belgium with the sole purpose of exposing Resistance helpers.

The Demarchez home, a two-story building, housed a working bakery on the first floor with living quarters on the second floor. In the closed-in backyard was a chicken coop with many chickens. An undetectable door was built into the floor of the coop, which led down a ladder to a ten foot by ten-foot space with a dirt floor. Here, in this room, were many weapons cached for the local French Resistance. It included guns, ammunition, grenades, and time bombs - all for use against the German occupiers, now and when the Allied invasion took place.

Bravery was in the blood of the French Resistance fighters. They were fearless combatants especially against an enemy they have warred with over the years and would do everything they could for France and for the Allies who fought to free France from *Les Boche*. Had my hiding place been discovered, I was certain that the Gestapo would have administered a torturous interrogation to squeeze out all that I knew of the Free French fighters and any military information that I would provide. I wondered if I could have weathered the torture.

My stay at the home of Pierre and Julienne Demarchez saw me enjoy two meals per day and a great rest for body and mind. They had no children of their own and treated me as a son, seeing to my every physical need. The aromas of the fresh baking bread from the bakery waft through the air tantalizing my nostrils and olfactory senses. How fortunate and smart the Germans were to allow Pierre to run his bakery for the whole community where they also could purchase their supply of the freshly baked bread.

Pierre had been a Lieutenant in the French Army and fought the German invaders in the early months of WWII, before America entered the war. He was captured and held prisoner, working as a baker. Pierre escaped from the German prison and returned to Chaumuzy, France where he started the bakery in the store. The Germans loved his products so much, especially his bread, that they permitted him to remain to run the bakery and where they could see his whereabouts and keep track of him.

When the British RAF dropped off supplies for the Resistance a short distance from the bakery, I was taken along with the cell members as a lookout for German patrols. A light machine-gun (Sten) was shoved into my hands.

Pierre took advantage of the cast I was wearing and introduced me to members of the resistance as his deaf and dumb nephew who suffered injury in an air raid on Paris, as he went out to pick up supplies that were air dropped. These supplies consisted of explosives, fire bombs, arms and ammunition for purposes of sabotage in blowing up trains, rail ties and bridges. These were quickly gathered up by the Resistance for distribution among the various geographical cells. Pierre's share was added to the secreted cache in the dugout below his chicken coop.

On each fly-by, I was told to be prepared to board the British plane in the event it landed to pick me up for return to England. I sensed that the S.O.E. was behind this operation. The British took risks but there was no need to compound the danger and blow the Resistance cell activity. I was ready and eager for flight but the opportunity to fly never presented itself as the drop off plane never touched down.

One day, Pierre returned to the bakery from making his daily rounds, in a state of excitement, to tell me of a downed American fighter pilot and an intact airplane. I asked for the make of the plane and Pierre shrugged his shoulders indicating he had no idea. At my request Pierre made a sketch of an airplane which convinced me that it was one of those new model P-51 Mustangs recently flown into England to provide escort for our bombers on combat missions. “I would like to see the plane,” I said. Pierre pointed out and from a distance we viewed the plane guarded by a German soldier. The plane definitely was a P-51. On returning to the house, I made a sign of explosion with both hands. I emphasized that the plane would be used against us by the Luftwaffe and must be destroyed, but Pierre had already decided to destroy the plane. Pierre wasted no time to go out to the munitions cache below the chicken coop to return with a time-bomb. He placed it on the kitchen table to examine the wiring and to check the timing device and together we returned to the site of the downed P-51 where the unsuspecting guard, previously befriended by Pierre, allowed close examination of the plane. Pierre introduced me as his nephew, wounded by British Bombers in a Paris air raid. We walked around the plane looking at it closely and on the opposite side of the plane, Pierre set the timer and placed the bomb under the pilot seat. “Have you seen enough?” Pierre asked. “Then let us be on our way”, he winked. One hour later, the bomb blew, and so did the P-51 with the German guard. These men of the Resistance had such courage.

P-51 Mustang.

This is how I appeared in the forged German ID card created by the Reims French Resistance, April 1944.

Very rarely would a downed Allied airman stay for an extended period at a safe-house - a day or two, maximum, and the airman was passed on to another safe-house. I was allowed to remain for a longer period because my undernourishment left me frail, and my wounds and emaciated body needed to rest in order to heal. My heart was full of gratitude for Pierre and Julienne, who sacrificed all to care for me, putting their lives at such risk. A grateful son could not ask more of loving parents; I was treated as a member of the family and was as comfortable as any son might be. My body gained some health and strength, and fear of discovery left me.

The day before my departure to another safe-house, my time with the Demarchez family already overextended, Pierre introduced me to a deaf mute friend and together we three had a photograph.

Pierre also introduced me to a local priest and coincidentally, the next morning, the day of my departure, while Pierre was away from the bakery making his delivery rounds, the fearful Gestapo appeared at the bakery to arrest me with Julienne and her mother. Were they tipped off? I had been in plain sight; how did they suddenly raid the bakery? We were taken downtown Reims, to a Gestapo Substation where we were questioned individually. After a short questioning, Julienne's mother, an old woman, was soon released.

I was the next to be questioned. The interrogators were surprisingly civil asking only questions about activities at the bakery. "Where had Pierre gone?" Who were his friends and their addresses"? "What is my name, what caused my injuries?" "Who provided me with medical attention and where"? Trained to give only my name, rank and serial number, this was the only information I supplied. They missed the opportunity to catch me in a lie, and fortunately they never asked to see my dog-tags, or I would have been in serious trouble. They were well aware of who I was, and how I got there because they had me recorded since the lock-up and shoot-out at *La Bonne Maison*. For the time being they ignored my stubbornness, and they left the room.

I could hear the yelling from the room adjacent and I knew they were leaning on Julienne, and then there was the blood curdling screams. Julienne was being pressured to talk but she gave them nothing, so they continued with their barbarism. While I felt pain for Julienne, the thought never left my mind that they were not through with me, and I was going to be put through the test. I wondered how much I could take; and if I gave in, how much could I tell them. The thoughts of giving up my friends of the Resistance gave me shivers. How in hell could I live with myself if I gave up my best friends and blew the cover of any cell and I knew a number of them? I decided that rather than "rat" that I would suffer the torture. These friends of the Resistance had proven their sacrifice, their honor to me. I could do no less. Perhaps, I would not get that far. As soon as they discover that I had no identification; dog tags which were taken away from me at *La Bonne Maison*, and was dressed in civilian clothes, I would be taken as an infiltrator and shot as a spy.

Pierre was warned by his friends of the local roundup at the bakery and went into hiding. His cache of military supplies hidden in the hole under the chicken coop floor was never discovered. He eluded the Gestapo for the remainder of the war.

Pierre Demarchez, his friend & John (Note: arm in cast.).

## CHAPTER 24
## Second Escape

Following my capture, two German soldiers were assigned as guards to transport me to another Gestapo prison for interrogation. On the way the German staff car was halted at a roadblock. Several official looking vehicles were in the vicinity, and I was mysteriously removed from the staff car and hustled into one of these vehicles. It soon became apparent that this car belonged to the Reims Chief of Police who had orchestrated this rescue in conjunction with the Resistance. No shots were fired. A deputy chief's jacket and cap were handed to me as we quickly drove away from the encounter. The drive ended at a Reims winery where a hideout several floors underground in a wine storage facility was revealed. I got my thoughts together, cleared my vision and realized that my only companions were a 30-watt bulb and thousands of bottles of wine. It was a typical wine storage cellar; cold, damp, resembling a dungeon, but a safe hideout.

I was at a loss as to how this had been arranged. The Resistance did not offer details. I never had occasion to meet the Police Chief again. After a period of time, the day still showing daylight, and arrangements solidified, I was taken from the wine cellar to board an inconspicuous looking auto and driven several miles north of Reims to a farmhouse, belonging to Mr. and Mrs. Bronis Korach. They had a very courteous three-year-old boy named Erhard, large for his age of three years old, which they addressed as, "Le Petite Gorilla". The farm was located next to a forest on a former WWI battlefield. Trenches were still visible with battle debris of that era, such as French helmets, guns, empty shell casings and other paraphernalia strewn about. These may have been great items for souvenir hunters, but my basic interest was survival and escape. Their home was a buried blockhouse, built by the French military during the First World War. Not having run into another Allied person did not seem strange, as my concern was about my own skin and I never thought about anybody else who arrived here under similar circumstances. Here at the Korach farm, I met with a British Lancaster bombardier, Jack Hoad, a night flyer who was shot down by enemy aircraft fire. He, too, was looking for an escape route.

Together we stayed at the farm several days during which time the embarrassed Gestapo were looking everywhere in the area for us, and had advertised in the local newspaper, offering a $10,000.00 reward for information as to the whereabouts of any Allied airmen. The Patriotic French did not think of betraying their liberators or themselves. No doubt my health together with the many problems incurred by the Gestapo, had given many headaches to the wonderful French people, especially the Resistance; but to expose an Allied escapee- *Navaire*!

The Korach farmhouse sat about one hundred yards from the road, and was so positioned as to allow observance of any activity leading to the house. Bronis Korach showed us two water wells, one of which was dry, and in which we could hide should the Gestapo come. We could be let down on a bucket to the well bottom, twenty or thirty feet below, and a cover placed over the well.

True to our luck, the Gestapo showed up the next day to inquire about certain activity of downed Allied airmen in the vicinity. Jack Hoad and I were quickly lowered into the dry well and for an hour we could hear the questioning of our hosts by the Gestapo up above. Of course, the questioning took place in French and right over the dry well in which we were hidden. We exhaled a sigh of relief when the talk ended, and the Gestapo departed. After a short wait, Bronis lowered the bucket, and we were raised. Our location outside the city of Bourgogne was learned from Bronis as he prepared to leave on his motorcycle to do an errand, stated, "*Me parti a Bourgogne*." Bronis had many animals on his farm. one was a ferret kept to catch rabbits in a hole. I never did see it make a successful hunt. In the forest, Bronis took us on a hunt for wild boar. The meat of the animal is delicious. I imagined tasting the succulent porker. However, the hunt was unfortunately not a success. Mrs. Korach served us escargot (snails) which I found unappetizing at first, but a little hunger changed my mind and then found them to be delicious. It did not bother the Korach family to have their animals, including goats, visit them in their kitchen during mealtimes. Jack and I also accepted the animals and dared not offend our protectors to whom we were greatly indebted. They took many risks to provide us safety and comfort.

## CHAPTER 25
## Café de Bourgogne

On the day Jack Hoad and I left the Korach home to go to another safe-house in Bourgogne, the Gestapo pulled a surprise, but anticipated raid just before curfew at the farmhouse. By then we were comfortable at our new safe-house with Mr. Gerhard Erhard and his wife who operated Café de Bourgogne, frequently visited by German airmen from the airbase located between Bourgogne and Reims.

Dog tags were a serious item for downed Allied airmen - for without them the enemy challenged one's identification. On 20 March, the day of my bailout, the Gestapo had taken one of my dog tags from me and I often wondered what happened to the other one. Here is where the mystery was uncovered. At the Café' Bourgogne, Mr. Erhard had a dog tag mounted on a large plate glass mirror back of the bar. He would brag that he knew the American flyer that was being hunted by the Gestapo. "Here is the dog tag," he would say. As I sat silently in the bar room, Mr. Erhard would introduce me as his partially deaf and dumb nephew from Paris who got injured in an Allied raid on Paris and had a cast on his arm. Try as I might to get my dog tag, Erhard had no mind to return it. If captured again, I would be in a serious predicament without this identification as proof of who I really am. I will forever remember when my loyalty was questioned at the Circus. That evening he introduced me to a German Colonel in the Luftwaffe, an ME110 fighter pilot, flying combat for seven years that also included combat flying in the Spanish Civil War. American aviators considered the ME-110 obsolete once the American P-51 Mustang was equipped with the British Merlin engine. In conversation, Gerhard mentioned, "Would the Colonel be interested in flying an American airman to England?"At the Café de Bourgogne the owner Gerhard Govin had befriended an unhappy, Luftwaffe Colonel who was flying combat for seven years. He knew the Allies would win the war and believed rightly that his "time was up". He was killed in combat two days after my helper Mr. Govin attempted to have the Colonel, fly me back to England, and he was somewhat receptive. Govin introduced me to him. We three had champagne together at the Café, to celebrate Govin's birthday. I don't really know if the Colonel knew it was me that would accompany him to England, as he never led us to believe he did. I was introduced as Govin's nephew, injured in a British air raid in Paris, who was deaf and dumb.

Photo of a German ME-110 fighter plane, similar to the one the German Colonel piloted.

The Colonel, a congenial guy, was much older and wiser than the younger German pilots and had stories to share of his flying exploits. He had seen much, and been through much; and perhaps “His time had come to hang it up,” he said jokingly in conversation. Some remarks were made that the Colonel might want to fly to England and take along an American flyer “piggyback” in his ME-110. That kind of talk was scary for me as I listened, even though the German showed no suspicion of anyone’s status. Shortly after meeting the Luftwaffe Colonel, he was shot down and killed by the American Air Force.

The German Military caught Gerhard along with an accomplice in the act of cutting enemy telephone lines. Gerhard was shot in escape and died of his wounds two days later.

The next day after the evening of small talk in the bar, Mrs. Levy, the doctor’s wife, a nurse by profession, came from the clinic in Reims for dinner at the Erhard’s upstairs over the Café de Bourgogne. While in conversation she tried without success to remove the cast on my arm. Mr. Erhard obtained a large pair of shears and with much difficulty, managed to cut off the cast.

Mrs. Levy told me that I would be transferred for one day, to the home of Mademoiselle Ramoge, the English speaking woman, and after a visit to a champagne factory, I will board a train to Paris. My dog tag remained in the back of the bar mounted on the large plate glass mirror.

The dinner was venison, meat that I had never seen, let alone eaten, and holding the knife in my right hand, now devoid of a cast, I was unable to cut the meat, as the knife blade kept snapping back. I did not understand. Was this a joke? No, it was a test. When I began to eat, the fork in the wounded right hand, Mrs. Levy whacked my fingers with the blade of a dinner knife, and told me that Europeans hold the fork in the left hand. Eating with the fork in the right hand is a dead-give-away that I was an American. I was embarrassed for the scolding, but became very careful at the dinner table; getting hit on the fingers hurt, but eating improperly was both foolish and dangerous. Being on the run required extreme caution in any of my activities. The next day I was taken on a tour through the champagne factory, which was interrupted by an air raid by the 8th Air Force on the marshaling yards at Reims. Several German soldiers entered the factory during the air raid and the tour group rushed me into the champagne cellar below ground to be safe from curious eyes. The thousands of champagne bottles in the factory shook violently, but not a bottle was broken. Being closed in damp quarters under these conditions, I felt totally defenseless and experienced a sense of fear and claustrophobia.

Several months after the war's end Sgt. Anthony DeFazio, a friend from Haverhill, was handed two bottles of champagne by the owner while touring the champagne factory - one to keep and one to be delivered to me on his return to the U.S.A. Tony delivered the bottle.

After the factory visit, I spent the night at the home of Mlle. Ramoge. At bedtime, she decided that I should take a bath and insisted to help. I was embarrassed for her assistance. In my physical condition with my arm now stripped of the cast and needing care, in addition to not having had a bath in two months, her help was most welcomed. After the bath, I hit the sack and slept comfortably and soundly all night. In the morning a crowing rooster awakened me, and after breakfast goodbyes were said. As preplanned I headed for the train station. I will never forget that night.

FRANCE JUNE 1944

John in Gendarme uniform. Paris 1944

Marcellin Villemont Paris 1944

Marie Villemont - Paris 1944

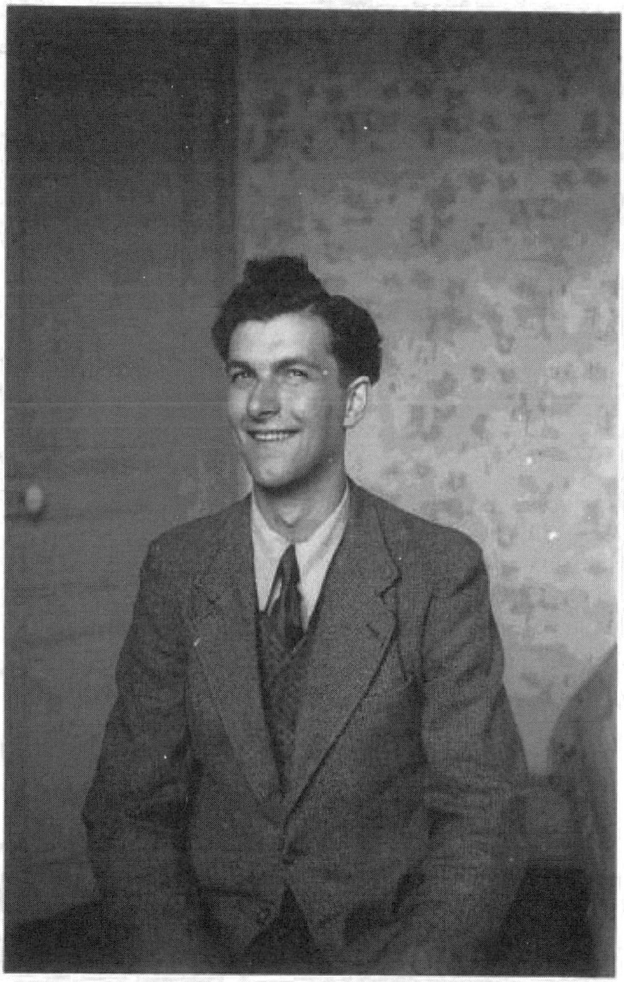

John in civilian attire - Paris, France May/June 1944

John Katsaros with
Members & family of Paris underground.
Mr. Marcellin Villemont..Paris, Franc

The lady in the photo is my Reims, France helper, Madeliene Felix at age 33, circa 1944 and Mr. Marcellin Villemont's third floor neighbor, name unknown, resistance fighter. He advised me of German "roust".

## CHAPTER 26
## Time To Move On

I arrived at the railroad station where again I met up with Jack Hoad and a French guide. The guide gave us new picture identification cards with our new names. My new name was Jean Gouloise, like the name of the French cigarette. I tried that brand once to find it was not to my liking. A small pipe was also given to me that I still possess with the memorabilia of my fugitive life during the war.

Security was enforced here at Reims and at every railroad station as Gestapo agents, recognizable in their long black leather coats, are posted at every train stop. Other agents were always in the area, unassumingly looking for Allied escapees, members of the Resistance, Jews, spies and other wanted, so they were not looking specifically for Allied Airmen.

We were cautioned to remain calm and unpretentious while waiting for the train; fidgeting was bound to draw unwanted attention and inquiry from the Gestapo. The train arrived, the guide boards, Jack and I followed, and he separated himself in a distant compartment. The train make a stop at Epernay, some 15 miles south of Reims, to pick up passengers and continued west to Paris, another 40 miles, to off-load its travelers. The boarded Gestapo was busy looking out for out-of-place individuals but did not disturb the passengers in any way between stops on the trip, nor ask for I.D. cards.

Our instructions were to follow the guides, and we spotted a young woman, accompanied by two men who made hand gestures towards us. We followed for a short distance when the woman, a young brunette, and all business, stopped, looked directly at me and spoke in perfect English, "My name is Genèvieve, follow me." Following at a distance, I am led by Genèvieve to the home of Gendarme Marcellin Villemont and his wife, Marie, who lived on a second floor apartment at 151 Boulevard Davout. Genèvieve now departed. The Villemont's introduced me to the couple who lived on the floor above and the man told me that he could be of assistance in the event of a "roust" (a roundup by the Gestapo and military in a closed-off of a section of homes with a quick search of a number of apartments to look for Allied airmen, spies and especially Jews.)

On occasion, young, healthy male citizens were rounded up for shipment to Germany to bolster the labor force used in the war effort.

Learning of a roust informed me that the German military was picking up Jews to be sent to concentration camps for extermination. A large yellow Star of David placed on their clothing, by the Gestapo, was an easy identifier of a Jew.

Dressed in one of his uniforms Gendarme Villemont and I would walk his rounds daily on the Champs L'Elysee. On occasion, because we were in gendarme uniform, German soldiers would stop us, to ask for the location of a pissoire, a light for a cigarette or request directions. I always deferred the questions to Marcellin to assist them. One day early evening, a German soldier, accompanied by his date, entered the pissoire and while relieving himself and talking to his date across the opening in the wall of the pissoire, turned to look at me and posed a question. It was the first time I was caught off guard and I answered, "Je ne sais pas", zipped up and made tracks to Marcellin. I made up my mind to think through my actions and movements to avoid danger. For me to be out on the town was to learn to be comfortable around people to avoid fear and to stay at Marcellin's elbow so he could respond to all inquiries.

Jean Moulars, the Paris Police Chief, and leader of the French Resistance, in Paris, was asked by Gendarme Villemont to check out my identification papers which the chief found to be flawed. He directed me to a photographer and expert forger of I.D. papers. The large yellow Star of David on her dress easily identified this woman as Jewish. She was the first person to confirm to me the details about the Holocaust and round up of Jews for torture and murder – men, women and children in the gas ovens of the extermination camps, in Eastern Europe and Poland.

The flawed I.D. papers I possessed, she informed me, would have been identified as forgeries had the Germans stopped me. She destroyed the old I.D., made new ones with a proper photo and handed them to Gaby, the new guide, who gave them to me.

New I.D. in hand, it was time to say "Good-bye" and many thanks to Gendarme Marcellin, Mrs. Villemont and the couple upstairs. I still think about the many times a roust took place in the area and consider myself fortunate that I was not involved in a roust.

Gaby and I walked to the railroad station where we met up with Jack Hoad and together we took the Metro (Paris subway) to the Electric building, which is a school building. It was good to see Genèvieve and several men of the Resistance there. Additional escapees and evaders were also there, making the count a total of seventeen in the group of Escape and Evaders of which seven were Americans, seven Jews, one British, one Polish and one Frenchman.

It became obvious to Jack Hoad and me, as it had to the Resistance that we had been together for an extended period of time, perhaps close to ten days. Our knowledge of names and places of the Underground posed too great a threat to them for us to remain together as travel companions. Our initial meeting was at the safe-house at the Korach farm where we hid out in a covered deep dry well and narrowly escaped detection by the hunting Gestapo who had a reward out for us. We had traveled together and were at the Café' de Bourgogne for three days after which we separated overnight, only to meet again in the morning at the Reims train station where we journeyed thru Epernay to Paris where we were split up again. I was taken to the home of Gendarme Villemont and several days later we are reunited at the Electric Building.

Sergeant Jack Stead, an American B-17 gunner, was my new travel companion. The threat posed by the Jack Hoad and John combination was at last broken up.

I met a Major Bufor Thacker, the highest-ranking officer, and there were Lieutenants Burgess, Ray Holtz and Charles McLain. A heavy-set humpback gentleman of the Resistance gave last minute instructions on comportment at the train station, in order not to foster attention to us. This train was to leave Paris destined for Toulouse, and hopefully good fortune would next take the group to the Pyrenees Mountains, the gateway to Spain and freedom.

With my new partner, Jack Stead, I connected with our guides to Toulouse, a short, good looking brunette and a slender, sickly looking man, wearing horn-rimmed glasses, whose appearance resembles that of a bookworm. We were slated to go to Pau, at the foothills of the Pyrenees, but things fell into disorder, as the guides were not wearing proper identification. Two men approached and said that his GI boots easily gave up Jack as a stranger, and they advised us to stay clear of Pau. It appeared as though these two men were creating a difficult situation.

We thought they were Gestapo, and Jack and I played deaf and dumb. During this confrontation McLain, Burgess and Holtz came on the scene and convinced the men that we were legitimate. Could these men have been Special Operations Executive (S.O.E.) plants?

It is important to note that after WWII, the AFEES (Air Force Escape and Evasion Society), of which I am a member, told us that we were fortunate to have left Paris when we did because two weeks after our departure, the Resistance forces were exposed by an informant who advised the Gestapo that the Paris Chief of Police, Jean Moulars, was the leader of the Resistance. The Chief was apprehended, along with two hundred U.S. Army Air Force and Allied airmen who were discovered to be awaiting orders to evacuate Paris for the Pyrenees. The Gestapo executed all. This was typical of the brutality and inhumanity of the enemy, particularly the Gestapo. It was horrifying to learn this shocking news.

From the Electric building, paired off with new travel companions, we walked to the Paris train station nearby, following the replacement guide who soon gave us the “slip”. We had no tickets and no boarding information. None of the other members of the group were visible. Jack Stead became anxious and now he felt the situation was getting desperate. Jack was a few years older than I, and married with a child. In order to calm Jack, I reminded him that we are dressed in civilian clothes and looked like Frenchmen, so to be calm and remain unobtrusive.

Now, no words are passed between us, just eye, head and hand signals. I signaled with my hands to wait and to keep our eyes open. An English speaking man walked by Jack and said, “Follow me.” Eagerly we followed his lead that took us to the train, where he discreetly passed train tickets to us and urged us to be careful, for the first guide has been picked up by the Gestapo for questioning. Jack and I boarded the train, Paris to Toulouse, tickets in hand, to discover that no seats were available, and the aisle was jammed with travelers, so, we stood along with other passengers in the aisle. A seat became vacant and Jack plopped himself down on it. Now, there was no communication between us at all. Several hours passed on this long journey to Toulouse, and I had been standing on my painful legs and aching feet. A woman arises and left her seat. Exhausted, I grabbed it tout de suite. The woman returned within a few minutes to stand right before me. I played the deaf and dumb. Jack rose to the occasion and offered his seat to the woman. She was grateful to Jack but cast me a glaring eye.

Some passengers began eating the food they brought along for the trip while Jack and I, without rations, remembered the delicious taste of the bread slice we each had for breakfast. We chose to ignore our hunger pains and savor thoughts of the coming of sweet freedom, more precious than food and drink. We arrived at Toulouse with no added problems from the German military. The Germans were unable to check passenger identifications on the overcrowded train.

French I.D. picture of John Katsaros taken by Jewish woman with "star of David" sewn to clothes.

## CHAPTER 27
## The Pyrenees

We traveled through Montauban to Toulouse, France where a new guide greeted us as we detrain. He directed us to the home of Mademoiselle Fernands Moulis, who was one of the leaders of the Resistance in the Toulouse area. Jack and I stayed one night.

The Resistance had outfitted me with a pair of dress shoes, at least two sizes too small, and Mademoiselle tried in vain to get me a decent pair of shoes in the proper size, suitable for mountain climbing. My other issued clothing consisted of a dress shirt, tie, trousers, short-sleeved sweater and a dress jacket. A hat or a pair of gloves essential to scale the mountains are not given to me. Early the next morning we reassembled at the train station and eventually boarded the train out of Toulouse and arrived at St. Girons, a small town at the foothills of the Pyrenees. A guide, presumably a Spanish Basque, was expected to meet the travelers at the station, and the trek up and over the Pyrenees was to begin at this point, but the guide did not appear. Without a guide the group was unsure about relying solely on the escape maps. We questioned our ability to venture through the thick forest without apprehension by the Germans. So, we decided to wait.

Finally, at dusk, after two days of nervous anxiety, the guide showed up to provide the leadership to enter the dark, unknown forest. Naturally, the group was elated, though nerve-spent; we had feared the Basque Guide would leave us to our own destiny. The group, in pairs, followed closely behind the Basque guide, possibly a prior WWII smuggler, and headed for the forest by a circuitous route. Our climb over the Pyrenees began by entering a narrow path, through thick brush and took the group into a descending valley heading to the base of the mountains. Suddenly, panic struck the group as the barking of dogs was heard up ahead and a search beam flooded the murkiness over our heads. God, we had already been discovered! The guide directed everyone to the ground to hide in the overgrowth. There were shouts directed through the dark to come forward; the guide put one finger across his lips, “Shh,” to be silent and gestured with his hands to stay put. A German patrol had heard our trampling through the brush and fixed their spot beam in our direction no advance movement was made to check out the noise. After a period of waiting, the lights went out and the patrol retreated with the dogs. The guide immediately recognized the peril in the continued travel along the valley floor and altered his direction to head for the mountains, to begin, sooner than planned, the arduous ascent up the mountainside, in single file.

After a quick, exhausting climb, the guide stopped for the group to rest and recuperate. Here he told us that the patrol offered no challenge because it figured the group to be a large, well-armed group of Resistance fighters and did not think it prudent for their little patrol to engage such a formidable force. Little did the Patrol know that the group had no weapons. After the quick breather, we added more distance between the patrol sighting and our group. The guide had us climbing half the night to make tracks, and to avoid possible detection by planes patrolling the area, looking for us. When daylight arrived, we stopped, exhausted, and fell asleep underbrush cover on the cold ground.

The Jewish men carried a heavy valise and after a day of exhaustive mountain climbing, were physically too tired to carry the bag and asked for assistance. The Major and one of the airmen volunteered to take on the chore of carrying the luggage. After several hours of exchange hauling between them, they, also, became tired, did not want to continue. Too weak to carry their own burden, the Jewish men pled for help with their precious possessions. The Major told them they must carry their own luggage, and the aged Jews continued to weep for assistance. The Major, tired of sharing the burden and mindful of the necessity to continue with our journey, tossed the valise, contents and all, into a ravine. The Jews were grievously pained by their loss and cried extensively. This was not a time for sympathy - life hung in the balance.

My feet were killing me from the tight dress shoes, and they gave me severe problems climbing the mountain rocks. I also needed help in climbing, having the use of only my left arm. Jack Stead, Charles McLain and the Major took turns, using a small tree branch to pull me up the mountains. To them, I am eternally grateful.

Feeling weak, sick and dispirited with my situation and not wanting to be a burden to the others, I requested to be left behind with a small compass in order for the group to continue moving forward without me. The group told me that I was one of them, and they would not leave me.

This gave me the encouragement I needed to continue, as they said, "We are getting closer to freedom and we are all going to make it."

The second morning in the mountains, a German spotter plane, probably a "Stork", flew close to our location and circled overhead in the manner of a hunter tracking deer; but we had taken cover under the trees and with dark clothing, we were not observed. The spotter hung around, circling, and seeing nothing of interest, flew away. Lady luck was holding out after having been spotted that once by a patrol on the first night in the mountains. The Basque guide, without whom we would not reach Spain and freedom, had packed a little food for himself. He ate from time to time and did not share with anyone. We did not consider him to be selfish or greedy, just looking out for himself. Freedom on an empty stomach would taste sweet. Freedom was a fleeting thing, especially in a nation like Spain, which remained neutral in WWII and owed allegiance to Germany for military aid to Generalissimo Franco during the Spanish Civil War, where Hitler tested his armament of planes, tanks and guns.

I had not eaten anything in two days and was extremely tired, as were the others, and I lacked the energy to continue the climb in this harsh environment. There were no roads or paths to follow and the high altitude made it difficult for me to breathe in my condition. Now and then we would come to a stream to cross and were able to refresh ourselves with clear, cool, fresh water. Not even wild berries were available to curb my hunger and on the third day in the mountains without a morsel of food and my stomach touching my backbone, some kind soul gave me two sugar cubes and told me to savor them slowly. This tasty tidbit and the kindness of the donor boosted my energy level enough to continue the challenge of the Pyrenees. Here we were scratching our way up a mountainside on our way to freedom, with no food, while back in France they were having their problems with the scarcity of food, and life's difficulties evading the Gestapo, steering clear of rousts and in constant fear of informants in their midst.

By the third or fourth night with no food and weary from the punishing mountain slopes, we asked the guide if this was the last mountain.

We asked again and again and his answer always was, "One more mountain". I was completely worn out and saw no end to our journey. I wondered if I could make it all the way to freedom. That magic word "freedom" gnawed on my empty stomach, yet, my great fellow travelers continued to bolster my weariness with encouraging words.

The guide knew our location and where we were going, and he headed to an empty barn. Exhausted, I lay down in the straw, out like a light within seconds, and had an uninterrupted night's sleep. In the morning, I was full of welts from biting bugs and could not stop scratching. At a nearby stream, fed by melting snow from the mountaintops, we all refreshed ourselves with clear cold drinking water before washing up. This was the first week in June and on our travels light snow had fallen, although at the tops of the mountain there had been heavy snowfall. Only a few climbers had proper climbing boots. My dress shoes had thin, smooth leather soles. They were too small for my feet and they got cramped and frozen. This gave me great discomfort. They also gave me great difficulty with the steep pitches on the icy slopes, the snow-covered rock areas, and on fording streams, and rivers with stone and gravel bottoms. Thankful for the rest under cover, the group left the barn and traveled for several hours when the absence of the P-51 pilot is noted. The guide refused to retrace our steps, as time would be lost and there was distance to travel. The Major, our senior officer, stated that in the future, a roll call would be taken, and added that the missing Captain, trained in navigation, had a compass with him and would find his way. After a short break, we continued to forge ahead when the guide gave the news, "Only one more mountain to climb". Alleluia! We would soon arrive at the border separating Spain from France. We trudged along for several more hours of stressful ascent through snow-covered ground and rocks, up to a small rock formation with carved lettering and arrows pointing, one, south to Spain, the other, north to France. The arrow, pointing to Spain, pointed downhill and the transgression over the border and down the Pyrenees proved to be very arduous. Happiness echoed in the group in a loud voice, and the guide admonished the group to be quiet and to speak in whispers, as the German military patrolled the border, and, if captured, although on the Spanish side of the Pyrenees, they will take prisoners. The Basque guide said, "Goodbye, good luck," and departed into the forest. Just like that.

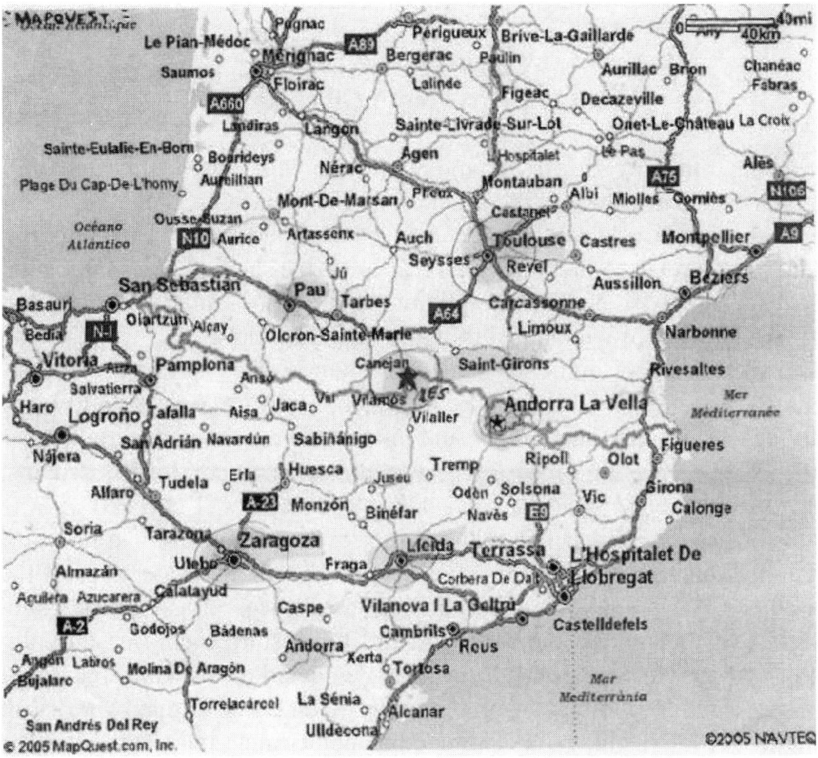


The "Long Escape", from Reims to Epernay, to Paris, Toulouse, St. Giron, France, over the Pyrenees Mountains to Les, Andorra, Lerida, Zaragoza, Madrid, La Linea Spain; to Gibraltar; to Bristol, London and Deenethorpe, England.

# CHAPTER 28
## From The Pyrenees to Gibraltar

We made our way down the mountainside with much difficulty and dragged ourselves towards the town of Les. The pace quickened to reach the thick underbrush where cover was taken for several minutes as the sound of a German spotter plane echoed across the canyon. The Major gave the "All clear." Arriving at the small town of Les, the Spanish Constabulary met us. They were sympathizers to the German cause and were not as friendly as first appeared. Escape and Evasion lectures had prepared each of us for just such a situation; the Major took charge, requested to meet with the mayor or town manager, and his request was honored.

From this meeting, the group was directed to comfortable rooms. Together with Jack Stead, as advised by our lectures, I checked out the room for listening devices, implanted to record conversations in hopes of obtaining valuable information, such as names, and meeting places of the Resistance. We found two tiny microphone devices (bugs) in the room behind two pictures on the wall, and did not disturb them but carefully monitored our conversation subjects. I remembered one instance regarding an Escape and Evasion lecture given to the 401st Bomb Group by a British General. He told us how they extracted some pertinent information from a ranking German fighter pilot who had been shot down near London. At the time of his capture, the German bomber aircraft had devastated London during the famous "Blitz" bombing. Many sections of London were reduced to shambles. In order for British Intelligence to obtain information from their prisoner they took him on a circuitous route around that part of London that had not been "blitzed" and to a famous restaurant where they had prime cuts of steak. The German pilot could not believe his eyes for he had heard that London was devastated by the German bombings and the people of England were living on meager rations. His information was correct, but he was led to believe otherwise. British Intelligence, in this devious manner, gathered a few secrets from this pilot.

Charles J. McLain, Lt. Colonel, (Ret.) - One escapee of several that climbed the Pyrenees into Spain with John Katsaros - June 1944.

Intelligence officers told the Luftwaffe pilot that the German bombers were actually bombing decoys in and around London and the British people were not on strict rations. Of course this was misinformation. The British General left the podium and an American officer was about to excuse us when the General/lecturer returned. However, his uniform was that of a British non-commissioned officer. He had tricked us. His final remark was, "If captured, give only your name, rank, and serial number because you will not know who is questioning you." Training and experience dictated your behavior.

Being forewarned by the hotel staff of unexpected companionship, we were not surprised at brunch to be accompanied by two Gestapo agents seated at a nearby table. And while at Les, it appeared that they were always in our company. We remained aloof yet cordial. In the evening, we strolled over to the Catholic Church, and looking up to the inside of the church dome, we were astounded to see the gold inlay. We looked at each other in disbelief and shook our heads. On return to the hotel from our stroll, we found the missing P-51 pilot left behind at the first barn stop on the mountaintop, there, to greet us, mad as a wet hen. The P-51 pilot was furious for our neglect and despite our embarrassment we were extremely happy that he made his way with the aid of his small compass to rejoin the group at Les. The Major was correct when he stated that the Captain had been trained in navigational aids. An escape kit holding money, maps and a small compass was installed on each parachute. The Gestapo on my first capture had taken my escape kit from me, or the distrusting Resistance group at "The Circus" in Reims confiscated the kit for its valuables. Only the French phrase booklet was returned to me.

The second night at Les, I got sick to my stomach, as did most of the others. In all probability, I did not know how to eat in this situation; not having eaten in five days, I ate and drank too much, too fast for my empty stomach. The chow was good, so barring food poisoning; it is unreasonable to put all the blame on the quality of the food and the water.

We stayed at Les for about forty-eight hours. In the morning of the third day, we were told that our next destination was Lerida via Andorra la Vella, and off we went, loaded on an old truck with a wooden bed. A ride down a mountainside in a rickety old truck was gratefully appreciated, especially when the stop was reached. At Andorra la Vella, we had a snack and visited the "horror" chambers in the mountain caves used during the period of the

Spanish Inquisition. Jews, Muslims and heretics were tortured, burned alive, and hung, garroted or otherwise executed for their religious beliefs. The morning after a night's sleep we mounted the truck to continue our journey to Lerida. The trip to Lerida was not a pleasant ride and immediately upon our expected arrival, the Spanish military greeted us and separated the group by national origin. The reception over, we were marched to prison and locked up. This is my fourth lock-up experience and it was becoming a bad habit.

The thoughts of the taste of the fresh air of Spain, that had kept me going on the hard climb over the Pyrenees, was hardly the savor of the freedom for which my expectations had prepared me. Not only was I frail, I was emaciated and having great difficulty with my weakness. The Major recognized the seriousness of my condition and requested a meeting with the prison commander, with whom it was agreed that I should be seen, under guard, by a doctor. I had no means or strength to escape, so the guard allowed me to enter the doctor's office by myself. The Spanish doctor's English was perfect, as he said to me, "You are an American?" "Yes sir," I replied. The doctor weighed me and began his examination. "You are in poor health and should be admitted to the prison dispensary." While held as a prisoner at the "Circus" my physical health took a turn for the worse and the exhaustive climb over the Pyrenees coupled with my deteriorating physical health through lack of nourishment accounted for my weight loss to eighty-seven pounds, weakening me considerably. A thought of comfort in a bright room in the dispensary was welcoming to me compared to being caged in a prison cell. Abruptly, the doctor continued to sputter, "The Allies invaded France and the shit will be kicked out of them."

"I feel better already – goodbye". Thinking to myself, "I've got to get away from this guy" and I headed straight outdoors to tell the Major of the invasion, which in all probability took place while we scaled the Pyrenees. When we returned to the prison, the Major asked for a meeting with the prison commander, and requested permission, in accordance with international law, to telephone the American Embassy in Madrid. The request was granted a couple of days later and the Major spoke to the American Ambassador who confirmed the Allied invasion of Europe at Normandy 6 June 1944. Our troops were preceding rapidly through France. The Ambassador asked us to remain calm, that he would send an official to Lerida to affect our release.

An Embassy Service Officer arrived the next day and had us released from prison unto his custody. It felt good to see an American civil official exert his influence where we had none. From the Lerida prison, the American flyers were herded onto an open, very old, Italian Fiat truck and placed under armed guard. A Spanish soldier proceeded to drive on the narrow dirt road up and down steep mountain passes towards our next destination. Whenever our driver met with another approaching vehicle, one or the other had to back up a considerable distance to let the other proceed. The truck had no sideboards to protect us from falling out, nor were there fences or barriers to keep the truck on the road. Our legs hung out of the truck sides, and on some turns our bodies suspended dangerously over cliffs of several thousand feet. This was a wild roller-coaster ride as the truck swayed from side to side managing the rough mountain road of stones, roots and hard pack, pitching violently on the many hairpin turns, as the driver sped along oblivious to the safety concerns of his passengers.

I was curious as to why we had armed soldiers guarding us, and if we were to be taken to another prison? So I asked one of the guards, "Are we to be released at the next city?" "Si", he answered. Their rifles appeared to be of WWI vintage, and I asked to examine one of them, and to my surprise a soldier handed me his rifle. It was WWI German vintage, all right, similar to our 1903 Springfield.

The Spanish government had provided us with meager services enough to satisfy the needs of the American Embassy without causing a diplomatic flap, but it was obvious that they had little love for America. The Spanish people however, viewed us with affection.

At the foothills of the Pyrenees I saw the damage to the buildings, bridges and roads, caused by the Spanish Civil War of 1936/1937, a few years before WWII. What impressed me most is how the government has repaired holes created by the aerial bombardment on the bridge roadways. The holes were covered with wood planks and nailed down on the road. The rickety old truck crossed over these bridges while the shaking of the structures gave the riders grave concern for their stability. Without further mishap, the rickety old truck took me to our destination, the city of Zaragoza, where the seven American airmen were escorted to a nice hotel. We were two to a room, except for the Major who had a separate room. We bathed, freshened up, and assembled later in the lobby. An American Embassy Official greeted us in the lobby and escorted us to a nearby men's haberdashery where we were outfitted head to toe with brand new mufti wearing apparel. Most important for me, besides the clean underwear and socks, was the selection of a civilian pair of shoes that fit my poor, tired, aching feet. The shoes were comfortable and to my amazement, smaller than my regular size, as my feet with my body had dropped in size and weight. That evening, dressed in new suits, shirts and ties, and all freshened up, we were guests of the American Embassy at dinner and we were now in American hands. This was a great day!

After this heartening experience, we were told that Madrid was our next destination. In the morning we were transported from Zaragoza to the American Embassy in Madrid where it was possible to catch a glimpse of Generalissimo Franco on his way to view the bullfights. Our request to attend the bullfights was denied - temporarily forgetting for a moment that the Spanish government owed allegiance to Germany for their assistance during the Civil War, we did not question the wisdom of our Embassy Service Office.

From the Embassy, we learned of a high ranking American fighter pilot who had been shot down, evaded capture by the Germans, and preceded us over the Pyrenees to freedom. This man was "Chuck" Yeager, the same American Test Pilot who became the first person to break the sound barrier. Chuck, after his career and retirement as a General from the USAF, spent many years as an aircraft engineer and government test pilot.

After spending a day in Madrid in the luxury of the fine Embassy Quarters, a bath with hot water, brand new wearing apparel and a banquet dinner, arrangements were made for the group to travel by train to La Linea at the base of the British Gibraltar on the Mediterranean Sea. Upon arrival at the La Linea train station, the British military met the group and gave escort to a military supply building on Gibraltar where our civilian attire was replaced by RAF military clothing consisting of a field cap, stockings, jumpsuit, jacket and RAF boots. Our visit on the Rock of Gibraltar was a pleasurable experience as we were well received and provided for as guests of the Commonwealth of Great Britain, eating and resting concerned only with our newfound luxuries. Forty-eight hours were spent touring the area and exploring numerous caves in the rocks inhabited by monkeys. Much of the area was cordoned off as "OFF LIMITS", where I assumed that arms, ammunition and military equipment were stored for defensive purposes. It was interesting and colorful to view the impressive British in "Changing of the Guard." Very impressive.

Gibraltar

The American Embassy in Gibraltar provided each of us with spending money in American dollars. I used a portion of the money at Gibraltar to purchase wristwatches, as I was told they could be sold for a handsome profit when I reached England. On the third day the group and I were provided transportation from Gibraltar to Bristol, England in an unarmed RAF C-47 cargo plane. I believed that the German Luftwaffe still patrolled the English Channel, so I had reservations about flying that great distance to England without machine-gun protection. I would have preferred escort by British or American fighter aircraft; however thankfully, our plane flew without incident to Bristol.

Soon after our landing and parking the aircraft, the ground crew rushed us looking for wristwatches. I had purchased four watches supposedly manufactured by Omega but did not carry the label. One was all I needed for a keepsake to replace my Air Force navigator watch, taken by the Gestapo, so I sold the other three for profit.

C-47 Transport - Gibraltar to England

# Escape Lines Memorial Society
## Calendar 2006

***For information on any of these Commemorative Walks, contact the ELMS Secretary, Roger Stanton, at 5 Tansy Road, Harrogate, North Yorkshire, HG3 2UJ, U.K.; Phone 01423 508667***

| | | | |
|---|---|---|---|
| 25 April – 02 May | ELMS Reunion week | Social/Visits | York/Malton |
| 28 April – 30 April | ELMS Memorial W/E | Parade/Dinner | York/Malton |
| 07 May | Nidderdale Walk | Moderate | North Yorkshire |
| 19 – 21 May | Aircrew Evaders | Meeting/Dinner | Stratford Upon Avon |
| 23 - 30 May | Cretan Freedom Trail | Difficult/Severe | Crete |
| May* | Italian Freedom Trail | Moderate | Barrea Italy |
| June 19 - 23 | Dutch Freedom Trail | Moderate | Arnhem Holland |
| June 19 - 23 | French Freedom Trail | Difficult/Severe | St Girons France |
| June* | Rossano Freedom Trail | Difficult/Severe | Rossano, Italy |
| July* | The Frankton Trail | Moderate | Bordeaux/ Ruffec |
| 6 – 9 July | French Freedom Trail | Difficult/Severe | St Girons France |
| August* | Danish Freedom Trail | Moderate | Seaby Denmark |
| August* | Shelburn Freedom Trail | Moderate | Brittany France |
| 7 – 12 September | Belgian Freedom Trail | Moderate | Pays Basque |
| 20 – 22 October | ELMS/Comete Memorial W/E | | Brussels Belgium |

NOTE: The Burgundy/French Freedom Trail we climbed, from St. Girons, France over the Pyrenees Mountains to Spain was rated, Difficult/Severe.(Each year the majority who attempt the Burgundy/French Freedom Trail, even with assistance, food, water, and proper clothing, fails the arduous climb. More moderate escape lines are generally chosen).

**Jack Stead Relives His Journey**

*"I write this, not as a tribute to any personal courage or glory, but at the insistence of my family, who for many years have urged me to set this down before it is lost either by a loss of memory or my demise.*

*Before I begin, I wish you to understand that for many years it was not possible to relate these events due to orders from the U.S. Army, that nothing be revealed until officially released. This was done to protect those brave people that aided in the hour of greatest need. Had they been discovered helping me, a B17 Flying Fortress gunner to evade capture, they would have forfeited their lives. The Germans would have seen to that.*

*About ten days passed, after my bailout and hiding in the Guyon family safe house, with no word on the progress to evade capture being made. Then we received word that I would be leaving the next morning and to be prepared to follow instructions to the letter. That night the Guyon family and I made our goodbye. I thanked them for all they had done for me to which they responded that it was nothing. Imagine that, they risked their lives, shared their meager food supply, searched out help when their cell was isolated and regarded it as nothing. I asked if there was anything they wanted from me and Paulette said she would like to have a ring I had that was a cameo and had been in my family for about eighty years or so. I immediately gave it to her and pleased to do so. We all hugged, kissed and Paulette cried a little. She then gave me two small religious mementos to take with me as a remembrance and wished me Godspeed and to please write after the war. Now, I could not carry their address with me for fear of being captured and the Germans finding it on me, so I left mine with them so they could hide it until after the war. They could write me, and I could reply.*

*The next morning Marcel and I left early and walked for about three miles in town to a church. We entered and found a man standing and about thirteen people sitting in pews. Marcel spoke to the man, came back to me and said in French, "I leave you now, and have a good journey", gave me a handclasp and departed. I sat with the others and the man began to speak to us in French first then in English. He explained the procedure to be used for the journey south. We were to travel in pairs from the church, always keeping the pair ahead of us in sight but we were not to stay too close as to make it noticeable we were together. We, above all, must never appear as a group.*

*The "Conveyors" were to be a young man and a young woman traveling as man and wife. They would arrive shortly, be introduced so we might recognize them, and then we would be on our way. They did arrive, and we then left the church together. We waited several minutes and then the first pair of us left, repeating this procedure until all were gone each pair keeping the pair ahead in view and the first pair following the guides. We had been given the train tickets prior to leaving and were instructed to surrender them only to the conductor on the train. We proceeded a short distance to the station and the train being there, we proceeded to board. To say it was crowded would be the understatement of the year. It was so jammed to the gills, as they say, with absolutely no place to sit and hardly a place to stand.*

*Now I had been paired with a young American flier about nineteen years old who had been seriously injured when he was shot down. His one arm was almost useless and he did not understand a word of French. We found a place to stand in the corridor not far from the bathroom and stood quietly casting an occasional glance down the line to keep the pair ahead of us in view. If they moved then we must do likewise. The train was so jammed that people were even in the bathroom, one sitting, and two standing with the door open. We were all mixed together, men and women, not many talking just keeping to our own thoughts. I could not talk to my partner, whose name I neglected was John Katsaros, because if we spoke we would give ourselves away, and who could be trusted?*

*Our group consisted of men from nineteen to seventy-five years of age, so we looked rather commonplace and this could only help... I later learned that half were Jewish and the rest of us were officers and enlisted men and French, English, American and, I believe, a Canadian. We had a real mixture.*

*The train finally started and we were on our way, packed like sardines lacking only the oil. After about two hours a man came struggling down the aisle, squeezing by person after person. Believe me there was a lot of complaining but he just said he had to get to the restroom. He finally gets there and finds three in it, and he had a fit. He carried on so much that the three in there decided they had to come out so he might get in. Now, let me tell you, there was hardly room for one extra person in the aisle let alone four. One was behind the door so the two had to come out so he could close the door; get around it and out of the room. They shuffled about and the desperate man finally got in and had his day. You will not believe this but that guy, and only that guy, came back three times on the first leg of the journey to use the room. Finally, on his last trip someone spoke up asking what his problem was and another voice from somewhere said in a loud voice that he must have taken a suppository. As grim as things were, believe me, this brought down the house. The corridor was not disturbed again. It was a long ride until we reached a few stations that relieved the crowding, as more got off than got on. John and I were by now standing near a compartment and at a stop, a seat became available. We only had to watch for the two ahead of us when the train stopped I sat down and figured I could relieve John shortly. Soon a woman got up and left (it turned out she was going to the rest room) so John came into the compartment and sat down, happy to have a seat. Lo and behold she reappears, marches up to John and says, in French, "Sir, you have taken my place." He gives her a big grin and sits there. I knew the woman was not going to give up easy and John had no idea what she wanted, so I got up and gave her my seat and that made her happy.*

*We proceeded south on the train not certain just what to expect, or just exactly where we were going. We knew we had to cross the mountains, but we had no idea how far south we could ride or even just how we could get into Spain. The people helping us escape could not risk the entire operation by some of us getting caught, and being forced to reveal how the operation was run. We were all aware how the Nazis could obtain any information they desired, it was simply a matter of would you die before you talked, and they were experts at their job.*

*The route we were taking, seemed to be in good repair, indicating that the Allies were not concentrating on this rail system, because we did not stop once for repairs to the rails. We made quite good time and now that we could sit down the journey was endurable. The only thing was, we had nothing to eat, and we had left very early that morning. But, all in all, an empty stomach is worth freedom anytime. Very late that day, we went through a town called Montauban. It was good-sized town, and after a short stop, we continued on south for about another thirty-five miles to Toulouse. This was a much larger town and proved to be the end of the journey. The two people ahead of us got off the train and John and I followed. We were inside a huge station with about four tracks across for servicing various routes to and from the area. As we had been instructed, we stayed together in twos but this time we could see our Conveyors. We all stood near the shops and along the wall of the station, keeping our eyes on the man and woman. They had taken up a position adjacent to the nearest tracks, upended their suitcases, and sat on them.*

*We had been advised, in our briefing, that someone would walk up to them engage them in conversation and that they would give us the all clear signal and then they would simply leave the station while we waited for the next act. We stood and they sat for hour after hour but nothing happened. We, John and I, felt in our bones that we were in deep trouble. This feeling got worse when the man and the woman got up and simply left with no signal to us. There were German soldiers all over the place, some on leave, I presume, as well as, Gestapo men because they were everywhere all the time and watched everything.*

*Again, we could not talk because of the fear of being overheard, so we communicated by eye contact and head nods. We moved inside a small coffee shop for a while to change our positions so as not to be quite so obvious. We could not stay there for long because no one could contact us those circumstances, so we moved back to the station proper. John was great, even though he was hurting, he never let on anything was wrong through the whole trip. Mind you, both of us were scared to death by the uncertainty of the situation. The two of us stood there, watching and waiting and finally a man came by, looked at me right in the eye, and said in English, "Follow the man with the pipe." He said this and quickly moved on. John and I looked at one another with a question in our eyes. Was this a contact that could be trusted? Was this the Gestapo trying us on for size? Should we move out or stay put? Now, none of the other people had made a move nor had anyone contacted them and we could not figure out why we had been spoken to but they were ignored. All of us around the station were keeping an eye on the others. We had to, we were all in this together, and what happened to one happened to all. We decided that moving and following the strange order the man had given us was much too risky so we waited some more. After about one half hour, the same man came by and again looked me in the eye and said the same thing but this time he was mad as hell and said it through clenched teeth as well as slightly louder. I looked at John, shrugged my shoulders, and nodded my head in the direction of the exit tunnel. We had to do something so let's go for broke. But believe me, I was scared to death. We strolled toward the tunnel trying to be nonchalant so as not to attract attention. A glance over my shoulder told me the others were now moving also. Was I condemning all of us to capture once we left the station? As we arrived at the tunnel, there stood a man of average height, smoking the largest pipe I had ever seen. He was leaning against the wall with a casual air, but as we approached, he turned and walked ahead of us, through the tunnel and outside. We followed for about two blocks when he then stopped, and allowed us to catch up to him. We stood there and he finally said, in English, "Are you people the shipment from Paris?" We told him that we were and asked about the other people with us. He said that they were being taken by twos by other men, and would be safe and that we would be together tomorrow if all went well. We asked why we had been left there so long and he said that his people knew a shipment was coming through that week but the men that handled that had been captured the week before and were either dead or in prison. He said that they had been going to the station everyday to meet the train from Paris but had no way to tell who was who or what was what. Today, he said, they had gone again and without much luck. They had seen the couple sitting at the tracks but it meant nothing to them so they were about to give up when one of their men indicated he wanted a meeting. They left the station and had a conference.*

*The man said he had spotted a young man with American Army shoes that had been dyed black and he felt it worth the risk to try and make contact. In fact he was so sure he was right he insisted they try. They were my shoes that I had bailed out with and had been wearing right along. We airmen had been advised in lectures regarding escape and evasion that shoes were the hardest item to get in Europe and that it would be wise to take ours with us as I had done. So, a pair of shoes, it turns out, moved us to the next part of our escape.*

*The man with the pipe took us to his house, (I never knew or asked his name) fed us, let us clean up and stay the night. He told us we would be leaving the next afternoon if things could be arranged. They were working on rebuilding the local organization to replace the operation lost by the capture of the other men. It was not so simple because they had to arrange connections all the way back to Paris and be sure those connections were safe. It felt good to have a decent meal under our belts as well as a place to sleep after the long train ride and the episode at the station. By checking a map now I can see where we had traveled some three hundred and fifty miles, as the crow flies, and by land more than that. I can see now why we had left so early in the morning. Chances are the trip we took might only go once a day or because of the war perhaps once a week. The impression that remains with me to this day about this house we were taken to is that it was a multiple dwelling with I think four floors. The building was very old looking from the outside, but when we entered the apartment itself, it was very modern and furnished well. There was no woman to be seen, the man did everything for us and did it as though he knew what he were doing. I often wondered if he was alone because he was single, or if he had sent his wife away because of the nature of his business. John and I were so exhausted and so hungry that the many things I think about now never occurred to either of us. We seemed to live from minute to minute and at the hands of other people. The best way to describe the feeling is to say; it was like a dream or a nightmare. We bathed and shaved and fell into bed to sleep the sleep of the dead. I thought I would never be that tired ever again, anytime in my life. Little did I know!*

*The next day we woke up very late, having been allowed to get all the rest we seemed to require. The man fixed us breakfast, even though it was afternoon, and when we had finished, he announced he was going out and see just what plans had been made. He told us they had a man to guide us over the Pyrenees Mountains into Spain and that everything had to be coordinated. We were left alone for several hours as he went about his business. Our only fear was that someone would come to the door looking for him because we sure did not know what to do. Not answer the door was what we probably decided but at this point I can't recall. He returned and advised us that everything was in order and we were to leave right away. He had train tickets, which he gave us, and then led us back to the station to join the others. Our instructions now were to pay no attention to our former companions but just ride the train to the end of the line and get off. We were to be met by someone and told what to do. Off we went, onto the train, found a seat, and waited. Soon the train started to move and once we were under way the conductor came through and collected the tickets. We either looked like natives or he just did not care but either way we attracted no attention and went on our way. There were not many people on this train and we were not sure if this was the best condition. Either way it made no difference because there was nothing we could do about it. We were not going as fast as the other train, and stopped at every little burg along the way. It was obvious it was a local line servicing all the little places in the south.*

*Eventually we reached the end of the line and got off, standing alongside the train by the tracks. The station was not much to speak of and we could see no life. A few people got off with us but they went their way without a backward glance. Here we were again, not knowing what to expect, when along comes a man walking quickly to the bunch of us. He never stops but motions us all to follow and goes by taking the lead he walks toward the front of the train and from there he branches off into the countryside. It was slightly hilly but not too bad so we had no trouble keeping up. After about twenty minutes he stopped in a small clearing in the woods and had us gather around. He then told us we had made it unscathed so far and also undetected by the Germans. We were, he said, to remain there until someone came for us. Under no circumstances were we to move or to do anything that might bring attention to ourselves such as lighting a fire or making any loud noise. He could not say exactly when our help would arrive, only repeating we must stay there. The man we had stayed with had given John and me some sandwiches so at least we had something to eat. Our fellow travelers also had been provided with something, not much, but something. Don't forget, food was short for the people and anything they gave us was less for them. So, not knowing how long we were to wait we settled down on the grass in small knots of people, those knowing one another together, the rest of us in random fashion. I am certain we all felt our savior would be along before nightfall and we would start the next phase of the escape. The sun went down, dusk came, the moon came out, and night was upon us in full force. I tried to sleep on the ground but, the dampness permeated my clothes and I was uncomfortable, as were all the others. There was much whispering, such as, "Is he coming? Did he get caught? Have we been set up? Should we strike out on our own?" We had only questions, no answers. This, I think, was the longest night of my entire life.*

*By morning I was so cold I thought I was going to freeze to death, it was June, and we were in the foothills of the mountains. I remember standing at the top of a small rise waiting for the sun to come up. A young Frenchman was standing alongside me he was in the underground and had made this trip before. He claimed he had information he wanted to get to England so the trip was necessary. I was famished and so was he. He asked if I had any food and I said no that what little I had had gone last night. He opened a knapsack and extracted a can of Pet Milk, poked a couple of holes in the end, tilted his head back, and poured some in his mouth. He offered me a swig and I gratefully accepted, getting it the same way he had. I had never tasted this canned milk before, but I can tell you, it was so high in sugar content; it was like a shot in the arm. I thanked him, returned the can, and he stowed it in his pack carefully so it would not spill. We both soaked up the warmth of the sun as it got higher and eventually warmed up and dried off... I had no idea what the others did to keep going, all I knew was, at last daylight had come, and now our man would be there any minute to care for us. Life was looking good again. Time, as such, is relative as I am sure you all know. Sometimes a minute can seem like an hour, another time the same minute does so quickly it seems never to have existed at all. Even days can follow this pattern of fast or slow flow. We all know the old saying, "The watched pot never boils," and it is so true to those involved in the time span in question. All we had to do was have patience and our troubles would be resolved in short order.*

*Spirits were up, life was good, and the next part of the adventure would certainly be less complicated than what had gone on before. The day wore on slowly and the sun got higher until we were at noon. Still no one approached us in our spot in the woods. We were not that far from the little town, so why didn't someone come for us? Oh, well, maybe one hour and we would be on our way because we certainly couldn't just sit here all day and risk getting caught. Someone said that perhaps the Germans had also broken the contact we were waiting for and we would be here forever. We discussed this possibility, agreeing that there might have been a problem, and that is someone did not show up by nightfall, we would strike out on our own, using our escape maps and head for the Spanish border. Having arrived at this decision we all tried to settle down and make the best of the situation.*

*The afternoon dragged along, each minutes like an hour, each hour like a lifetime. Mix this with a dose of scared, and you know how we felt. Hungry? Oh yes, but there wasn't anything to eat so we just endured, but not like hero's, no sir, we complained to whomever would listen. It sure didn't do any good, but we felt better just getting it off our chests. Had we known that it would be four more days before we had anything to eat, I am sure we would have given up on the spot. Finally, everyone got tired of complaining so we just sat and passed the time. We could not speak with the Jewish people very well, so they kept to themselves, talking among them. We did find out, through the French fellow that the old man with his group was seventy-five years old, and we assumed that the Underground was charging them all a lot of money to get them out. Right here, before I forget, I want to mention that this old man made the entire trip under his own power and I never once heard him complain. What happened to them all, once we got to Spain, I have no idea, but I hope they lived to tell of their ordeal?*

*This is how the afternoon passed, just waiting, until at last the sun started to go down. We were quickly reaching our hour of decision as to whether to wait some more or proceed on our own. All through the day, as odd as it might seem, we had been quite quiet, always speaking softly so as not to attract any attention should someone pass near. At last we heard some footsteps on the trail leading to our lair and our pulses quickened as we watched to see who it might be. It was our man. Finally he had arrived. He explained to the French fellow that he had never had any intention of coming to us in daylight and that we should have been told. Who cares? He's here. We are going at long last. "Did he have any food for us?" someone asked. He merely said that he did not, even though he had a knapsack on his back. He carried his own food and we must shift for ourselves, as he did not have enough for everyone. I have since thought that this man must have been a Basque since he obviously was a mountain man and knew his way around the Pyrenees Mountains. He wasted no time, getting us all on our feet and under way. By now it was quite dark and the guide led us down to the valley and along a road that led deeper into the mountains. We were told to form a single line, keep the person ahead in sight, and above all, not to talk. The guide set a rather fast pace and it quickly became obvious that the civilians could not keep up the pace as they were carrying suitcases. The guide stopped and instructed us younger people to carry the luggage. We did this and started off again. Although we were younger, it was not an easy task to carry this stuff, so, when we came to a small bridge some time later we all threw their things in the river. I have always wondered what was in those suitcases. Was it money, jewels, or just clothes? Later on when they found out what we had done, they could have killed us, they were so mad. But as it turned out, we would have lost them anyway, or at least had to abandon them because of events that followed.*

*We were really making good time down the valley and things seemed to be at their best, until all at once a huge search light came on down the road, and a car started up, pulling out of a side road onto our road, and headed towards us. There was a short road to our right leading to the foot of a hill; it was about a quarter of a mile long, dead- ending at the hill with a field on both sides of the road. The guide ran back down the line of people, headed up this short road and ducked into the tall growth and threw himself on the ground. Needless to say, we all did likewise, lying as still as dead men. The car turned up this road and stopped almost opposite us. They never left the car, just sat there with the motor running for maybe three or four minutes. Finally they backed down the road, never having flashed a light into the fields, and went back where they started. We laid there for about five more minutes to be sure everything was safe, then followed the guide as he abandoned the road and the valley and started to climb the hill at the road's end. It was tough work since the hill was about a 45-degree incline and grassy so the shoes slipped as we worked our way up. We would climb a little and rest a little and after a few hours of this we were all exhausted so that every time we rested we would fall asleep for a few minutes. We would be so hot from the work of climbing but after a few minutes of sleep we would wake up shivering from the damp and cold. It was miserable. Our easy journey through the valleys was all over. From now on, it is, climb up and slide down, and climb up again. We were among the trees, so that helped some as it gave us something to grab on to if one was in our path.*

*We asked the Frenchman why the people in the car didn't come into the field after us and he said the guide told him he was surprised also but felt that they may have been afraid that the people in the field were the French Underground and heavily armed and were afraid they might get hurt.*

*Little did they know how close they were to collecting a group of unarmed, frightened people?*

*We continued in this fashion all through the night. Poor John Katsaros, my partner from Paris, was having a terrible time trying to climb with only one arm; the other as I said before, was badly shot up and of no use to him. I broke a branch from a small tree and used it to help pull him up. Of course, the only time we had to do this was when it was very steep. He never complained, but I knew it was very painful for him to twist and turn in attempting to climb the hills. As daylight approached, the guide located a barn and we spent the day there sleeping in the straw. At nightfall he roused us and we went at the mountain again. Everyone was so hungry but there was no food. We were able to get water from the many streams we crossed, but after taking a drink and climbing awhile one got thirsty quickly and we had no way to carry water with us. How do you keep going like this? I don't know, but go we did. If it was tough on us, imagine the older people; imagine the old man, how did he do it? I don't know but by God he did. The will to live is powerful.*

*As I look back on this, I am amazed at the lack of conversation that went on during this trip. It must have been because it took all our strength just to keep going. But I'll tell you one thing, our guide never once faltered and walked as easily at the end as he did in the morning. We later felt he had made this trip many times and that as a matter of fact, he probably was a smuggler in peacetime and made his living carrying contraband over the borders. This was conjecturing but quite believable and it at least seemed like a good guess.*

*I could belabor the journey, but suffice to say, it took four days and four nights to get over to Spain. One day was quite like the preceding, a lot of hard climbing by day and luckily sleeping in barns at night. It might help to mention here that although there were barns to be found, there were no farmhouses. It seems that the natives, in the summer take their livestock up into the mountains for grazing but do not stay there with them all the time. The barns are not large and are used to store hay, straw, feed and other incidentals they do not want left out in the weather. So there was no one to bother us and moreover it was early in the season so nothing had been brought up as yet. Our next worry would be when we approached the border we might be seen by German guards with dogs because they were on continual patrol looking for anything amiss.*

*The third day out we had a catastrophe in that when we got up in the morning in the barn we had slept in, we thought we had roused everyone from the straw before we set out on that day's climb. Around noon, as we rested, we discovered we had left one of our men behind. There was nothing we could do for him at this point, only agreeing that in the future to make a good head count before leaving for the day. We could only hope that poor fellow could find his own way into Spain. Rested, we continued climbing and that day we climbed above the tree line as well as the usual mountain streams we used for drinking. By the end of the day we were all parched with thirst. We continued up until finally the guide called us together and pointed to a huge pile of rocks banded together with chicken wire. When you stood by one and looked off into the distance, you could just make out another one. These were the markers for the boundary between France and Spain.*

*He indicated that we must be very careful of planes flying the border as well as soldiers on foot patrolling. The planes, if they spotted us, could notify the soldiers by radio of our position. He also indicated that they would come into Spain after us if we were seen. He waved us to go on and turned and walked away from us down the mountain to our right. He obviously was finished with his job and now we were on our own. Even though it was late enough in the season, there was snow for us to deal with, but there was a large depression in the ground, maybe fifty feet around and it was full of water. We didn't even stop to think whether it might be poisoned or at the very least dirty. I guess it was good water since no one got sick.*

*We gathered ourselves together and proceeded to climb past the rock markers so as to be in Spain as quickly as possible. We continued up for several hours, made the top, and proceeded down to Spain. We had made it. We kept walking down the hills but couldn't see any signs of life. We walked until it started to get dark and as luck was with us we found another barn, the first we had seen that day. We spent the night there as we had in others. When morning came we would have to devise a plan of action since we were now without a guide. The barn provided the shelter we needed from the chill and the dew of the mountain. Sleep was no problem, because we were worn out from the day's activities. When you think about it, it is odd that being in the situation we were in, one might wonder how anyone could sleep. There is no doubt we were all frightened, unsure of what was going to happen next, yet our bodies need for rest apparently superseded our mind's need to worry. The night passed without event, so everyone got a good night's rest. We did discuss the man we lost, wondering where he might be, and if he might catch up with us. Our hearts and minds were with him and we all wished him luck. I, myself, thanked God that it wasn't me who was wandering out there somewhere lost and alone. Frankly, I had enough problems as it was, I sure didn't need another batch of them to carry.*

*Now it was daylight, and decisions had to be made. We had no set leader to make decisions, so it became a general discussion meeting, and those of us that could communicate did so. There were not a whole lot of options for us to consider but we knew we must press on until we found some help in Spain. Here we were in another country and we had entered it illegally by crossing the border where there were no border guards. It was a moot question because we doubted the guards would have admitted us if we did confront them. It became obvious there was only one real course of action to take, and this was to strike out in small groups, going down the mountain and let nature take its course. So off we went sliding and walking when it was possible, the grade was very steep, until we came to the road. No sooner had we reached the road than the local police were upon us. There were no pleasant greetings and smiles, just some orders we could not understand. The language was not to be understood, but the gestures certainly were not in doubt. They all had pistols at their waists and I am sure if we had given them any trouble, they would have used them. They kept us there as other policemen rounded up the others as they appeared at the side of the road at various points. We were all more or less in the same area so they had us all in short order. No one tried to escape, rather we were happy to be found because we felt that now the authorities had us and the proper steps would be taken to get us on our way to England. WRONG!*

*They marched us all to a good-sized barn along the side of the road, lined us up and one by one had us turn out our pockets, taking everything we had of value. As each one was relieved of their valuables they were ordered into the barn. They took all our watches; wallets, maps, coins and rings, if a person had one. Soon everyone was inside, the doors closed, secured and a guard was posted outside. Why they took everything we could not understand, but after a little discussion we decided the police were going to keep this stuff for themselves. Why not? There was nothing we could do one way or the other. Again, it would have to be a wait-and-see game.*

*We were locked in the prison for quite some time, just sitting on the floor, letting our minds process the possibilities of the next chapter in the unfolding dramas. Suddenly the door was flung open; an officer strode in, followed by two policemen. One man had a small table and chair, and the officer sat down. The policemen looked a little unhappy, the officer looked mad. He spoke some English, telling us to come up one at a time and reclaim our property. He did not apologize, but sat by the box as each person found their stuff. Now, although I have not mentioned it, we were all starving to death, and by the time everyone's goods were reclaimed, it was noon or a little after. Remember now, it had been four days and four nights since we had eaten. We had been expending energy like a ditch digger, and had about reached the end of our rope. How the old man suffered all this and kept going, I'll never know.*

*Once everything had been returned, the officer motioned for all of us to follow him. We went out the door, across the road, up a flight of steps and into a hotel building. A long room was already set up with a table and the number of settings to accommodate all of us. We had been expected! Quickly sitting down, we waited for some food. Before eating, they came, poured some clear liquid into a glass for each of us, and then filled the glass with water. The liquid turned cloudy and it tasted like licorice. We drank it but it really knocked us for a loop. We were in no shape for drinking. Finally we got some food, just what I cannot recall, and when we finished we were shown to some rooms with nice clean bedclothes. That ended the day for the whole group. A real bed, clean sheets, a full stomach and, at least it seemed nothing more to worry about. We were on our way home.*

*The next morning we were able to clean up, and it felt good to be washed even though there was nothing we could do about our clothes. They were dirty and had to stay that way. We were not about to ask for a washing machine or give anyone any trouble. We were fed and then taken down the road a mile or two. It seems to me we walked because I don't recall riding in or on any type of conveyance. I recently checked with my companion, Jack Katsaros, and he recalled that the town they took us to was Les. We had been apprehended down the road from this town, held in that immediate area, and transferred to Les. When we arrived there we were given a room in an inn and there were two of us to each room. We were then called together and a man that spoke English advised us that we were free to move about the small town during the day.*

*We were not to leave the town proper and were to be in the inn by nightfall. At this point, an officer that was with us requested permission to try and contact the American Embassy in Barcelona. The man was not very friendly, but he also was not cruel. He gave his permission, told us how we could contact him if we needed him, and left the inn. The officer set about trying to contact the Embassy and after some little while he succeeded in getting through. The Embassy told him they could not help us from Barcelona because the area was too mountainous and the way the mountains were situated it would take days for them to get to us. They told us that the main Embassy was in Madrid and that they would contact them for us and arrange to try and get us out of there. Now all we could do is wait.*

*We all walked the town to take in the sights, such as they were. It consisted of one main road with most of the buildings along this on both sides of the road. I recall a bridge built of stone over a rather small run of water. We sat on the bridge and soaked up the sun, enjoying the first real relaxation for many a day. We returned to the inn for lunch and dinner and as I recall, the food was not too bad. But then, four days and four nights without food can make anything seem good. We had learned not to be too fussy. We never could figure out who was paying for our keep. It is true that in our case perhaps the Spanish government had been assured by the United States that they would pay for our keep, but what about the civilians that were with us? We had no money to speak of, and I am fairly certain the others also were in the same position. That night we went to bed early because we were still exhausted as well as the fact that there was nothing to do to amuse ourselves. The next morning we awoke, John and I, in the same bed. I took one look at him and had a fit. He was a mass of red welts all over. I thought he had caught something so I told him about his condition. He just looked at me and said I didn't look any better. It turned out that the place was alive with bed bugs so from then on we slept with the lights on.*

*The second day we heard someone shouting outside and we rushed out to find some of our people walking with the man we had left behind in the barn. Believe me, he was a mess. The poor fellow was tired beyond belief and looked like the devil. Unshaven, gaunt, wide-eyed and also very mad, he was a sight to behold. We really thought we would never see him again. He felt we had abandoned him and indeed he was right. We did not follow proper procedure prior to leaving the barn that morning, but then consider that we had never been through anything like this before and we had never been briefed on how to handle the situation. We admitted we were wrong; that it was not intentional, and he could see for himself the concern we had for his well-being. So when he calmed down, he forgave us and said he now understood. I sometimes think he kept going because all he wanted to do was get to all of us and perhaps kill us. The amazing thing about his arrival was the fact that being alone and not knowing the area, he merely proceeded straight ahead uphill and down, trying to maintain a straight line to the south. Our guide knew the best way and I am sure saved us a lot of hard climbing. Our journey was not easy, but we were appalled at what our comrade must have gone through. Another odd thing about this is that he arrived so close to our final destination. It makes you think that perhaps someone was watching over him, at least I like to think that this was the case.*

*Later, we were all called together and informed that arrangements had been made for us to be transported to another place and that we should be ready to move out early the next morning. We had nothing to pack so we could move at a moment's notice. We had been able to bathe but we had not been able to wash any clothing, including our underwear so we were a little ripe.*

*The next morning, after breakfast, we were told to go to the road and wait. We did. After a short time, a truck came along with a load of logs. They were piled high and tied down with ropes to keep them in place. This was our ride out of here. Not first class, but better than walking, so we climbed aboard and off we went. We had two more to our group at this point, a young couple, but who they were or why they came out with us I never knew and since they were Spanish, we were not able to talk to them. The ride was not the most pleasant trip I have ever taken, but in that rugged terrain it sure beat walking.*

*We rode most of the day, passing men at work in the fields, and sighting quite a few wrecked vehicles, tanks and trucks, just abandoned in the ravines. These were left from the Spanish Civil war, left to rot and rust as a monument to man's inability to get along, even with his own people. The truck was old, very slow, and the road was quite steep both up and down. The day was most pleasant and not too hot, even though we were right out in the sun. We proceeded in this fashion until late in the afternoon finally arriving at a place with a wall around it. Some people came out, ordered us down and into the walled area. We sat on the ground or walked around to stretch our legs, waiting for the next episode to unfold. Each time things seemed certain, we were faced with a new situation, and our nerves would begin to get raw again.*

*It wasn't long until a man appeared and ushered one of our people into the building. In about five minutes our man reappeared and another person was taken inside. We were all crowded around the first man, asking what was going on in there. He said he had been questioned as to his identity and why he was in Spain. He had explained that he was an American airman and was escaping the Germans and wanted to rejoin his unit in England. This presented no problem, he said, until they had him turn out his pockets and discovered his French Identity book. This, of course, had his picture but another name, place of birth and occupation. They did not seem happy with this but kept the book and told him to go back into the yard. His advice to us was, get rid of the book, and fast. We all, that are military people, got out our books and heaved them over the wall. I really hated to do this because it would have been a beautiful souvenir to keep for remembrance. Soon enough, my turn came, and I was taken before a man at a table in the house. He spoke very good English, questioning me as the first man had said as to why I was in the country in an illegal fashion. I also explained why I was there and having nothing in my pockets to contradict my story, I was quickly returned to the yard.*

*When everyone had been interrogated, the military personnel was directed to the gate and we left the walled area to find a bus waiting, along with a small dark haired man that proved to be a Spanish fellow that worked for the American Council in Madrid. Our Jewish companions were left behind to their fate, and until today, I often wonder what happened to them. It would be painful to even for a moment consider the possibility that they were turned back into the hands of the Germans. We were all aware that Spain had leaned toward Germany all through the war because of aid Franco had received from Hitler during Spain's Civil War.*

*The bus started up and off we went, in style this time. We were taken a short distance to a town by the name of Zaragoza. The bus went to the center of town, stopping in front of a large store of many floors. It was, in fact, a department store. Our man from the Embassy told us we were to get new clothes and because it was so late in the day, all the clerks were gone but the store was being held open for us. Unbelievable! We all went in the store and up to the men's department. We were all instructed to pick out a suit, new shoes, and two pairs of socks, two sets of underwear, two shirts and one tie. A man in the store listed our selection, and we were ushered back to the bus for another short ride.*

*We were taken to a spa-type resort that had springs baths with high sulfur and the odor to go along with it. We were given nice clean, albeit small rooms and the view of the surrounding area was beautiful. We could come and go as we pleased but again, had to be in at dark and stay within the confines of the spa. How we forget the small pleasures of life. What a treat to take a bath and get into fresh clothes. My shoes, which were G.I. issue but dyed black, were held on by a series of small rayon pieces oj shoelace. The only laces we could get to replace the brown laces were made of rayon. Now, rayon, when wet, gets weak and breaks so I wound up with small pieces to hold the shoes on. You think this was a problem? John Katsaros was walking in shoes a couple of sizes too small for him. He had big feet and the people that helped him did the best they could. Imagine walking for weeks in shoes a couple sizes too small. At last he had a pair that fit. I must tell you here that at no time during the entire trip, from Paris to the spa, did John ever complain that his feet were killing him. I guess the poor guy was so shot up he hurt worse elsewhere. The food was good, and there was plenty of it, the only problem was, they used oil for all their cooking. Have you ever seen fried eggs, beautiful to look at, sliding around on the serving plate in a sea of oil? We tried to get them to cook the eggs and other stuff with butter, but they acted as though they didn't understand what we wanted. I'll tell you this, between the oil and the beautiful, big, ripe cherries and other fruit we could get, we were in a bad way. Our systems could not handle all this and we more than paid the price.*

*Things were starting to move fast now because we were not at the spa very long, perhaps a day or two and left Zaragoza by train and off we went to Madrid. Upon arrival in Madrid, Spain we were taken directly to the American Embassy and one at a time, again questioned. This time our people wanted to hear about any information we might have regarding troop movements, German emplacements, tank deployment, and other related information. When this was finished, we were told that we would be moved right along, the next day, to the British in Gibraltar. Consequently, we never were able to see anything of the city of Madrid.*

*The next morning we were again put on a train, which proceeded, to Granada and on to La Linea de la Concepcion, or as it is generally called, La Linea. This little town is right near the entrance to the Gibraltar fortifications held by the British, even to this day. We actually walked from the town to the gates of Gibraltar and were passed through with no delay. This indicated to us that we were expected. At last we were safe and again among our own people.*

*The records I have obtained from the government show that we arrived at Gibraltar on the 13th of June. I thought we might have a chance to see some of this famous Rock, the monkeys, the gun emplacements the caves, and whatever else might be of interest but that was not to be the case. We were ushered into a room and told to get out of the civilian clothes we were wearing. We were to turn in the clothes we had received at Zaragoza in the store and we were issued G.I. underwear, shoes, socks, pants, a shirt and a fatigue jacket. We were allowed to spend the rest of the day as we pleased as long as we did not venture into any areas marked "OFF LIMITS".*

*As I wandered about looking at the rocks and the sea, I came across a sailor, and he was carrying a brown bag full of watches. He said that he had come from Africa where he had been able to get these watches for a song, and did I want to buy one? Now I had given my watch to the French people that helped me, so I was in need of one. I asked him the price and he said twelve dollars. I looked at the watches and did not recognize the name and thinking he was a fast dealer, I decided not to buy. The name on the watches was OMEGA. I later learned this is one of the finest watches made. Such is life.*

*It was getting dark so I returned to the area we had been assigned only to learn we were to fly out the next day, if the weather permitted. We had dinner in the mess hall and went to bed.*

*The next day was bright and clear, real flying weather, so we were driven to the airfield, put on a plane and told we were bound for England. The flight was uneventful, and we landed at Bristol where we were put on a bus, under guard, and taken to London. We were installed in a large manor house that was used by the American Military Intelligence Service.*

*We were held and interrogated in detail. They wanted to get as much information as they could from what we could remember and also our individual stories of escape or evasion for their future use. We were not allowed to leave the building until someone that actually knew us and could identify us arrived. For me this was a two-day wait and fortunately for me our tail gunner on our crew was still at the base. The rest of my crew had been shot down while I was in France trying to get back. The man's name was Chuck Pryne, and was I glad to see him. He vouched for me and signed some papers to indicate he was telling the truth. We were allowed to leave the building for an afternoon of relaxation and we did just that. As a matter of fact, we hit several bars and got stiff as a billy goat. Chuck went back to the Group the next day, and I was sent to Eighth Air Corps headquarters to get my records, and then I went to my group to have the records brought up to date and to be paid. My instructions were to return to London and prepare to try and find a seat on a plane home."*

# CHAPTER 29
## Air Intelligence

During my escape and evasion through German occupied France, the Resistance had given me the code name "Burgundy" which proved to be very interesting and informative to Allied Intelligence. On landing at Bristol, we mounted staff cars and were immediately driven to London where American Air Intelligence at ETOUSA Headquarters was waiting to interrogate us. An Intelligence officer introduced himself to the group and spoke candidly on our heroics and stated that each airman was to be debriefed by an Air Force officer of the Intelligence Staff, that intelligence wanted to get a complete picture from each airman of everything that transpired from what happened to him on his last mission and his travels through the Underground to include names, locations, times, dates, and places, up to the landing here at Bristol, England. The call goes out, "Who is Burgundy?" I raised my hand. ETOUSA Intelligence was amazed to learn that this young skinny, 20 year old Sergeant was the individual code named "Burgundy," who had such harrowing experiences, escaping and evading the enemy with the aid of the French Resistance. They were well acquainted with the Special Operations Executive (S.O.E.), a clandestine warfare and sabotage group founded by Prime Minister Churchill in the summer of 1940. Their secret agents parachuted behind enemy lines, trained and shared intelligence with the French Resistance. John's travels thru France, his encounters and the daring and ingenuity of his rescuers in his escapes from the Gestapo, were well known to Headquarters. He endured through an amazing story something of a movie epic - Unbelieving, yet this one is real, a jaw dropper. John's return to his home base at Deenethorpe was not as welcoming and he soon learned that Intelligence at Headquarters ETOUSA had not passed down any intelligence information to Division intelligence - where he was raked over the coals for the "truth" of the fate of "Man-O' War" and its crew.

In August, Lt. Ted Krol, the bombardier, returned to England to provide verification of John's story as to the fate of "Man-O' War" and its crew. Division intelligence was now satisfied with John's Story.

An Intelligence Officer escorted each of the seven airmen to a private room to be interviewed. I was asked to give an account of every step of my ordeal to include the nature of my crew's mission, the mission date, number of mission flight hours, names of crew members, type of aircraft that shot us down, KIA's and wounded, parachute out or crash land, where captured, how escaped, names of helpers, names of Resistance fighters, location of safe-houses and medical treatment received. The questioning went on for hours and hours until I was now drained mentally as well as physically. Intelligence asked for any information that could aid the invasion forces, including types of German troops and locations of installations. I told them all that my memory brought forth about my travels through France and Spain and especially intelligence that could be of military value. A formal request for the information I provided Intelligence was recently granted. The surprise was that the secret document was partially declassified without my knowledge, 11/31/81 and reads as follows: 11/31/81: Declassified per Executive Order 12356 Section 3.3 by RLB/LLB, NARA Date APPENDIX "B" to E and E Report No. 755

a. Hearsay that there is an airfield at Juvincourt (N of Reims) where as many as 125 A/C of all types can be seen on the ground at a time.

b. The results of Allied bombing at Courcy and Juvincourt (NW of Reims) in early May 1944 were good. On 23 May 15 new JU88's were observed on the field at Courcy, while up to 43 FW 190's were flying formation over the field earlier in the week. Many ME 109's, with belly tanks were observed at Courcy.

c. Early in May a gun emplacement 1 mile E of Courcy was destroyed by a P-47. The gun is since replaced.

d. When the RR station at Reims was bombed on 1 May a trainload of Germans was hit and many killed. However many bombs missed the target by 1 mile. The station was in operation 3 days later. There is usually an ammunition train on the siding, but 1 May was an exception. The Fortress bombing of 23 May had much better results.

e. At intervals of a few miles, light AA guns, with very little camouflage, is stationed along the left side of the RR tracks from Epernay to Paris.

f. Hearsay that Red Cross RR cars in Paris are equipped with AA guns, which have been used against the USAAF.

g. The RAF bombing of the Toulouse munitions plant and bridges south of Toulouse was a thorough job. The plant is believed to have been permanently, knocked out.

APPENDIX “D” to E and E REPORT NO. 755
1.1 AIDS BOX: My aids box was taken while I was unconscious.

1.2 PURSE: My purse was taken while I was unconscious.

1.3 PHOTOGRAPHS: I carried 8 photographs, I used one and gave the rest as souvenirs, which meant that I had to be re-photographed later.

1.4 LECTURES: I was lectured by S-2 at squadron and by evaders. I was given help before I had time to use anything they taught me.

1.5 SUGGESTIONS: I carried my GI shoes on my parachute harness and I think this is a good arrangement. Mine were taken while I was unconscious and I often wished for them later. The seriousness of my wounds or my ill health seems to be of no concern to anyone but me, and I am in need of medical attention.

Major Wilfred B. "Pop" Fry,

Luckily, the name, Major Wilfred B. "Pop" Fry, the Bomb Group 401st Intelligence Officer whom I had previously met came to mind. Major Fry was summoned from Deenethorpe to my hearing at ETOUSA Headquarters in London to confirm my identity and when "Pop" saw my physical condition and heard my story, he was astounded that I was able to escape. When I attempted to salute him, he said that it was not necessary and in the future he would salute me. It was admirable of Major Fry to make this statement. Years later; Major Fry wrote a letter to me restating the above quote. I could not believe that he remembered. Major Wilfred B. "Pop" Fry, a WWI "retread" and no youngster, deserved special mention. After completing Intelligence School in Harrisburg, Pennsylvania, "Pop," volunteered for overseas duty. He went on bombing missions over Germany with the 401st Bomb Group whenever he was able to obtain permission. "How can I brief our crews on flak, targets, enemy fighters and other intelligence matters if I don't join them in their experiences over enemy territory?" he argued. He was a class act.

The interrogation completed, I am required, as is each of us, to sign a document of secrecy, dated 15 June 1944, stating I will never divulge the details of my escape and evasion to anyone, including family members.

I now belong to the Air Force Escape and Evasion Society (AFEES) as do many of the others of my escape group.

Because of the signed oath, my family has not learned the details of my story. I requested a copy of my debriefing in the Intelligence Report (IO) of 17 June 1944 from the government and my request was honored with a short unclear document, which touched on my travails. The facts of my interrogation not having been confirmed by Intelligence remained classified until July 2005.

I was promised by the government to be released from the signed oath decades ago, and in response to my latest inquiry in August 2004 a copy of Headquarters ETOUSA memo AG383.6 dated 15 June 1944, declaring my oath of secrecy to the U. S. Government, was returned to me date stamped declassified per Executive Order 12356, Section 3.3 NND 745001, dated 10/31/89.

At Intelligence Headquarters, I ran into Ken Terroux, a hometown friend. We exchanged greetings and I learned that he, also, was a B-17 gunner and got shot down by enemy flak. Ken was fortunate to have been downed without wounds and was immediately picked up by the Belgium Resistance who arranged for his return to England by an English gunboat within forty-eight hours.

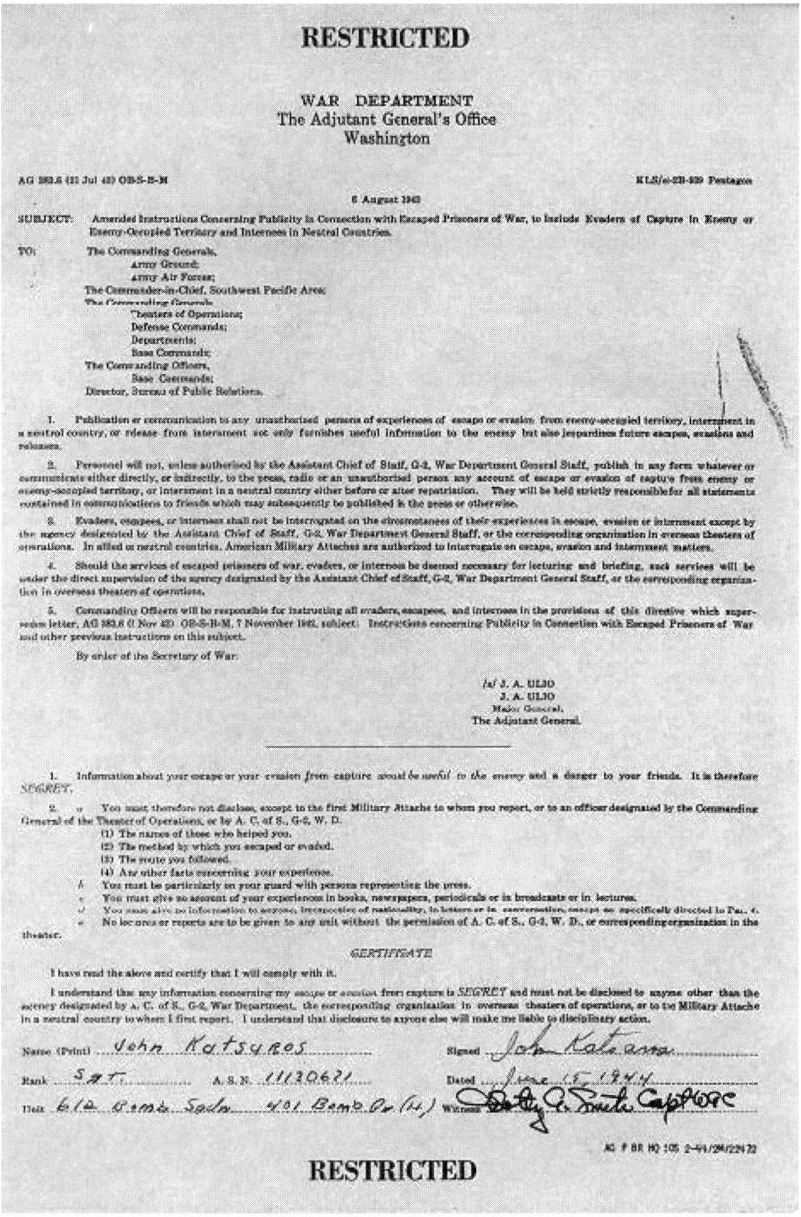

**RESTRICTED**

WAR DEPARTMENT
The Adjutant General's Office
Washington

AG 383.6 (21 Jul 43) OB-S-B-M KLS/el-2B-939 Pentagon

6 August 1943

SUBJECT: Amended Instructions Concerning Publicity in Connection with Escaped Prisoners of War, to include Evaders of Capture in Enemy or Enemy-Occupied Territory and Internees in Neutral Countries.

TO: The Commanding Generals,
Army Ground;
Army Air Forces;
The Commander-in-Chief, Southwest Pacific Area;
The Commanding Generals,
Theaters of Operations;
Defense Commands;
Departments;
Base Commands;
The Commanding Officers,
Base Commands;
Director, Bureau of Public Relations.

1. Publication or communication to any unauthorized persons of experiences of escape or evasion from enemy-occupied territory, internment in a neutral country, or release from internment not only furnishes useful information to the enemy but also jeopardizes future escapes, evasions and releases.

2. Personnel will not, unless authorized by the Assistant Chief of Staff, G-2, War Department General Staff, publish in any form whatever or communicate either directly, or indirectly, to the press, radio or an unauthorized person any account of escape or evasion of capture from enemy or enemy-occupied territory, or internment in a neutral country either before or after repatriation. They will be held strictly responsible for all statements contained in communications to friends which may subsequently be published in the press or otherwise.

3. Evaders, escapees, or internees shall not be interrogated on the circumstances of their experiences in escape, evasion or internment except by the agency designated by the Assistant Chief of Staff, G-2, War Department General Staff, or the corresponding organization in overseas theaters of operations. In allied or neutral countries, American Military Attaches are authorized to interrogate on escape, evasion and internment matters.

4. Should the services of escaped prisoners of war, evaders, or internees be deemed necessary for lecturing and briefing, such services will be under the direct supervision of the agency designated by the Assistant Chief of Staff, G-2, War Department General Staff, or the corresponding organization in overseas theaters of operations.

5. Commanding Officers will be responsible for instructing all evaders, escapees, and internees in the provisions of this directive which supersedes letter, AG 383.6 (1 Nov 42) OB-S-B-M, 7 November 1942, subject: Instructions concerning Publicity in Connection with Escaped Prisoners of War and other previous instructions on this subject.

By order of the Secretary of War:

/s/ J. A. ULIO
J. A. ULIO
Major General,
The Adjutant General.

---

1. Information about your escape or your evasion from capture would be useful to the enemy and a danger to your friends. It is therefore SECRET.

2. a You must therefore not disclose, except to the first Military Attache to whom you report, or to an officer designated by the Commanding General of the Theater of Operations, or by A. C. of S., G-2, W. D.
(1) The names of those who helped you.
(2) The method by which you escaped or evaded.
(3) The route you followed.
(4) Any other facts concerning your experience.
b You must be particularly on your guard with persons representing the press.
c You must give no account of your experiences in books, newspapers, periodicals or in broadcasts or in lectures.
d You must give no information to anyone, irrespective of nationality, in letters or in conversation, except as specifically directed in Par. 4.
e No lectures or reports are to be given to any unit without the permission of A. C. of S., G-2, W. D., or corresponding organization in the theater.

*CERTIFICATE*

I have read the above and certify that I will comply with it.

I understand that any information concerning my escape or evasion from capture is SECRET and must not be disclosed to anyone other than the agency designated by A. C. of S., G-2, War Department, the corresponding organization in overseas theaters of operations, or to the Military Attache in a neutral country to whom I first report. I understand that disclosure to anyone else will make me liable to disciplinary action.

Name (Print) John Katsaros Signed John Katsaros

Rank SGT A.S.N. 11130621 Dated June 15 1944

Unit 612 Bomb Sqdn 401 Bomb Gr (H) Witness [illegible] Capt WAC

AG F BR HQ 105 2-44/2M/22472

**RESTRICTED**

Secrecy document signed by John Katsaros

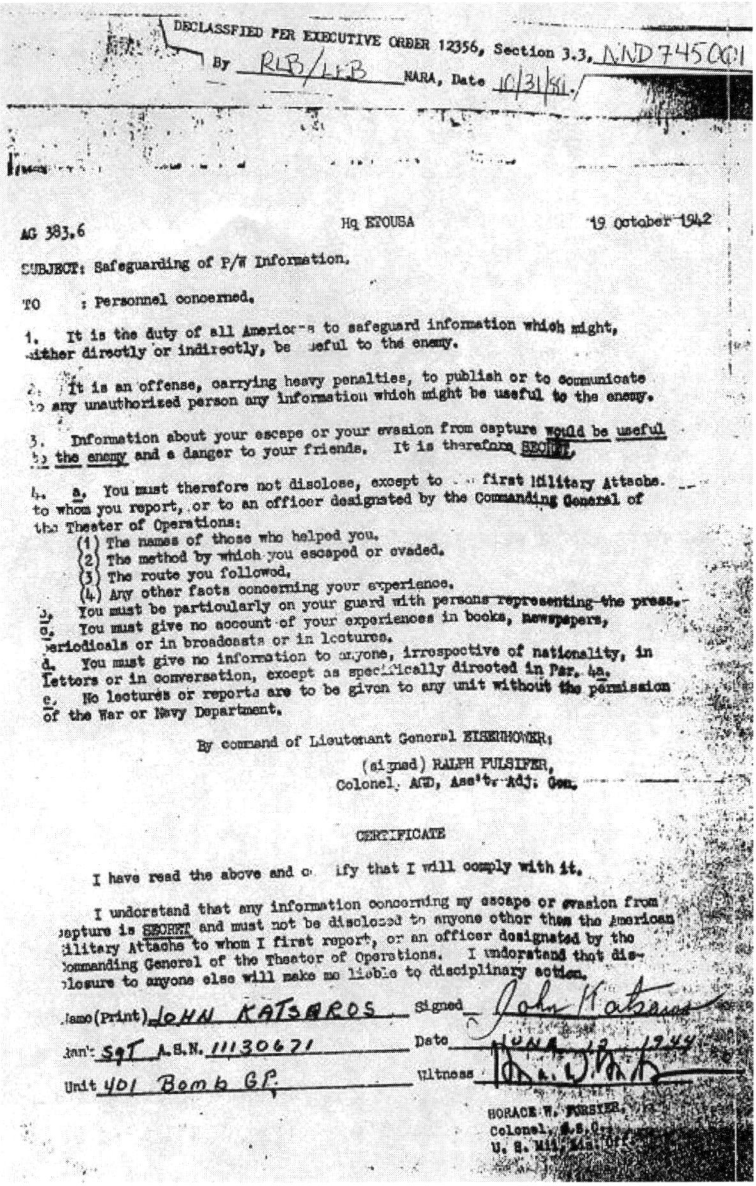

DECLASSIFIED PER EXECUTIVE ORDER 12356, Section 3.3, NND745001
By RLB/LFB NARA, Date 10/31/91

AG 383.6 Hq ETOUSA 19 October 1942

SUBJECT: Safeguarding of P/W Information.

TO : Personnel concerned.

1. It is the duty of all Americans to safeguard information which might, either directly or indirectly, be useful to the enemy.

2. It is an offense, carrying heavy penalties, to publish or to communicate to any unauthorized person any information which might be useful to the enemy.

3. Information about your escape or your evasion from capture would be useful to the enemy and a danger to your friends. It is therefore SECRET.

4. a. You must therefore not disclose, except to the first Military Attache to whom you report, or to an officer designated by the Commanding General of the Theater of Operations:
(1) The names of those who helped you.
(2) The method by which you escaped or evaded.
(3) The route you followed.
(4) Any other facts concerning your experience.
b. You must be particularly on your guard with persons representing the press.
c. You must give no account of your experiences in books, newspapers, periodicals or in broadcasts or in lectures.
d. You must give no information to anyone, irrespective of nationality, in letters or in conversation, except as specifically directed in Par. 4a.
e. No lectures or reports are to be given to any unit without the permission of the War or Navy Department.

By command of Lieutenant General EISENHOWER:
(signed) RALPH PULSIFER,
Colonel, AGD, Ass't. Adj. Gen.

CERTIFICATE

I have read the above and certify that I will comply with it.

I understand that any information concerning my escape or evasion from capture is SECRET and must not be disclosed to anyone other than the American Military Attache to whom I first report, or an officer designated by the Commanding General of the Theater of Operations. I understand that disclosure to anyone else will make me liable to disciplinary action.

Name (Print) JOHN KATSAROS Signed John Katsaros
Rank SGT A.S.N. 11130671 Date JUNE 13, 1944
Unit 401 Bomb GP. Witness [illegible]

HORACE W. FORSTER,
Colonel, A.S.C.
U. S. Mil. Att. Off.

The secrecy document was signed under sworn oath that mentioned heavy penalties if details of my story are revealed.

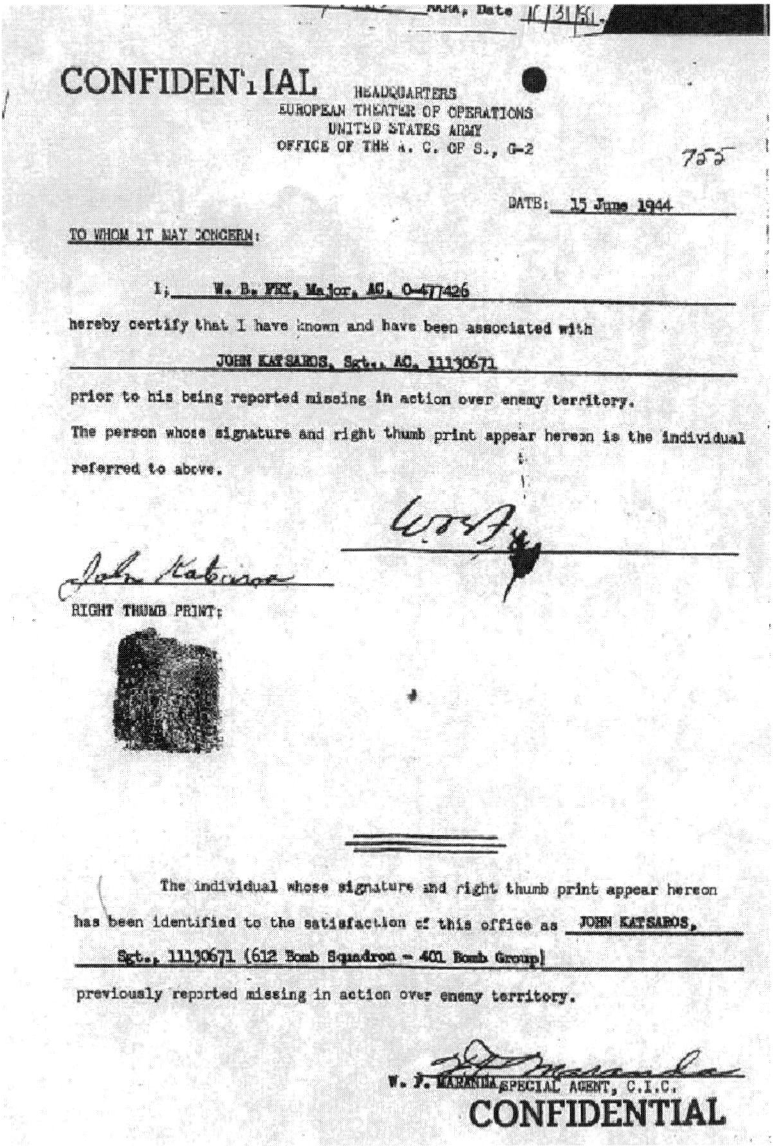

NARA, Date

CONFIDENTIAL

HEADQUARTERS
EUROPEAN THEATER OF OPERATIONS
UNITED STATES ARMY
OFFICE OF THE A. C. OF S., G-2

725

DATE: 15 June 1944

TO WHOM IT MAY CONCERN:

I, W. B. FRY, Major, AC, O-477426 hereby certify that I have known and have been associated with JOHN KATSAROS, Sgt., AC, 11130671 prior to his being reported missing in action over enemy territory.

The person whose signature and right thumb print appear hereon is the individual referred to above.

RIGHT THUMB PRINT:

The individual whose signature and right thumb print appear hereon has been identified to the satisfaction of this office as JOHN KATSAROS, Sgt., 11130671 (612 Bomb Squadron - 401 Bomb Group) previously reported missing in action over enemy territory.

W. J. MARANDA SPECIAL AGENT, C.I.C.

CONFIDENTIAL

Major "Pop" Fry, 401st Bomb Group Intelligence Officer was contacted to verify my identity and sign the above document appearing with my right thumb print.

## CHAPTER 30
## Return to Home Base

After Major "Pop" Fry confirmed my identity, he and I drove back to base at Deenethorpe where we met with Colonel Bowman, the Group Commander. Our meeting lasted a few minutes when he asked me to go on a speaking tour to several air bases to address Escape and Evasion issues. He said that my experience would be helpful to any airman shot down in enemy territory. I agreed to help my fellow airmen. Then Colonel Bowman asked me to wait, as he stepped out of the room. A high-ranking officer entered the room and began to grill me. I had no idea who this officer was or that I was going to be interrogated again. For some reason, my story of our getting shot down was not only not believable but pure fiction to him, so he put pressure on me, becoming hostile; similar to the arrogance displayed by the Gestapo in their trying to break me. He practically accused me of a counterfeit story and wanted to know the truth, the real story of what happened on our mission to Frankfurt. So, that was the reason for his hammering, to get the answers he wanted to hear. I learned that there were reports that there were bomber crews, after participating on a mission that did land in a neutral country to be interred for the duration of the war. This officer must have come from Division, to get the truth. Somewhere up the line of organization, there was serious doubt that this one aircraft out of the Division solely took on the target at Frankfurt. There is doubt in my mind on knowledge, if anything, was learned by this officer from Intelligence Headquarters 8th Air Force in London.

I reminded the interrogating officer of the bad weather conditions from the start before we left England that the mission was held up because of foul weather when finally the word came to "Go". I related how our bomber crew's predicament began when a bomb loaded aircraft, out of control; fell from the formation above, endangering our aircraft. Our pilot, Lt. Jack Dunaway, exhibiting outstanding professionalism to avert collision with the falling aircraft and other aircraft adjacent and below, put our plane in a sharp dive and pull to the left. This maneuver put the plane in a rough, turbulent downdraft and the plane dropped over a thousand feet before the pilot recovered control. The lost altitude was regained to return the ship to formation; it was nowhere to be found. Unaware of the group recall, because of radio silence, due to bad weather conditions, the pilot decided to continue to target, expecting to meet up with the Group.

1st Division Headquarters did not believe this strange story and they sent a bully to get the real facts. The story of the action of the plane must have been passed to them as told to Air Force Headquarters in London. Where did the bully believe you got shot up? Why did not Intelligence confirm the bombing of Frankfurt on 20 March 1944?

Major "Pop" Fry, although outranked by the interrogating officer, interceded, coming to my defense, to vouch for my honesty, training and veracity. His mediation got me released from the brutal grilling.

After being raked over the coals by the Division Intelligence Officer, I ran into Lt. "Bid" Fitchett and his crew who were preparing to depart for the U.S.A. They were one of the "lucky" crews who survived the completion of their thirty-five hazardous missions over Europe without having been shot down. We reunioned on base and off base and they were to learn of the many surviving members of my crew who were being held as POW's at undisclosed German camps. We relaxed, recounting stories of our exploits from the beginning in the U.S. to the present.

The next day I was assigned to the lecture tour and spent a few days visiting various groups in the 8th Air Force in England, lecturing on Escape and Evasion to the air crews, giving helpful hints injected with bits of humor on behavior, table manners and guttural speech. The G.I.'s were receptive and they asked a lot of questions.

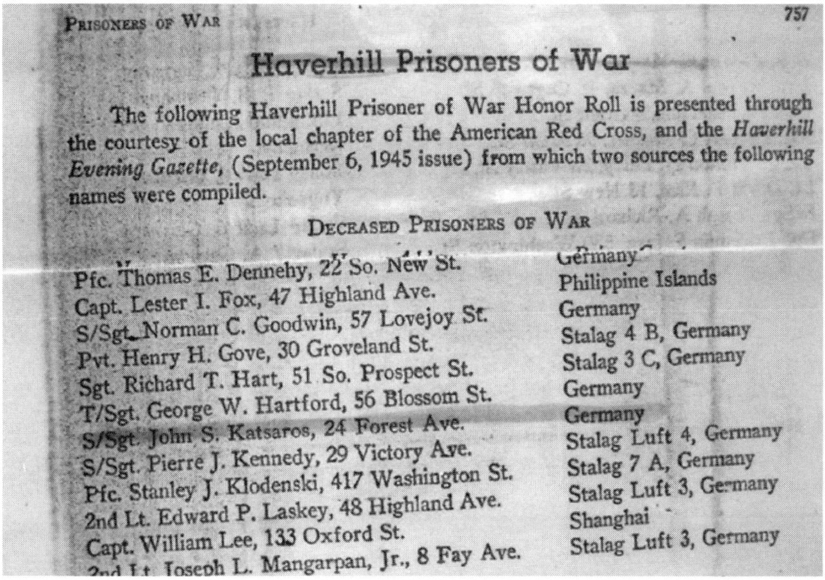

PRISONERS OF WAR 757

## Haverhill Prisoners of War

The following Haverhill Prisoner of War Honor Roll is presented through the courtesy of the local chapter of the American Red Cross, and the *Haverhill Evening Gazette*, (September 6, 1945 issue) from which two sources the following names were compiled.

### DECEASED PRISONERS OF WAR

| | |
|---|---|
| Pfc. Thomas E. Dennehy, 22 So. New St. | Germany |
| Capt. Lester I. Fox, 47 Highland Ave. | Philippine Islands |
| S/Sgt. Norman C. Goodwin, 57 Lovejoy St. | Germany |
| Pvt. Henry H. Gove, 30 Groveland St. | Stalag 4 B, Germany |
| Sgt. Richard T. Hart, 51 So. Prospect St. | Stalag 3 C, Germany |
| T/Sgt. George W. Hartford, 56 Blossom St. | Germany |
| S/Sgt. John S. Katsaros, 24 Forest Ave. | Germany |
| S/Sgt. Pierre J. Kennedy, 29 Victory Ave. | Stalag Luft 4, Germany |
| Pfc. Stanley J. Klodenski, 417 Washington St. | Stalag 7 A, Germany |
| 2nd Lt. Edward P. Laskey, 48 Highland Ave. | Stalag Luft 3, Germany |
| Capt. William Lee, 133 Oxford St. | Shanghai |
| 2nd Lt. Joseph L. Mangarpan, Jr., 8 Fay Ave. | Stalag Luft 3, Germany |

Haverhill Gazette article erroneously listing John Katsaros as deceased.

RESTRICTED

GENERAL ORDERS )
No. 132 )

EXTRACT

Hq 1st Bombardment Division,
APO 557, 29 June 1944.

Under the provisions of Army Regulations 600-45, 22 September 1943, and pursuant to authority contained in Section I, Circular I, Hq ETOUSA, 3 January 1944, the PURPLE HEART is awarded to the following-named__________ *

* *

JOHN (NMI) KATSAROS, 11130671, Staff Sergeant, 612th Bombardment Squadron, 401st Bombardment Group (H), Army Air Forces, United States Army. For wound received in action on a bombardment mission in the European area, 20 March 1944. Home address: 24 Forrest Avenue, Haverhill, Massachusetts.

* * * * *

By command of Major General WILLIAMS:

BARTLETT BEAMAN,
Brigadier General, U. S. A.,
Chief of Staff.

WAR DEPARTMENT

OFFICIAL:
ROBERT P. JOHNSON, JR.,
Lt. Col., A.G.D.,
Adjutant General.

RESTRICTED

A TRUE COPY

John M. Weidner

JOHN M. WEIDNER
Captain, MAC
Registrar

Purple Heart Award

SGT. JOHN KATSAROS
. . . reported safe

# Sgt. Katsaros Reported Safe

## Interned In Neutral Country After Raid

(Special to The Gazette)

WASHINGTON, D. C.—Security reasons were given by the War department today for its firm policy of denying any information, other than to members of a soldier's family, as to his internment in a neutral country.

This was the explanation made today in connection with the case of Sgt. John Katsaros, of Haverhill, Mass., reported now in a neu-

(Continued on page three)

The text of the article reads as follows: "Washington, D.C. - Security reasons were given by the War department today for its firm policy of denying any information, other than to members of a soldier's family, as to his internment in a neutral country. This was the explanation made today with the case of Sgt. John Katsaros, of Haverhill Mass., reported now in a neutral country after having been reported missing March 20 in a raid over Germany. The International Red Cross and the U.S. military attaché in the neutral country have authority under international law to care for such interned soldiers. Reports from time to time indicate that they actually enjoy a very pleasant status and are acclaimed as heroes by natives of these countries. All mail from or to such internees is rigidly censored by the neutral country. Details of such forced landing for military reasons are held secret by the War department. The department did report that 39 U.S. planes have been forced down in Sweden, and the planes and personnel are required to remain there so long as the country is neutral. Sergeant Katsaros, son of Mr. And Mrs. Speros Katsaros, 24 Forest Ave., was an aerial mechanic attached to the USAAF. He was graduated from Haverhill High School in 1942 and before his enlistment he was employed at the Portsmouth Navy yard. He enlisted Dec. 7, 1942. The War department, in a telegram to his parents, April 6, reported that he had been missing in action over Germany since March 20."

Several years after WWII, the 612th Squadron, 401st Bomb Group, wrote a history on the life of the Squadron. It tells of its beginning in the U.S., it's assignment of air crews and their development in training together as individual crews, to grow into a combat-ready Squadron team punctuated with the ability to fly precision formation with the other Squadrons in the makeup of a Group Combat Machine. The history continues as the Squadron ships overseas to the combat base at Deenethorpe, England and relates how the training is picked up for mastery of flying the combat formation with many groups of B-17 aircraft.

Every combat mission is summarized, and my crew's last mission on 20 March 1944 to Frankfurt, Germany is spotlighted in the squadron history: "Finally, after wondering since 20 March 1944 just why Lt. Dunaway and his crew had not returned from the mission to Frankfurt, Germany when they stalled out of the Group formation, the story came to light on the 17th June when Sgt. John Katsaros returned to Group. He was flying as Left Waist Gunner on the ill-fated aircraft and sustained wounds from 20mm cannon fire from enemy aircraft, which had attacked after it had become separated from the Group formation. This was the cause of the aircraft not returning as enemy aircraft fighters knocked it down. Sgt. Katsaros parachuted to safety with a badly mangled right arm. Fortunately, he was able to get assistance from the Underground and was spirited away for safekeeping from prowling German soldiers. Here begins the most amazing story about the magnificent work of the French Underground. It was necessary for them to furnish a skilled surgeon, and they did, to perform three separate operations before Sgt. Katsaros was well enough to make the hazardous escape to Spain and eventually to England. A copy of his complete escape and evasion story that is pertinent to the details will be appended in a subsequent month's history.

Another story came to light during the month of August 1944 when Lt. T.J. Krol, who was a member of Lt. Dunaway's crew which was lost 20 March 1944 returned from France to tell a remarkable story of practically five months in enemy occupied territory. His story confirmed one by Sgt. John Katsaros, a member of the same crew who managed to evade from France earlier. Reaching the ground by parachute, after leaving the aircraft at a remarkably low (800 to 1,000 feet) altitude, Lt. Krol took a free fall, similar to that of Sgt. Katsaros and "popping" his chute at low altitude enabled him to hide from the searching German Patrols.

Later he contacted some friendly Frenchmen after painfully crawling with a broken foot away from the scene of his hiding place. The French took him in and provided excellent medical attention for his broken foot, which remained in a cast for thirty days. During this time they put him in contact with the Underground Organization, which clothed and fed him competently. Later he was moved to Paris where he spent several weeks in an elaborate apartment right under the noses of the Boche. During his stay Lt. Krol manages to see most of Paris and learned a lot about French activities. Finally he moved out of Paris with the Marquis and remained with one of their units in the field for another good while doing various works that proved to be extremely troublesome for the Germans. Here again the story within a story, which can't be repeated, about living conditions, supplies, etc., and the other things he dealt with. Finally he and the others were able to contact some advance American patrols from the Invasion Area and their return to England was arranged. Unfortunately the details of such an experience are restricted for publication of any kind. However his experience has already proven of great value for lecturing to other crews who might be in a similar position sometime. Besides the wealth of intelligence he was able to provide to our Higher Command.

After completion of the Escape and Evasion lecture tour, I was summoned by Lt. General Robert B. Williams Commanding General of the 1st Air Division to Bushy Park an underground facility in London, code named, "Wide-Wing". The 401st Bomb Group was part of the 1st Air Division. This was the European Theater of Operations (E.T.O.) of the 8th Air Force, Headquarters of the Commanding Lt. General Ira Eaker and later Lt. General James H. Doolittle and their staffs.

Upon meeting General Williams, he asked to tell my story and especially the helpful experience given me by the various cells of the French Resistance, I was taken by surprise, as he handed me a special pass to any and all U.S. Army Air Forces facilities and English cities in the United Kingdom (U.K.), which he personally signed, and I used exclusively and often. I spent a few days at "Wide-Wing" in a room next to General William's office where I met and had conversations with many of the General Officers on my visit there.

During the London Blitz all military ran to the nearest Underground (Subway) to pass the time with the English people deep in the tunnels, singing patriotic songs. Later, during a blitz, American soldiers and aircrews spent their time in the local pub, as an act of foolish bravado.

One night around 15 January 1944, during the London blitz our left waist gunner, Jack Crowley and I, on pass before starting our combat missions, were trapped nearby #10 Downing Street, the residence of the Prime Minister Winston Churchill. While the German Luftwaffe was bombing the city, we could not locate a shelter, forcing us to body press against a brick building. The bombs and fragments of British flak fell near us. This was the first of many experiences we had during the London Blitz. Although neither one of us was injured, it was most memorable. We learned to avoid such occurrences by passing liberty time indoors. There were times when we assisted the London Fire Department in fighting fires after a bombing and it was not unusual to see Prime Minister Winston Churchill pitching in with the firemen.

London was a frightened city in the spring and summer of 1944. For more than a month the pilotless, jet-propelled V-1 bombs dropped in urban areas had killed thousands of Londoners. For the second time since 1939, schoolchildren were evacuated into the countryside away from danger. A million children were on the move to safety. The rest of the capital's population waited in dread for the now familiar drone of the rocket engine overhead and the awesome silence as the motor cut out - and those in the homes and shelters below counted out fifteen seconds to elapse before the "doodlebug" hit the ground and exploded. There was just enough time to pray that the bomb did not fall in this vicinity.

It was always of concerned interest to watch the RAF airplanes attacking the German V-1 unmanned bombs from above and to the rear of the bomb. If the attack were successful, the bomb would explode in the flight path of the RAF airplane. The RAF pilot would fly through the explosion, praying that the explosion would not destroy their aircraft. Whenever the V-1 bomb penetrated the Allied defense, one would listen for its engine. When it ran out of fuel, the bomb descended rapidly. Within a few seconds it would crash with a devastating explosion killing or wounding the inhabitants and doing great damage to buildings.

The V-1 rocket attacks were relentless. Prime Minister Churchill stated that the flying bombs were coming in at a rate of 100 to 150 per day; yet in public he was full of enthusiasm, bolstering the spirit of the British people. In private he showed great concern for his people, knowing that Allied victory required not only air superiority but also elimination of the rockets, which were devastating the English cities. More than 2,750 buzz bombs launched from Luftwaffe bases in northern France laid waste to major cities, especially London, killing about 3,000 and injuring 800 people.

The object of the use of the non-guided bombs was to create death and destruction, to demoralize the people and to take away their will to fight.

The V-2 bomb flew at an altitude too high for our fighters to reach much like the present day rockets. The V-2 would drop quickly and without a sound. It also carried a much larger bomb load than the V-1. These were two of Hitler's secret weapons that were aimed directly at London and other large British cities, creating death and devastation to the inhabitants and property. However, the V-1 and V-2 bombs along with the Luftwaffe's new jet fighters and bombers were introduced too late in the war to change the outcome of WWII.

Had Hitler's top secret weapon, the Jet bomber, and especially had the ME-262 Jet Fighter been mass produced earlier during WWII, the Allies would not have had anything in the air to compete with the faster flying German jets. Even the American P-51 Mustang fighter was no match for the speed of these jets. Whenever our fighters shot one down, it invariably took place as the jet was on landing approach, almost out of fuel.

German ME-262

German V-1 unmanned bomb-striking London July 1944.

The V-2 Bomb

## Hitler's Stealth Bomber

By Marcus Dunk, Mail Online, last updated July 8, 2009

With its smooth and elegant lines, this could be a prototype for some future successor to the stealth bomber. But this flying wing was actually designed by the Nazis 30 years before the Americans successfully developed radar-invisible technology. Now an engineering team has reconstructed the Horten Ho 2-29 from blueprints, with startling results.

Blast from the past: The full-scale replica of the Ho 2-29 bomber was made with materials available in the 40s.

The stealth plane design was years ahead of its time. It was faster and more efficient than any other plane of the period and its stealth powers did work against radar. Experts are now convinced that given a little bit more time, the mass deployment of this aircraft could have changed the course of the war.

The plane could have helped Adolf Hitler win the war

First built and tested in the air in March 1944, it was designed with a greater range and speed than any plane previously built, and was the first aircraft to use the stealth technology now deployed by the U.S. in its B-2 bombers. Thankfully Hitler's engineers only made three prototypes, tested by being dragged behind a glider, and were not able to build them on an industrial scale before the Allied forces invaded. From Panzer tanks through to the V-2 rocket, it has long been recognized that Germany's technological expertise during the war was years ahead of the Allies. But by 1943, Nazi high command feared that the war was beginning to turn against them, and were desperate to develop new weapons to help turn the tide. Nazi bombers were suffering badly when faced with the speed and maneuverability of the Spitfire and other Allied fighters. Hitler was also desperate to develop a bomber with the range and capacity to reach the United States. In 1943 Luftwaffe chief Hermann Goering demanded that designers come up with a bomber that would meet his '1,000, 1,000, 1,000' requirements – one that could carry 1,000kg over 1,000km flying at 1,000km/h.

A full scale replica of the Ho 2-29 bomber made

with materials available in the 1940s at prefilght.

A wing section of the stealth bomber. The jet intakes were years ahead of their time.

Two pilot brothers in their thirties, Reimar and Walter Horten, suggested a 'flying wing' design they had been working on for years. They were convinced that with its drag and lack of wind resistance such a plane would meet Goering's requirements. Construction on a prototype was begun in Goettingen in Germany in 1944. The centre pod was made from a welded steel tube, and was designed to be powered by a BMW 003 engine. The most important innovation was Reimar Horten's idea to coat it in a mix of charcoal dust and wood glue.

Vengeful: Inventors Reimar and Walter Horten were inspired to build the Ho 2-29 by the deaths of thousands of Luftwaffe pilots in the Battle of Britain.

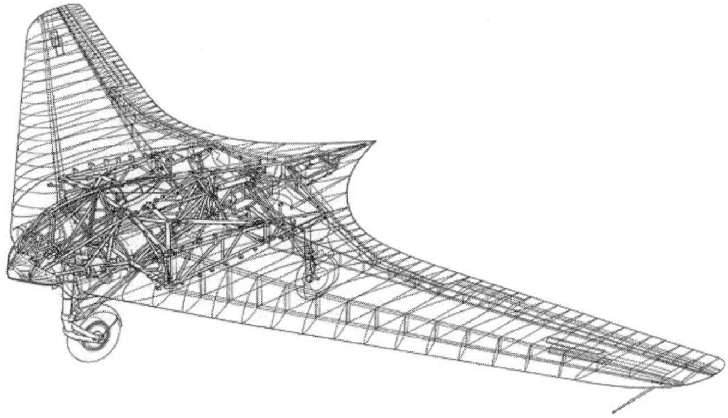

The 142-foot wingspan bomber was submitted for approval in 1944, and it would have been able to fly from Berlin to NYC and back without refueling, thanks to the same blended wing design and six BMW 003A or eight Junker Jumo 004B turbojets.

He thought the electromagnetic waves of radar would be absorbed, and in conjunction with the aircraft's sculpted surfaces the craft would be rendered almost invisible to radar detectors. This was the same method eventually used by the U.S. in its first stealth aircraft in the early 1980s, the F-117A Nighthawk. The plane was covered in radar absorbent paint with a high graphite content, which has a similar chemical make-up to charcoal. After the war the Americans captured the prototype Ho 2-29s along with the blueprints and used some of their technological advances to aid their own designs. But experts always doubted claims that the Horten could actually function as a stealth aircraft. Now using the blueprints and the only remaining prototype craft, Northrop-Grumman (the defense firm behind the B-2) built a full-size replica of a Horten Ho 2-29.

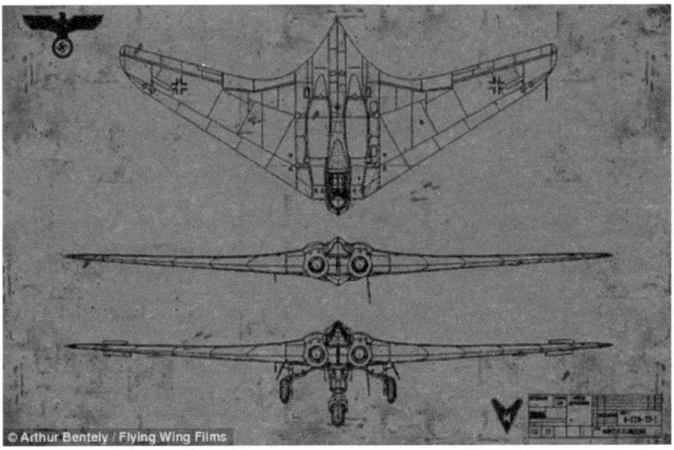


Luckily for Britain the Horten flying wing fighter-bomber

never got much further than the blueprint stage, above.

Thanks to the use of wood and carbon, jet engines integrated into the fuselage, and its blended surfaces, the plane could have been in London eight minutes after the radar system detected it. It took them 2,500 man-hours and $250,000 to construct, and although their replica cannot fly, it was radar-tested by placing it on a 50ft articulating pole and exposing it to electromagnetic waves. The team demonstrated that although the aircraft is not completely invisible to the type of radar used in the war, it would have been stealthy enough and fast enough to ensure that it could reach London before Spitfires could be scrambled to intercept it. 'If the Germans had had time to develop these aircraft, they could well have had an impact,' says Peter Murton, aviation expert from the Imperial War Museum at Duxford, in Cambridgeshire. 'In theory the flying wing was a very efficient aircraft design which minimized drag. It is one of the reasons that it could reach very high speeds in dive and glide and had such an incredibly long range.' The research was filmed for a forthcoming documentary on the National Geographic Channel.

By Marcus Dunk, Mail Online, last updated July 8, 2009

HEADQUARTERS
1ST BOMBARDMENT DIVISION
APO 557
Office of the Commanding General

A-A-1

11 July 1944.

MEMORANDUM:

TO : All Combat Wing and Group Commanders, 1st Bombardment Division.

I am in receipt of a letter from a senior member of the Allied Combined Chiefs of Staff concerning the operations of this Division on D Day. The following is a quotation from this letter and will be brought to the attention of the personnel under your command.

"An outstanding impression of my entire trip to the European Theater was the remarkable show on D Day, wherein your entire very large force moved with excellent timing and bombed objectives on instruments which they had never seen, without so much as scratching the paint on a rowboat in the squirming Channel below. That amazing display of scientific and training achievement was most impressive. I have described it to the Commanding General of Second Air Force in glowing terms as an end result of the training effort in that organization."

Robert B. Williams

ROBERT B. WILLIAMS,
Major General, USA,
Commanding.

D-Day MEMORANDUM To: 1st Bombardment Division, 94th Wing 401st Group

R E S T R I C T E D

GENERAL ORDERS )
NUMBER 127 )

E X T R A C T

Hq., 1st Bombardment Division.
APO 557, 27 June 1944.

III. Under the provisions of Army Regulations 600-45, 22 September 1943, as amended and pursuant to authority contained in letter, Hq Eighth Air Force, File 200.6, 1 June 1944, subject, "Awards and Decorations," an OAK LEAF CLUSTER is awarded to the following-named Enlisted Man for wear with AIR MEDAL previously awarded.

* *

JOHN KATSAROS, 11130671, Staff Sergeant, Air Corps, United States Army. For meritorious achievement while serving as left Waist Gunner of a B-17 airplane on a heavy bombardment mission over Germany, 20 March 1944. On this date the aircraft in which Sergeant Katsaros was flying was intercepted by hostile fighters enroute to the target. Numerous attacks were driven home. During one of these a .20mm shell exploded near him causing a painful arm wound. Another burst damaged the ball turret and the gunner was trapped inside. The order to bail out was given but Sergeant Katsaros, despite being wounded and suffering pain, remained. Completely disregarding his own safety, he was instrumental in freeing the gunner from his turret before abandoning the airplane. The courage, coolness and devotion to duty displayed by Sergeant Katsaros reflect great credit upon himself and the Armed Forces of the United States. Entered military service from Massachusetts.

* * * *

By command of Major General WILLIAMS:

BARTLETT BEAMAN,
Brigadier General, U.S. Army,
Chief of Staff.

WAR DEPARTMENT

OFFICIAL:
ROBERTS P. JOHNSON, JR.,
Liet. Colonel, A.G.D.,
Adjutant General

R E S T R I C T E D

A TRUE COPY

John M. Weidner

JOHN M. WEIDNER
Captain, MAC
Registrar

Two commendations were awarded to John: one for saving the life of Marvin Benz, the tail gunner, and the second, together with Frank Mastronardi, the radio operator, for extricating Walter Rusch, the ball-turret gunner who was trapped in his damaged turret by expended shell casings jammed in the gear track, making him a prisoner.

TECH. SGT. EDMUND S. SALAS
. . . veteran of 29 bomb raids

## Salas Modest About Feats

### River St. Youth Silent On Experiences

A 19-year-old River st. boy, who came home this week for the first time in 14 months as a veteran of 29 daylight bombing raids over Germany, France, Belgium and Holland, wearing the air medal, three oak leaf clusters, distinguished flying cross and two battle stars, minimized those experiences with the remark: "No, I didn't even have any experiences."

Tech. Sgt. Edward S. Salas, U. S. A. A. F., radioman-gunner in B-17 Flying Fortresses, is the young man who "can't single out any one of the raids as especially dangerous or thrilling." He's the son of Mr. and Mrs. William Salas, 279 River st.

He spent nine months overseas and took part in the pre-invasion, invasion and post invasion bombings of enemy held territory on the European continent.

The youthful sergeant flew in the Fortress, "Galyon's Stallion," in important operations of the Eighth Air Force's 388th bombardment group in shuttle missions to Russia, when oil refineries near Berlin were bombed. He took part in attacks on military targets in Berlin, on oil supplies in Leipzig, Merserburg, Madgeburg, Brux and Zeitz, chemical plants at Freidrichshaven and Munich, a ball bearing plant at Scheweinfurt, marshalling yards at Cologne and Osnabruck and military targets in Rostock and Brunswick, in addition to D-day action. All this is a matter of war department record, but the modest youth shrugs it off.

Sergeant Salas is now at home on a delayed en route leave until Jan. 2. He is a graduate of Haverhill High school, class of 1942. He was a shoe worker before entering the air forces.

Article reads as follows:

A 19-year-old River St. boy, who came home this week for the first time in 14 months as a veteran of 29 daylight bombing raids over Germany, France, Belgium and Holland, wearing the air medal, three oak leaf clusters and two battle stars, minimized these experiences with the remark: 'No, I didn't even have any experiences."

Tech Sgt. Edward S. Salas, USAAF radioman-gunner in B-17 Flying Fortresses, is the young man who 'can't single out any one of the raids as especially dangerous or thrilling." He's the son of Mr. And Mrs. William Salas, 279 River St.

He spent nine months overseas and took part in the pre-invasion bombings of enemy held territory on the European continent.

The youthful sergeant flew in the fortress, "Galyon's Stallion," in the important operations of the Eighth Air Force's 388th bombardment group in the shuttle missions to Russia, when oil refineries near Berlin were bombed. He took part in attacks on military targets in Berlin, on oil supplies in Leipzig, Merserburg, Madgeburg, Brux and Zeitz, chemical plants at Freidrichshaven and Munich, a ball bearing plant at Schweinfurt, marshalling yards at Cologne and Osnabruk, and military targets in Rostock and Brunswick, in addition to D-Day action. All this is a matter of war department record, but the modest youth shrugs it off.

Sergeant Salas is now at home on a delayed en route leave until Jan. 2. He is a graduate of Haverhill High School, class of 1942. He was a shoe worker before entering the air forces.

Photo June 1941: My best friend, Tech. Sergeant, Eddie Salas, arrives home after flying twenty-nine hazardous bombing missions, as a crew member on a B-17 in the E.T.O. Eddie got through the ordeal unscathed but sensed a premonition, having gone through hell that "his time was up." He had experienced many close calls in flying combat and felt that his luck cannot go on forever, and one day it will run out. Eddie and I chum out together while on furlough, and we both get stung with bad cases of poison ivy. His furlough is about to run out and he is scheduled to continue with his flying duties at Tampa, Florida. I pled with Eddie to let me speak to my doctor to get an infection report and extend his furlough that he might heal properly, but Eddie insists on adhering to his military pocket orders to travel on time to his next station. Within a week of his departure, Eddie was reported to have crashed and is killed in a Lockheed AT-18, an old type training aircraft. That knowledge puts the damper on my furlough, and as his best friend, I am asked to be a pallbearer at the funeral of my good friend, Eddie Salas, not quite twenty-one years of age.

## CHAPTER 31
## Homeward Bound

My last night in England, prior to departure for Scotland and on to Stateside, was spent at the London Red Cross sleeping facility. I signed the register, and there on the line above, was the name Arthur Papachriston. We were friends and schoolmates in my hometown of Haverhill, MA. I asked the Red Cross clerk at the counter for Arthur's room number. And she said, "He did not sign in last night and he just left minutes before you arrived." Dumbfounded, I muttered," I missed Arthur by minutes."

The time had come for me to say "goodbye" to all the guys at the 401st Bomb Group, and to my new friends at London Headquarters. Major General Robert B. Williams befriended me and, issued the access pass, which gave me entry to any American Facility in the E.T.O. Later, he provided me with first-class transportation on the overnight sleeper train from London to Prestwick, Scotland, from which President Roosevelt's constellation, the "Sacred Cow", was to fly many dignitaries and me back to America. I had no idea as to who the civilians or officers were and had no conversation with any of them. I was going home, Happy! The plane took off from Prestwick, made a quick re-fueling stop in Greenland, and flew then non-stop to Mitchell Air Field at New York City. I felt like a free bird but with all the hustle and bustle and the excitement to see my family, my jaw dropped when I was held up from my plans, to submit to a necessary stateside physical examination. Now, a 30-day furlough in hand, I could finally head for Massachusetts. I phoned my parents from Mitchell Air Field. In disbelief upon receiving my phone call, I was asked, "What neutral country are you being held in?" I replied, "New York City." They were ecstatic, full of surprise and joy, to hear my voice, alive, and back in the U.S. and not in the E.T.O. war zone. They had read the second War Department notification, my youngest brother 'Chuck' had received on 15 June 1944, that John Katsaros was in a neutral country. Little did they know the state of my injuries, but then, they could overlook injuries when they saw the life in me. My folks did not receive my cablegrams from Gibraltar or from England, so my live personal contact, here in America, took them completely by surprise. My folks couldn't wait for me to get home and I was dancing on a cloud.

My folks told me that my younger brother, "Chuck", was visiting in Hoboken, New Jersey, where an aunt and uncle ran a restaurant down by the shipyards.

I bused into Hoboken and spent a happy day with Chuck and our New York City Aunt and Uncles the Kyriazes and Harbilas families, then take the train to Haverhill.

By the time I arrived night has already fallen and being the only person on my coach when the train stopped, I let myself off in the dark; a single bulb shines at the distant station. It was pouring rain and the fog was heavy (pea soup) so I braced myself and proceed, with collar upturned, to walk through the wet and the fog towards the light at the station, a man in a naval uniform emerged out of the fog to directly approach me, and he appeared somewhat startled as he looks me in the face. It was a former high school teacher, Jackson George, now a Navy Lt., who knew that I was listed as "missing-in-action", and thought he was seeing my ghost. His shock, near over, I gave him knowledge of my return to the living. Our chance meeting had been a subject of remembrance and conversation over the years.

My "Long Escape" finally ended at home, happily with my family, relatives and friends. Joseph Azzarito was discharged while recovering from a broken back, after a crash landing somewhere in Brazil. Eddie Salas returned from flying combat raids as a radio operator and gunner on a B-17, with the 8th Air Force, in England. My attempts to contact the families of my crew met with no success. My intent had been to reassure the families of my crew that had survived, but the Air Force Headquarters had not contacted me with new addresses or phone numbers.

My furlough time up, I traveled, on orders, to Atlantic City, New Jersey for a breather, called rest and recuperation. While at "R&R", I tried again by telephone and the postal service to contact the families of my crew members reaching only the families of the Pilot and Co-Pilot to tell them what happened to their loved ones.

All rested up in sunny Atlantic City, my week of R&R over, I was transferred to the Air Force Recruiting Center on Commonwealth Avenue in Boston where I did recruiting officer duty for several months.

# Sgt. Katsaros Missed Death

## Got 'Chute Open As Plummeted Earthward

Five short seconds were the margin between life and death for a young Haverhill airman when he plummeted 25,000 feet from his Fortress, with shrapnel wounds in his right arm, and five broken ribs,to a land spot in Nazi-held Europe.

And they included, too, his chance to escape from the yoke of Nazism for if he had not regained consciousness long enough to pull the rip cord of his parachute, he would never had lived to find his way out of German-held country back to his base in England.

It's not hard to understand, after talking to Staff Sgt. John Katsaros, age 21, U. S. A. A. F., engineer and gunner on a B-17 Fortress, why he considers himself "just plain lucky" and also, why "it's great to be home."

He's one of 10 men who came back. The other nine, all close friends, survived the crash but, for all the staff sergeant knows, may now be confined to some German prison camp.

It happened after the first of the year. Dates and places and some facts have to be omitted in Katsaros' current story for reasons of military necessity. There's too much at stake and too many individuals involved.

The Haverhill soldier's big bomber was on a mission deep into Germany. It was the ninth since his unit went into action with the Eighth Air Force of England to continue the aerial assault on Hitler's roofless fortress and to pave the way for D-day, June 6.

Katsaros and his mates made the target run. They dropped their load squarely on their target and headed back for the base in England.

The sergeant recalled they hadn't gone far on the return trip when Messerschmitts picked out their fortress. Machine gun fire terrific, coming from all sides.

Finally, the ship was no longer able to stay aloft. The orders came to abandon it. But before they were sounded, Katsaros had been hit by shrapnel. His right arm was badly injured, fractured in two places, and his ribs were smashed.

"We attended to those fellows we could," he said, "and prepared to bail out. Five of us went down by the way of parachutes, the other five crash-landed."

Katsaros, himself, is not conscious of leaving the ship. It was miles in the air when he must have jumped but he doesn't remember it.

"I don't remember anything," he said, "until I got down to about 5000 feet. Then I came to for about five seconds and managed to get my 'chute open. I went out again and the next thing I remember was being on the ground and seeing a couple of German planes dropping earthward in my direction.

"I figured they were going to strafe, but they didn't."

Those five seconds proved time enough for the Haverhill staff sergeant to realize his position. He had already dropped more than three miles and if he didn't get the 'chute open, he would never make it for the ground was coming up extremely fast. The shock of the opening of the 'chute is believed to have rendered him unconscious again.

But he made it and that was "what counted" and it's the reason he is back home today.

From then on Sergeant Katsaros could tell a story thriller. Censorship, however, requires him to remain silent. All he can say is that he landed in Europe and made his way back to England eventually. He can't tell about anything, at least not until this war is over.

He did get back to England and underwent long weeks of treatment. And finally he returned to this country. And Thursday, his 21st birthday anniversary, he came back to Haverhill—back to his parents, Mr. and Mrs. Speros Katsaros, 24 Forest ave.

"I'm telling you," he said, with a broad smile on his face, "there's no place like Haverhill."

He's happy to be home—a trip that seemed unlikely not many months ago.

The young airman, who worked as a Gazette newsboy for nine years, is recovering from his arm and rib injuries. He looks to be in good condition and said he's feeling a lot better. He'll remain in Haverhill long enough for a good rest and will then report back to Atlantic City, N. J., for assignment.

He's through flying with the Eighth Air Force. They don't send fellows who get out of Nazi-held Europe back. Sergeant Katsaros will probably become an instructor. He went into air forces in December, 1942, and went across in December, 1943. He has two brothers in the Air Forces—Lt. Sotiris Katsaros, now in Ohio, and Pvt. George Katsaros, Camp Crowder, Mo.

This Haverhill Gazette newspaper article was published after my return to home in July 1944.

(Gazette Staff Photo)

**WAR BOND SALEMEN—Three Haverhill residents, just back from the fighting fronts, were salesmen at the War bond rally last night in St. Apostles Greek church. The rally was sponsored by Acropolis chapter, Order of Ahepa. Left to right: Pfc. James Georgian, U. S. Marine Corps, veteran of the Marshall Islands campaign; Staff Sgt. John Katsaros, U. S. A. A. F., who was shot down and wounded over German occupied Europe and made his way back to England, and Aviation Chief Radioman Michael Capetanelis, veteran of the sea battles in both oceans.**

John, Past President of the local AHEPA Chapter & Sts. Apostles Church, with military friends, speakers at the sponsored $4,000,000 Haverhill, MA War Bond Rally July 1944.

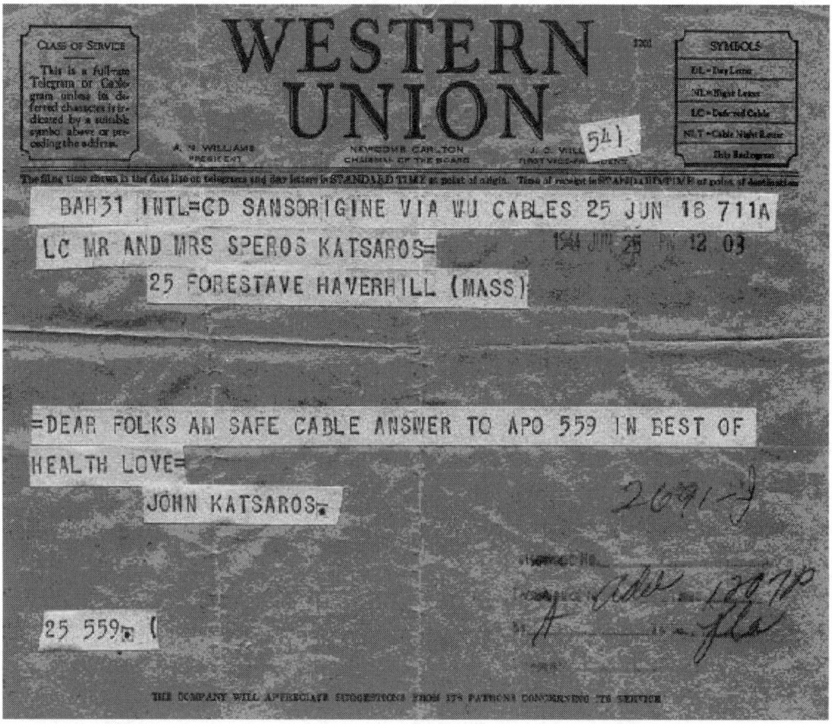

WESTERN UNION

BAH31 INTL=CD SANSORIGINE VIA WU CABLES 25 JUN 18 711A

LC MR AND MRS SPEROS KATSAROS= 1944 JUN 25 PM 12 03

25 FORESTAVE HAVERHILL (MASS)

=DEAR FOLKS AM SAFE CABLE ANSWER TO APO 559 IN BEST OF HEALTH LOVE=

JOHN KATSAROS.

25 559. (

The 25 June 1944 telegram sent to parents that I was safe. My arrival home July 6, 1944 came before the telegram. It reads: "Dear folks am safe cable answer to APO 559 in best of health love John Katsaros."

John (L) with the Boston USAF Recruiting Team in New Bedford, Ma.

S/Sgt. John Katsaros circa. Dec. 1944.

John and Spiros (father) 1944

My need for medical attention takes me to the Waltham Regional Hospital/Murphy General for removal of several pieces of shrapnel still imbedded in my arm, leg, and body. At the hospital, a surgeon decides that my tonsils need removal and he proceeded to remove them with a local anesthetic. I told the doctor that I was allergic to anesthesia, and he said, "You are frozen down to your toes." During the operation I felt the knife cut me, like raw meat, giving me great pain; the local anesthetic did not successfully numb the tonsils. Several days later, Mother and her friend came to see me. They visited a while and I called the nurse to tell my visitors that visiting hours were over. Shortly after they left, I have a blood hemorrhage that spewed blood over several beds in the ward. My routine tonsillectomy turned into an emergency - requiring the head surgeon to perform a second operation. This procedure went smoothly. The head surgeon who relieved him of his duty at the hospital learns the name of the first doctor, who botched the operation. That doctor had been the source of many complaints regarding his surgical procedures and his indifferent attitude as reported by many patients and hospital staff.

Prior to receiving my separation from the Army Air Force, I was asked to come to Boston for a physical examination, and to bring along my father. I kept the appointment, taking along dad, and several doctors performed the examination. When they had completed the exam, they showed grave concern for my emaciated physical condition, especially the healing of my right arm. My 201 file (Army records) shows engagement in sports activities prior to enlistment, and the doctors advised dad to encourage me to continue with sports activities, which would help me physically, in that my present condition would not make any progress without effort.

Believing to be a candidate qualified to apply for admission to West Point or the Naval Academy, I told the doctors about my wishes and they reminded me that I could not pass the physical examination. My many shrapnel wounds, and near frozen extremities, suffered during missions at high altitude cold and bone chilling climb over the Pyrenees with scant clothing and shoes too small were too severe for entry into a military academy. My application was denied!

Furthermore the doctors informed me that I would not be reassigned to any branch of the Air Force, disappointing me as my desire was to become a career military officer. I was advised this was not possible and was promptly discharged.

My final interview with the doctors was not a complete wash-out. They advised me of the new G.I. Bill of Rights Program that would pay for my college education and encouraged me to take advantage of the program to further my education.

Attending college was not an easy task, either, for a deaf man, as I began to realize that I had more personal problems to overcome. I was only twenty-one years old and my hearing had become impaired, apparently from the constant cacophony generated by the deafening roar caused by the four huge B-17 Flying Fortress engines and the constant ear-piercing explosions of the many .50 caliber machine guns firing in unison to repel the attacking enemy fighters. A deaf man would be rejected by a flight physical examination, and the wearing of ear protectors in combat was prohibited as the airmen needed the ability to listen and to communicate over the intercom at all times. At times like these, there was a lot of chatter going on, and it was all business. Other than that the communication lines were left open and clear.

My first semester at Boston University was a disaster, due to my hearing problems. Fortunately for me, my professors understood my problem, and permitted me to sit in the first row in all classes to be able to hear the lectures. My hearing got increasingly worse until the Veterans Administration provided me with hearing aids for both ears and from that time to this day a hearing aid in each ear is necessary for me to communicate. The Veterans Administration tests my hearing regularly and updates my hearing aids as improved models become available.

Nightmares were and still remain a constant problem with combat aircrew men. Dad observed me in a sleepwalking trance one night and he became ever watchful to check on me during the night, for fear of hurting myself. His vigilance to do this kept me from sitting on a hot stove and on another occasion, from bailing out of a second story window. The nightmares persisted, but the sleepwalking ceased a couple of years after discharge from the U.S.A.A.F.

Recently my youngest brother, S. Charles 'Chuck' Katsaros informed me that upon my discharge from the US Army Air Force, he remembered me speaking while sleeping and having nightmares. We shared the same room, and I would keep him awake. Chuck said, he never spoke to anyone about what he heard. However, on reading the 1st edition of 'CB-TLE', Chuck remembered those nightmares and dreams and related to many of the stories that appeared in the book.

As a youngster, heights or close quarters were not a problem for me. Today, I dare not look down from a high building or take an elevator without feeling a sense fear that got to me in the cellar of the champagne factory during bombing of the marshaling yards at Reims. What amazes me is that despite all my phobias I am able to fly on commercial airliners provided it is an aisle seat up front.

In March 1944, the month of my fatal mission, brother George, out on business to New Hampshire, had a strange premonition of my plane being shot down, he abruptly ended his trip to rush home where he finds a telegram on the kitchen table, delivered that very day, stating "The U.S. Government regrets to inform you that Sgt. John Katsaros 11130671 has been reported missing in action."

My folks received another unpleasant U.S. Government telegram that their son, my brother, Lt. Sotiris “Sot” Katsaros, while attached to the Nuremberg, Germany War Crimes Trials of the “Nazi” German accusers, was reported missing in action. A few weeks later my parents were advised that his crippled airplane was forced to land in a Russian Zone. The Russians considered him a spy and held him prisoner. Fortunately, the U.S. Army Air Force proved otherwise and secured his release.

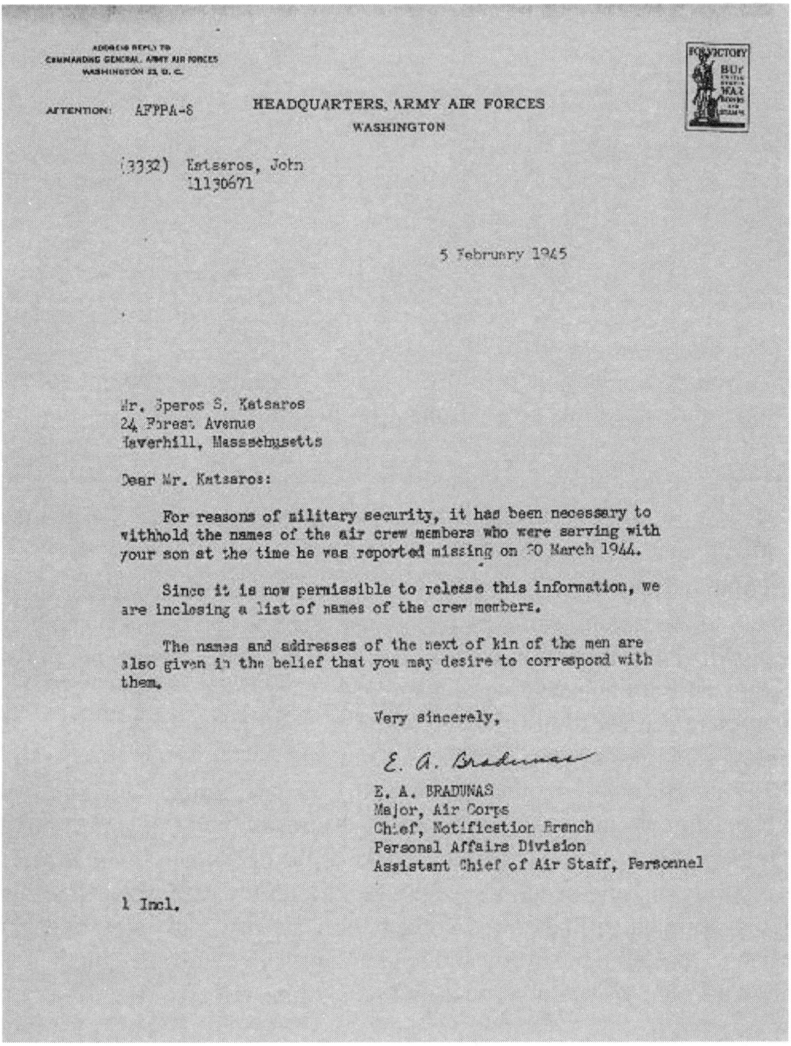

ADDRESS REPLY TO
COMMANDING GENERAL, ARMY AIR FORCES
WASHINGTON 25, D. C.

ATTENTION: AFPPA-8

HEADQUARTERS, ARMY AIR FORCES
WASHINGTON

(3332) Katsaros, John
11130671

5 February 1945

Mr. Speros S. Katsaros
24 Forest Avenue
Haverhill, Massachusetts

Dear Mr. Katsaros:

For reasons of military security, it has been necessary to withhold the names of the air crew members who were serving with your son at the time he was reported missing on 20 March 1944.

Since it is now permissible to release this information, we are inclosing a list of names of the crew members.

The names and addresses of the next of kin of the men are also given in the belief that you may desire to correspond with them.

Very sincerely,

E. A. Bradunas

E. A. BRADUNAS
Major, Air Corps
Chief, Notification Branch
Personal Affairs Division
Assistant Chief of Air Staff, Personnel

1 Incl.

Upon receiving the March 1944 MIA telegram; my folks had requested the names and addresses of my crew members. Because of security measures the assistant Chief of Air Staff Headquarters Army Air Forces could not release this information for almost one year later.

# Army of the United States

## Honorable Discharge

*This is to certify that*

JOHN KATSAROS

Staff Sergeant, 11 130 671, Headquarters, Army Air Force Redistribution Station, Atlantic City, New Jersey.

**Army of the United States**

*is hereby Honorably Discharged from the military service of the United States of America.*

*This certificate is awarded as a testimonial of Honest and Faithful Service to his country.*

*Given at* Waltham Regional Hospital, Waltham 54, Massachusetts.

*Date* 14 December 1944.

Elton L. Titus

ELTON L. TITUS
Colonel, MC

166✓

W. D., A. G. O. Form No. 55
January 22, 1943

11995

## ENLISTED RECORD OF

KATSAROS (Last name) JOHN (First name) (Middle initial), 11 130 671 (Army serial number), S/Sgt. (Grade)

Born in Haverhill, in the State of Massachusetts

Enlisted 7 December, 19 42, at Boston, Massachusetts

When enlisted he was Nineteen and five-twelfths (19-5/12) years of age and by occupation a Student

He had Brown eyes, Brown hair, Medium complexion,

and was Five feet Ten inches in height.

Completed Two years, No months, Eight days service for longevity pay.

Prior service:[2] None

FINANCE OFFICE, WALTHAM, MASS. Dec. 14, 1944
Final Statement Paid in the amount of $ 154.69
Account of H. S. RUTH, Colonel, F. D. made by
A. C. MAYNARD, Captain, F. D. Agent Officer.

Noncommissioned officer Sgt., 3/6/43 - S/Sgt., 3/23/44.

Military qualifications[3] Sharpshooter, 8/26/43 - .45 Cal. Pistol, 1M, March 1943 - '03 Rifle, Feb. 1944 - Carbine, Feb. 1944 - Thom.Sub, Feb. 1944

Army specialty AM (B-17 Type) Gunner (B-17)

Attendance at None (Name of noncommissioned officers' or special service school)

Battles, engagements, skirmishes, expeditions Missions over Germany, Frankfurt, Leipzig, Frankfurt, (3) Wilhelmshaven, Erkner, Augsburg, Landsburg, Frankfurt. D/ JON, BERLIN, BERLIN

Decorations, service medals, citations European African Middle East Theater Ribbon, 10/29/43, One Bronze Star to SAME Rib. - Aviation Badge, 12/11/43 ***

Wounds received in service Wounded in B-17 over Germany.

FINANCE OFFICE, WALTHAM, MASS.

Date and result of smallpox vaccination[4] 7 December 1942, Immune

Date of completion of all typhoid-paratyphoid vaccinations[4] 14 January 1943

LAPEL BUTTON ISSUED BY: A C Maynard Capt FD

Date and result of diphtheria immunity test (Schick) None

Date of other vaccinations (specify vaccine used)[4] Tetanus, 5/3/43 - Yellow Fever, 9/25/43 - Typhus, 10/11/43

Physical condition when discharged Poor Married or single Single

Honorably discharged by reason of[5] CDD, AR 615-361.

*Character* Excellent JMW Periods of active duty[6]

Remarks[7] Entitled to Travel Pay. No time lost under AW 107.

*** Air Medal and one Oak Leaf Cluster - Purple Heart.

Certification made for Mustering-out Payment in amount of $ 300.00
H. S. RUTH, Colonel, F. D.
BY: A C Maynard Capt FD

(Print of Right Thumb)

Signature of soldier John Katsaros

John M. Weidner
JOHN M. WEIDNER
Captain, MAC
Registrar

### INSTRUCTIONS FOR ENLISTED RECORD

[1] Enter date of induction only in case of trainee inducted under Selective Training and Service Act of 1940 (Bull. 25, W. D., 1940); in all other cases enter date of enlistment. Eliminate word not applicable.

[2] For each enlistment give company, regiment, or arm or service with inclusive dates of service, grade, cause of discharge, number of days lost under AW 107 (if none, so state), and number of days retained and cause of retention in service for convenience of the Government, if any.

[3] Enter qualifications in arms, horsemanship, etc. Show the qualification, date thereof; and number, date, and source of order announcing same.

[4] See paragraph 12, AR 40-210.

[5] If discharged prior to expiration of service, give number, date, and source of order or full description of authority therefor.

[6] Enter periods of active duty of enlisted men of the Regular Army Reserve and the Enlisted Reserve Corps and dates of induction into Federal Service in the cases of members of the National Guard.

[7] In all cases of men who are entitled to receive Certificates of Service under AR 345-500, enter here appointments and ratings held and all other items of special proficiency or merit other than those shown above.

### INSTRUCTIONS FOR CERTIFICATE OF DISCHARGE

166✓

AR 345-470.

Insert name; as, "John J. Doe," in center of form.

Insert Army serial number, grade, company, regiment, or arm or service; as "1620002"; "Corporal, Company A, 1st Infantry"; "Sergeant, Quartermaster Corps."

The name and grade of the officer signing the certificate will be typewritten or printed below the signature.

U. S. GOVERNMENT PRINTING OFFICE: 1943 O - 530071

Note: Physical condition on December 14, 1944 reported as "**POOR**."

CATERPILLAR CLUB

Membership Certificate

This is to certify that

JOHN KATSAROS

Is a member of the Caterpillar Club whose life was spared the 20 th day of MARCH 1944 because of an emergency parachute jump from an aircraft. This certificate is bestowed to the end that this safety medium in the art of flying may be furthered.

CATERPILLAR CLUB

Caterpillar Club Membership

## CHAPTER 32
## Visit to France

I have been fortunate to visit France, three times, to renew friendships made over many years since the cessation of hostilities. After the war, Pierre and Julienne Demarchez and family moved to Boulogne sur Mer, France and opened one of the best bakeries of breads and desserts in the country, supplying their products to the French railway system and to Air France, as well as to the local population. This is a great upgrade of the small bakery in Chaumuzy, well deserved for their fine products over which they heartily labor.

On one of the visits, Pierre handed me a key chain that General Charles de Gaulle had minted and handed to him in person, in honor of his Resistance efforts. I refused to accept it and told him to give it to his son, Didier, who was born after WWII. Pierre said he considered me his oldest son and insisted that I must accept it. I did accept the key chain and still treasure this great honor to this day. Pierre also presented me with a copy of a parchment that depicts his Croix de Guerre, France's highest award, and honors from the American government to him and his wife, Julienne for aiding dozens of Allied airmen and fighting for the liberation of France. USA President Franklin Delano Roosevelt and General Dwight D. Eisenhower signed these awards. Several of his mementos, identification documents and their FF armbands of their days with the Free French are in my possession for safe keeping, and perhaps one day they can be turned over to Pierre's grandchildren.

Years later, I asked Pierre if that suspected priest had turned us in for a reward of $10,000.00. His answer was, "The person who turned us in no longer exists." Need I say more? Mary made two of the three trips with me during which time we visited Paris, Reims and Boulogne sur Mer. While in Paris, we paid a visit to Boulevard Davout where my friends and helpers, Marie and Gendarme Marcellin Villemont and their upstairs neighbors lived. (Their names remained unknown because of fear of retribution by the Gestapo).

Many years have passed since the war days and my running with the Resistance, and many of my friends who endangered their lives to shelter me from the Gestapo, are long gone now but nostalgia drew me back to cherish that time, those friends and that place. Ted Krol, my bombardier, had told me about his bailout and the kind people who helped him in his hiding-out from the Gestapo, and in tending to his wounds, so Mary and I paid a call to Ted's helpers, Bertranne and her husband, Jean Auvert, where we got together like old friends.

Bertranne was a college student of medicine during the war and was assisted by Andre Molhos in the nursing of Ted Krol's leg, injured on contact with the ground after bail out. Bertranne was descended from royalty, and had royalty been in vogue, she would have been in line to be Queen of France. She became a Doctor in Ophthalmology, and her husband, Jean, a Doctor of Internal Medicine. Andre Molhos, a medical student at that time, became a Doctor of Medicine. Drs. Jean and Bertranne, with their son Geoffrey, paid several visits to our home in Haverhill. Sadly, Bertranne, Andre Molhos, and Mr. And Mrs. Ted Krol have now passed on.

The 401st donated this stained glass window to a Weldon, England church. Note our B-17 etched in the middle.

John with: Jean Joly, Julienne Demarchez, Madaleine Felix, & Pierre Demarchez, Photo taken at a 1987 reunion, City Hall, Reims.

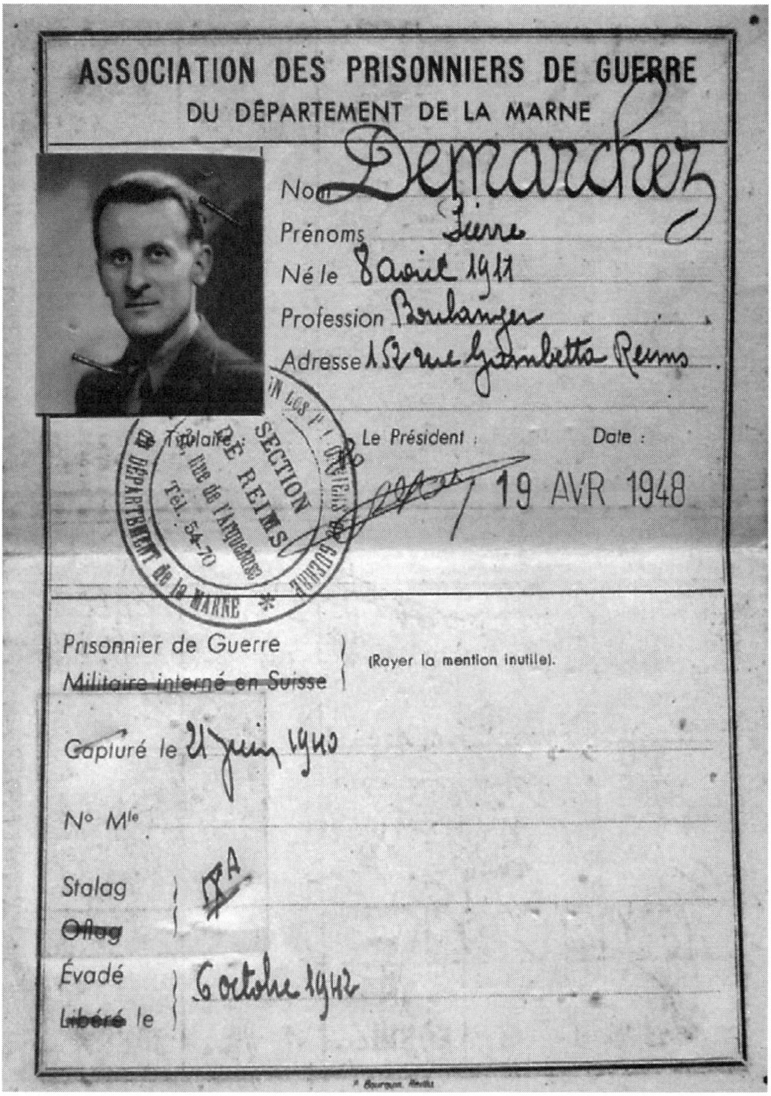

ASSOCIATION DES PRISONNIERS DE GUERRE
DU DÉPARTEMENT DE LA MARNE

Nom Demarchez
Prénoms Pierre
Né le 8 août 1917
Profession Boulanger
Adresse 152 rue Gambetta Reims

Titulaire : Le Président : Date :
19 AVR 1948

SECTION DE REIMS
Tél. 54-70
DÉPARTEMENT de la MARNE

Prisonnier de Guerre
~~Militaire interné en Suisse~~
(Rayer la mention inutile).

Capturé le 21 juin 1940

N° M^le^

Stalag IXA
~~Oflag~~

Évadé
~~Libéré~~ le 6 octobre 1942

Pierre Demarchez was issued this certificate in 1948 showing he was captured on June 21, 1940 and escaped on October 6, 1942.

1987 photo at John's dedication Mayor of Reims, France escorted by helpers, Chauvin, Demarchez, Joly & a female interpreter.

Helpers at dedication: Mr. & Mrs. Joly in fur coat & son, Mr. & Mrs. Demarchez, Madame Felix, Dr. Molho.

Henri in sweater, Mrs. Chauvin, John hugging Pierre, Frank Mastronardi on right.

A few of my French Resistance helpers at *La Bonne Maison* Farm reunion.

Julienne and Pierre Demarchez & I hugging, Henri in sweater.

John Katsaros with his helper, Madeliene Felix, taken at our B-17 *Man O' War* Crews, 1987 French Resistance Reunion at City Hall at Reims, France

My visit to Pierre, & Julienne Demarchez's home,
Boulogne ser Mer, France.

John & Julienne Demarchez

Jean Sirot

United States Reunion of John's French Resistance Helpers, the late, Julienne and Pierre Demarchez's son, daughter-in-law and grandson. Left to Right: Jonathan Cirome; the late Jacqueline Demarchez; John, Didier Demarchez; Atty. Alfred J. Cirome; Mary and Laurie Katsaros (John's wife and daughter); Frederic Demarchez and Cynthia Cirome.

Didier Demarchez, the son of Mr. & Mrs. Pierre Demarchez, holds a German issued ration coupon required to purchase a loaf of bread. John hid out in the safe house above the bakery at Chaumuzy, France.

L to R: The late Jacqueline Demarchez, John, Didier Demarchez, son Fredric, and Mary Katsaros.

My reunion with Jean and Suzanne Joly and their son, Andre at their home in Reims, France.

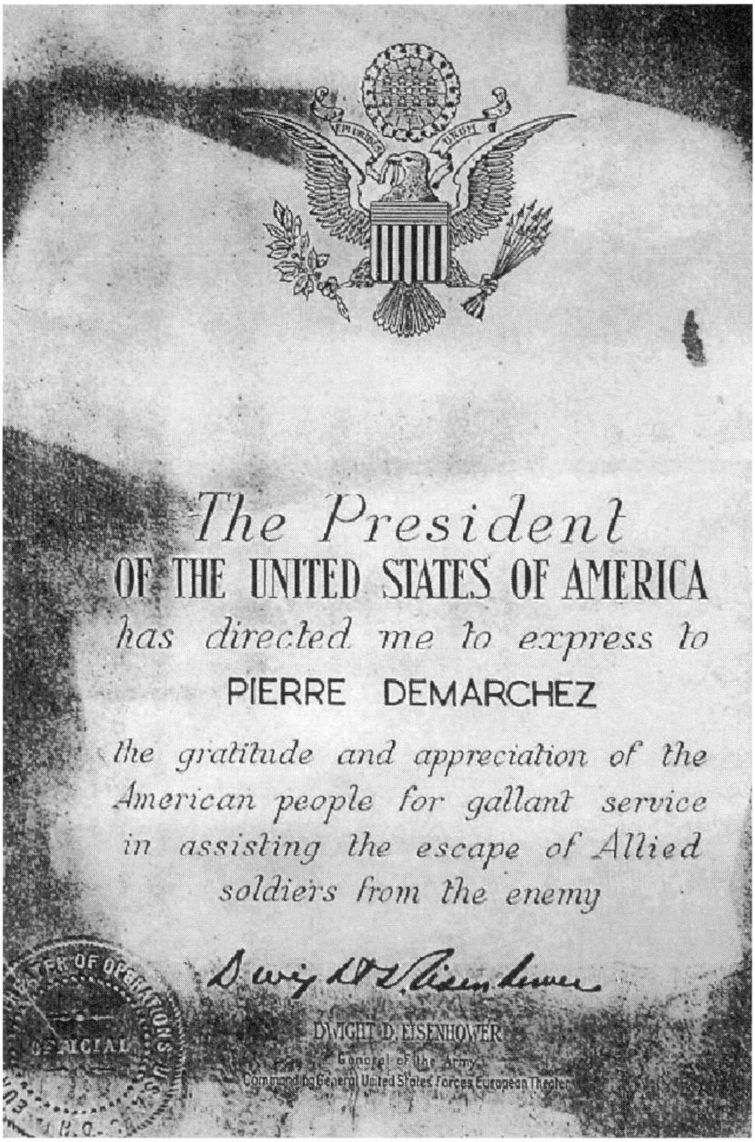

The President
OF THE UNITED STATES OF AMERICA
has directed me to express to
PIERRE DEMARCHEZ
the gratitude and appreciation of the American people for gallant service in assisting the escape of Allied soldiers from the enemy

Dwight D. Eisenhower
DWIGHT D. EISENHOWER
General of the Army
Commanding General United States Forces European Theater

Awards presented to Mr. & Mrs. Pierre Demarchez from General Charles de Gaulle.

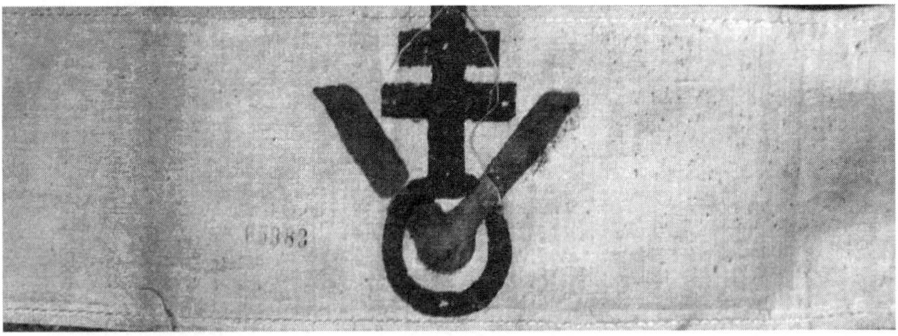

Armband Worn by Pierre Demarchez for French Resistance after D-Day.

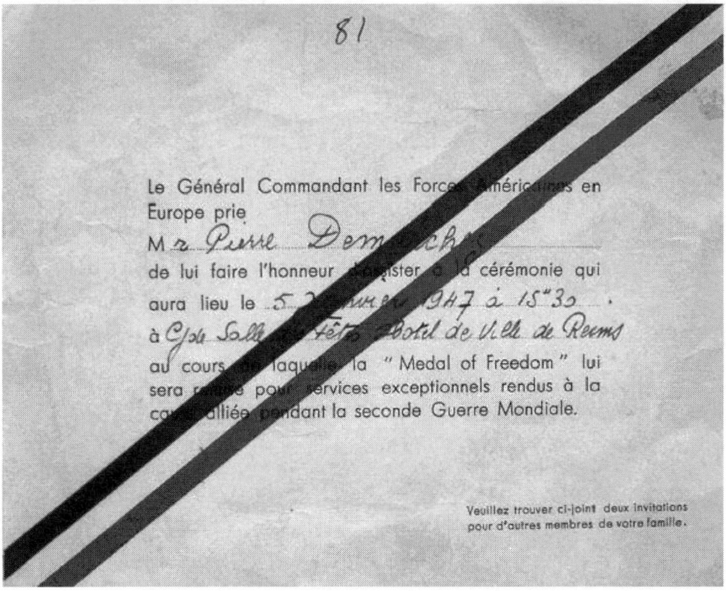

81

Le Général Commandant les Forces [illegible] en Europe prie

Mr Pierre Dem[illegible]

de lui faire l'honneur [illegible] cérémonie qui aura lieu le 5 [illegible] 1947 à 15"30 .

à Gde Salle [illegible] Hotel de Ville de Reims

au cours [illegible] la " Medal of Freedom " lui sera [illegible] services exceptionnels rendus à la [illegible] alliée [illegible]dant la seconde Guerre Mondiale.

Veuillez trouver ci-joint deux invitations pour d'autres membres de votre famille.

Awards presented to Mr. & Mrs. Pierre Demarchez

I was honored by the leaders of the French Resistance with the medal of the French Resistance 18 Juin 1972, (*Les Medalles De La Resistance Francaise 18 Juin 1972*).

I was made a Honorary member of the "*11 Demi Brigade Parachutiste De Choc*" by Jean Joly, head of Reims Resistance & Pierre Demarchez.

John's wife, Mary, with arms around Pierre, Julienne and son, Didier, with his wife Jacqueline, son Frederic and interpreter.

Mary Katsaros standing with Jean Sirot and the homeowner beside *Man O' War* B-17 prop at Reims, France.

## CHAPTER 33 AFEES,
## "Air Force Escape and Evasion Society"

Those airmen who escaped and evaded capture by the enemy, upon return to base, were issued escape and evasion identification numbers by the 8th Air Force Intelligence. I belong to the 401st Bomb Group and the Air Force Escape and Evasion Society (AFEES). The Military Intelligence Service at Headquarters ETOUSA established a report file number for each escape and evasion returnee, my AFEES file number is EE755.

One AFEES reunion was held in Savannah, Georgia, the site of the 8th Air Force beginning. Wives were invited, and Mary and I visited the mighty 8th Air Force Museum. We were surprised to view a beautiful diorama of the 401st Bomb Group based at Deenethorpe, which had been selected for viewing of approximately forty WWII bomber bases in England.

A section of the museum is set aside, specifically, to honor AFEES members. Visitors to the museum learn that while some of our downed airmen escaped and evaded the enemy, others, not so fortunate, were shot on sight and/or interrogated before execution. On one such occasion, just two weeks after our boarding the train from Paris to Toulouse, two hundred Allied airmen, mostly American, were hunted down and shot in Paris. The Gestapo had infiltrated the French Resistance and used the valuable information, which proved fatal to cell activities and the Paris cell leaders including Jean Moulars, the Paris Chief of Police, who were apprehended, tortured and executed by the Gestapo during May of 1944. These are the brave people who helped me to escape and evade from enemy hands; they sacrificed their lives for mine.

Ted Krol, Bombardier of my crew revealed to me the existence of the Air Force Escape and Evasion Society (AFEES), and I quickly provided the documentation required to become a member.

I attended my first AFEES reunion at Pittsburgh, PA where I met Mr. Gil Millard, who had made a listing of all the society members on his computer. Gil introduced me to Leslie Atkinson of Banyuls -S/Mer, France, who had researched and located hundreds of names of aircrew members who were shot down over Europe, and the names and locations of those friends who helped our airmen to hide out and evade the enemy.

Mr. Louis Collard was among the Chiefs of the Underground that I met in Reims, France. Now deceased, he was President of Daro -Voyages in Canada and helped the U.S. airmen to organize the AFEES's on their visit to Canada in 1969, and hosted a wonderful reception in Epernay -Champagne, France. I regret not being a member at that time and missing out on that get together.

Virginia Krol, John & Mary Katsaros & Leslie Atkinson.

Leslie Atkinson & John at AFEES reunion Savannah, GA

Jack Stead & John at AFEES Reunion, Pittsburgh, Pa.

My meeting up with Leslie Atkinson produced the full names of all the Americans in my escape group.

| | |
|---|---|
| EE 752 | Charles J. McLain, Lt. Col. (Ret.) 359B Squadron 303 BG MIA 28 February 1944 |
| EE 743 | Royston T. Covington, Lt. 544 B Squadron 384 BG MIA 8 February 1944 |
| EE 754 | Jack Stead, S/Sgt. 709 B Squadron 447 BG MIA 22 April 1944 |
| EE 755 | John Katsaros, S/Sgt. 612 B Squadron 401st BG MIA 20 March 1944 |
| EE 756 | Merlin K. Burgess, Lt. 575 B Squadron 391 BG MIA 26 April 1944 |
| EE 757 | Bufor Thacker, Major 479 F Squadron 474 FG MIA 7 May 1944 |
| EE 805 | Raymond K. Holtz, Lt. 359 F Squadron 356 FG MIA 27 April 1944 |

John Katsaros, back row, 2nd from left
Major Bufor Thacker, back row, 3rd from left
Lt. Colonel Charles J. Mclain, back row, last person on the right
S/Sgt. Jack Stead, Kneeling in front row, 1st on left
I could not remember to identify and name 3 out of the 7 escapees
Photo taken at the American Embassy in Madrid, Spain May 1944

Dear John and Mary 11th July 1989

I'm sorry that we couldn't talk more in Pittsburgh, it is the trouble with these meetings, too much good things in too short a time.

You were in the hands of "Réseau Bourgogne" and the "Genevieve" you mention is Mme Genevieve CAMUS - SOULIÉ, 260 Boulevard VOLTAIRE, 75011. Paris. France, Mr Georges BROUSSINE, 40 Rue VANEAU, 75007. PARIS was her chief and the head of "BOURGOGNE", both were guest of AFEES in the CHANTILLY's meeting of 1985 and Mr Broussine attended the ORLANDO's meeting.

In Reims, among the chiefs of underground you met was Mr Louis COLLARD, deceased who was, in 1969, President of DARC-Voyages in CANADA, he organized a part of the Afees visit in 1969 and a wonderful reception in EPERNAY - Champagne -

Mr Brunot The owner of the safe house in the forest was Mr BRUNICE CARACH. The owner of the café in the village near Bourgogne was Mr ERHARD GOUIN?

For the gendarmes who helped you and Jack w Stead I'll write to the Gendarmerie Head-Quarter in Paris and will write to Mme Camus-Soulié to know if she remembers and still knows some of your helpers.

The US airmen who crossed the Pyrenees with you and Jack Stead were:

E/E 452 Lt Col. CHARLES J. McCLAIN - Afees member 305-6390007?
6265 ANCHOR LANE, ROCKLEDGE, FL. 32955. tel 305 639 or?

E/E. ROYSTON T. COVINGTON. 544 BS. 384 BG. MIA 8 Feb 1944
E/E. MERLIN K. BURGESS - 575 BS 391 BG. MIA 26 April 1944
E/E. BUFOR THACKER - 479 FS 434 FG. MIA 4 Mar 1944
E/E. RAYMOND K. HOLTZ - 354 FS 356 FG MIA 27 April 1944

Mr Gil Millard can have received more details on them since May 1988

In your talk with Mr J. Stead and with Lt Col C. McClain if you can get more details for me it'll help my research.

PS and please, point my out the people you specially want and give the address of the ones with whom you are already in touch. Thanks

Warm Regards to you and Mary

Leslie

Sadly, both Gil Millard & Leslie Atkinson, two wonderful gentlemen and AFEES members have passed away.

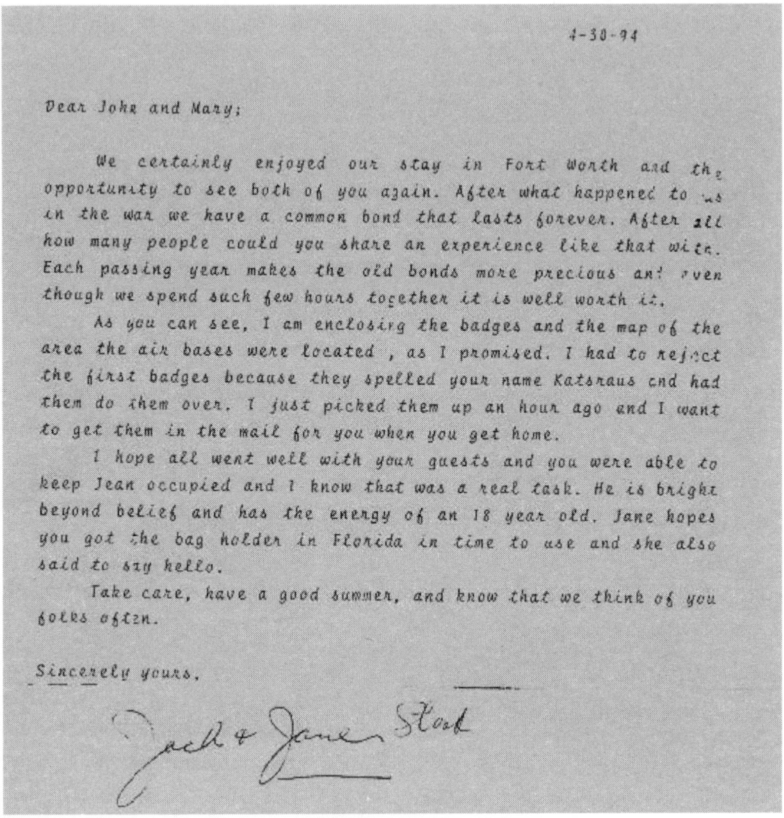

4-30-94

Dear John and Mary;

We certainly enjoyed our stay in Fort Worth and the opportunity to see both of you again. After what happened to us in the war we have a common bond that lasts forever. After all how many people could you share an experience like that with. Each passing year makes the old bonds more precious and even though we spend such few hours together it is well worth it.

As you can see, I am enclosing the badges and the map of the area the air bases were located , as I promised. I had to reject the first badges because they spelled your name Katsraus and had them do them over. I just picked them up an hour ago and I want to get them in the mail for you when you get home.

I hope all went well with your guests and you were able to keep Jean occupied and I know that was a real task. He is bright beyond belief and has the energy of an 18 year old. Jane hopes you got the bag holder in Florida in time to use and she also said to say hello.

Take care, have a good summer, and know that we think of you folks often.

Sincerely yours,

Jack & Jane Stead

Letter from Jack Stead

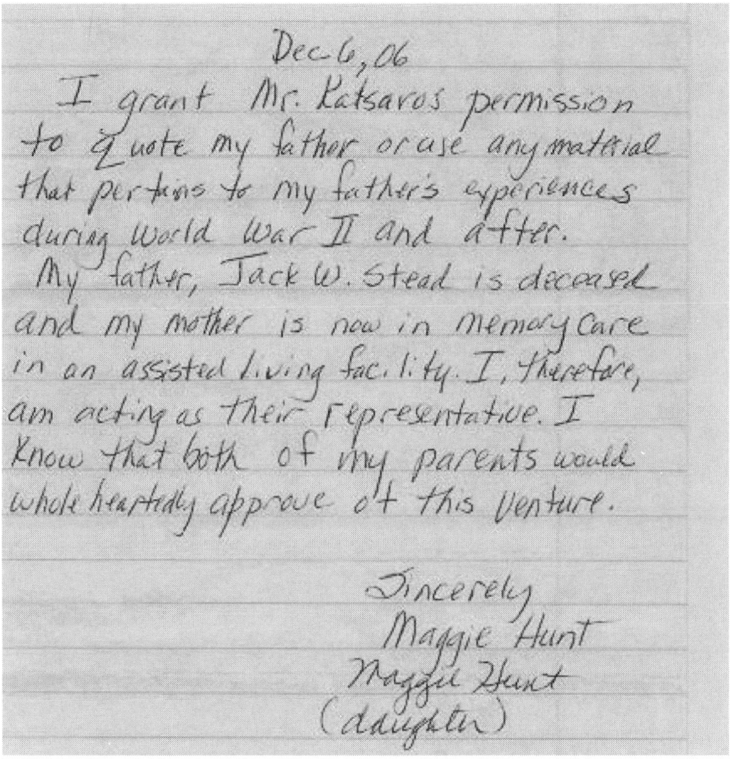

Dec 6, 06

I grant Mr. Katsaros permission to quote my father or use any material that pertains to my father's experiences during World War II and after.

My father, Jack W. Stead is deceased and my mother is now in memory care in an assisted living facility. I, therefore, am acting as their representative. I know that both of my parents would wholeheartedly approve of this venture.

Sincerely
Maggie Hunt
Maggie Hunt
(daughter)

Release from Jack Stead's daughter.

Ted Krol, Bertranne Auvert, AFEES President Ralph Patton .

John, AFEES President Ralph Patton, M/M Ted Krol.

Jack Stead, John, Unknown & Ted Krol at AFEES Reunion.

## Origin of AFEES Excerpt from "History of AFEES"

*During WWII, thousands of pilots and aircrew members were reported Missing In Action; more than half of those MIA's from the 8th Air Force were finally reported killed in action. Those that survived became Prisoners Of War for the duration.*

*A small percentage of those who survived in enemy territory Evaded or Escaped capture to eventually return to their units.*

*When they returned they were debriefed and "Sworn to Keep Secret" the details of their experiences and identification of those who helped them Escape and/or Evade. No notification was ever sent to these men and women lifting their "Pledge To Secrecy". Some individuals, for love of country, carried that pledge to their grave.*

*Many persons resisted the enemy by helping downed flyers. If caught, they stood to be executed or sent to prison where survival was most difficult. A number of American Airmen lost their lives attempting to escape from capture; but that was all in the line of duty, as they were under military orders to attempt Escape if downed behind enemy lines.*

*When an individual walks the fine line between life and death, with a Helper or a fellow flyer, a bond develops between them which is never severed in his mind. It is that bond which brought the AFEES Society into existence and perpetuates it today through those Escapers and Evaders and Helpers who still live, the spouse's offspring and new friends dedicated to keeping the spirit alive and well.*

*Prior to 1961, Leslie Atkinson, a Captain in the French Air Forces Reserve, inspired by the work of the British Royal Air Force, organized the Air Force Rescue Association in France in order to bring together Escaped American Aviators with their European Helpers. Many American names and addresses of Escapees by way of Operation Bonaparte was provided by Mathurin Branchous, a Resistance Leader, to Ralph Patton, who became the chairman of the AFEES Board. Patton, with two men, John T. Emery and Fred T. Schmitt, planned the first reunion in Buffalo, N.Y., 15-16 May 1964. The U.S. Air Force Escape And Evasion Society was born.*

*Leslie Atkinson plowed ahead with making contacts throughout Europe, into France, Belgium, Holland, Norway, Italy, and beyond. Thanks to Belgium's WWII Comete Escape and Evasion Line sent a delegation of 61 to the 1974 celebrations in Detroit, Washington D.C.. and New York City. Gill Millar, a professional computer programmer, took the information available about individual Escapers, Evaders and Helpers, and entered it into a database to help the AFEES, until his death.*

*AFEES Membership Chairman Clayton C. David and his wife "Scotty" by 1986 had located 400 members. The current list of Helpers exceeds 600.*

*The 2006 roster shows 288 members from the 8th AF, 93 the 15th , 29 the 9th , 9 the 12th , 5 the 14th , one from each of the 5th , 10th , 13th AF, The British Royal Air Force (RAF) and the Royal Canadian Air Force (RCFA).*

*For a group of pilots and aircrew who have had trouble getting any official recognition from the U.S. Congress, AFEES continues to achieve much, just as the members did when they served their country during WWII by Escaping or Evading.*

*In the year 2010 The US Air Forces Escape and Evasion Society honored John Katsaros to lead the AFEES Organization their, President*

## THE FAMILY

John Katsaros, 109 Crosby Street, Haverhill Massachusetts 01830
U.S.A. Telephone 978-374-7357.

Mother, Eleni Helen Christos Christopoulos, born in 1891, immigrated at age seventeen to the United States of America in 1908 with port of entry at Boston, Massachusetts. She settled in Peabody, Massachusetts with her family about twenty miles northeast of Boston. Dad had entered the U.S. at Boston in 1894 at age twelve traveling with Mrs. Schinopoulos and put down in Haverhill, Massachusetts about thirty miles due north of Boston. All these families were acquaintances in their hometown of Patras, Greece.

Dad, as a teenager, had a fire for business in his blood, and after three restless years in Haverhill, at age fifteen, he returned to his beloved Patras to open a grocery store. During these early years he became acquainted with Mr. Claus, a German expatriate, maker of wines who recognized Dad's acumen for business and invited him to come work at the winery. Dad saw his opportunity, and after eighteen months with the grocery, passed off the business to his brother, and went to work in the wine business where he soon became the head vineyard master of Greek fine wines, i.e., Demesticas and Mavrodaphne, and other brands of Archia Claus Winery. The name Archia Claus wines flourishes to this day. While working at the winery, Dad was stricken with malaria which caused a severe nose bleeding problem, and was advised by his Doctor Uncle to seek treatment in America where he would also find a better environment for recuperation. Mr. Claus was heartbroken to learn that Dad, the only son and family he had ever known, was to leave him and would pass up the promised inheritance of the winery. It was a tearful goodbye.

At age twenty-three, Dad immigrated back to Haverhill, Massachusetts where he sought the medical attention he so desperately needed. After two years of medical treatment, and restless again, Dad went to Providence, Rhode Island and ventured into the restaurant business. Whatever his dissatisfaction or yearnings, Dad, after two years returned to Haverhill to learn the flourishing shoe business. In 1912, at age 30, he started his own shoe factory, until the "bust" of the world depression during the "20s" brought closure to many factories. Dad's knowledge and exceptional skill earned him managerial positions with Greenstein and Brindis, two local large shoe manufacturers where Dad continued to work until his retirement in 1960 at age 78.

John's mother & father, Eleni Helen & Spiros S. Katsaros.

Mother and Dad married on 18 December 1915, ages 24 and 33 respectively, at Peabody, Massachusetts, and established their home in Haverhill where Dad had to look after his shoe factory. Soon, their happiness was fulfilled with Dad operating the shoe manufacturing business and a home filling with children. Six children, two girls and four boys were born to Spiros and Eleni Helen Katsaros: Sotiris, "Sot", the first was born in 1917; George in 1919; Ann in 1920; Madalene in 1921; John in 1923, named after his maternal Uncle John, an officer in the Greek Army, killed by a German sniper bullet one week before the ending of hostilities in World War I; and S. Charles "Chuck", the youngest, entered the world in 1932.

Mother passed away at the age of 78. Dad lived a vigorous and enjoyable life until the ripe old age of 100.

Regretfully, Chuck and Madalene are the only family members to learn of my story at this late date; U.S. Military Intelligence did not release me from the Secrecy oath until 1986, years after most of the family had passed away.

Now, I have been requested to write and lecture this story for the benefit of those that had not known of its existence and for the records in our national archives. POW Groups at Boston and Lowell, MA. and friends Capt. Joe Lovoi, author, 'Listen My Children,' and Colonel Steve Chirigotis, editor, both of whom served with the U.S. Army Air Force during WWII, prompted me to write the book. The book, *Code Burgundy –The Long Escape* reflects the code name given to me by S.O.E. British Intelligence, who also established 'Burgundy', as the name of the escape line for downed allied airmen, and spies from the Toulouse French Resistance.

Front row: My wife, Mary, my sisters, Ann & Madalene. Second row: grandchildren Corey, Caroline, Cameron. Back row: daughters Lynne & Laurie, grandson Craig, son-in-law Christian, brother Chuck & John. Photo taken 2003.

**Below are recently obtained secret German and American Intelligence reports by Michael and Joseph Belmonte, brothers of Reading, Massachusetts from the US Government, on "what happened to our *Man O' War* crew after bailout."**

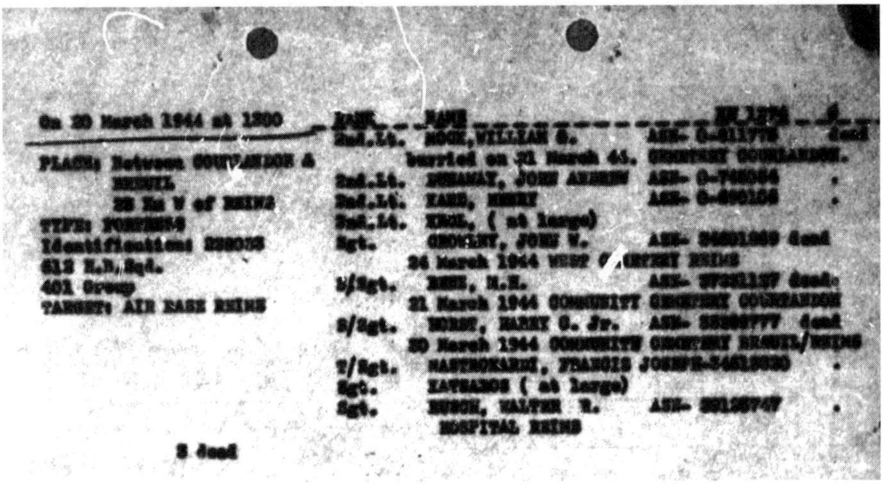
On 20 March 1944 at 1200
PLACE: Between [illegible] & [illegible]
25 Km W of REIMS
TYPE: FORTRESS
Identification: [illegible]
612 B.S.Sqd.
401 Group
TARGET: AIR BASE REIMS

8 dead

RANK NAME [illegible]
2nd.Lt. MOCK, WILLIAM G. ASN- 0-[illegible] dead
burried on 21 March 44. CEMETERY [illegible].
2nd.Lt. DUNAWAY, JOHN ANDREW ASN- 0-[illegible] "
2nd.Lt. KAHN, HENRY ASN- 0-[illegible] "
2nd.Lt. KROL, ( at large)
Sgt. CROWLEY, JOHN W. ASN- [illegible] dead
24 March 1944 WEST CEMETERY REIMS
S/Sgt. [illegible] ASN- [illegible] dead
21 March 1944 COMMUNITY CEMETERY [illegible]
S/Sgt. [illegible], HARRY G. Jr. ASN- [illegible] dead
20 March 1944 COMMUNITY CEMETERY [illegible]/REIMS
T/Sgt. [illegible], FRANCIS JOSEPH [illegible] "
Sgt. KATSAROS ( at large)
Sgt. BUSCH, WALTER R. ASN- [illegible] "
HOSPITAL REIMS

On the 20th of March 1944 Enroute to the briefed target our formation was flown directly into a deep overcast over France. Flying directly at slow speeds it was difficult if not impossibly to stay with the formation in the tail position. Falling out we continued alone to the target and bombed as briefed. In an attempt to rejoin the formation we flew the prescribed course keeping to the overcast for protection. Approximately 12 miles northeast of Rheims France at 1300hrs, we broke out of the overcast and were immediately attacked by lurking enemy aircraft. Our ship was disabled and set on fire, forcing the remaining live men to abandon it in midair. As a result of the encounter four men have been reported killed. One mans death was witnessed by me. The bombardier and one waist gunner managed to return to allied control without internment. Four men including myself were captured immediately and interned in Prisoner of War Camps.

Henry Kane
HENRY KANE
1st Lt. AC

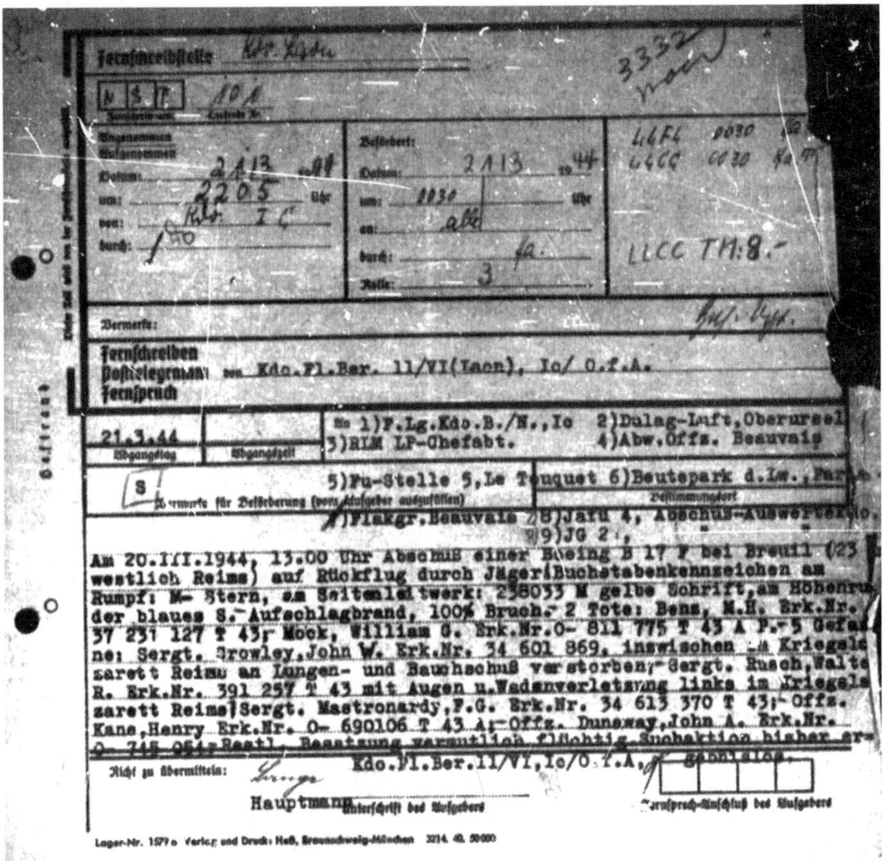

Fernschreibstelle

Datum: 21.3.44

um: 2205 Uhr

Befördert: Datum: 21.3. 1944

um: 0030 Uhr

Rolle: 3

LLCC TM:8.-

Vermerke:

Fernschreiben / Postelegramm / Fernspruch von Kdo.Fl.Ber. 11/VI(Laon), Ic/ O.f.A.

21.3.44

Abgangstag | Abgangszeit

an 1)F.Lg.Kdo.B./N.,Ic 2)Dulag-Luft,Oberursel 3)RLM LP-Chefabt. 4)Abw.Offz. Beauvais

S

5)Fu-Stelle 5,Le Touquet 6)Beutepark d.Lw.,Paris

Vermerke für Beförderung (vom Aufgeber auszufüllen) | Bestimmungsort

7)Flakgr.Beauvais 8)Jafu 4, Abschuß-Auswertekdo. 9)JG 2,

Am 20.III.1944, 13.00 Uhr Abschuß einer Boeing B 17 F bei Breuil (23 km westlich Reims) auf Rückflug durch Jäger; Buchstabenkennzeichen am Rumpf: M- Stern, am Seitenleitwerk: 238033 M gelbe Schrift, am Höhenruder blaues S.- Aufschlagbrand, 100% Bruch.- 2 Tote: Bens, M.H. Erk.Nr. 37 231 127 T 43; Mock, William G. Erk.Nr.O- 811 775 T 43 A P.- 5 Gefangene: Sergt. Crowley, John W. Erk.Nr. 34 601 869, inzwischen im Kriegslazarett Reims an Lungen- und Bauchschuß verstorben; Sergt. Rusch, Walter R. Erk.Nr. 391 257 T 43 mit Augen u. Wadenverletzung links in Kriegslazarett Reims; Sergt. Mastronardy, F.G. Erk.Nr. 34 613 370 T 43; Offz. Kane, Henry Erk.Nr. O- 690106 T 43 A; Offz. Duneway, John A. Erk.Nr. O- 745 064; Restl. Besatzung vermutlich flüchtig. Suchaktion bisher ergebnislos.

Kdo.Fl.Ber.11/VI,Ic/O.f.A.

Nicht zu übermitteln:

Hauptmann

Unterschrift des Aufgebers

Fernsprech-Anschluß des Aufgebers

Lager-Nr. 1577a Verlag und Druck: Heß, Braunschweig-München 3214. 43. 50000

FORM LEAF 81 KU 1274

STATEMENT ON CAPTURE OR RECOVERY OF MEMBERS OF ENEMY AIR FORCES

REPORT IS MADE THROUGH:

OFFICE OR STATION: Air Base Headquarters A 33/XI

LOCATION: Reims

DISTRIBUTOR:
Air District Headqu. Belgium-NorthFrance Ic
Transit Camp, Oberursel
Air Base Headquarters Ber.
OFFICE OF APPRAISAL-VALUES:

REGARDING: DOWNED / EMERGENCY LANDINGS / CRASH } 1 B-17-F DATE AND TIME: 20 March 1944 1830

AT: NEAR: between Courlandon and Beuil (23 Kilometer westof Reims)

PERSONAL RECORD OF MEMBERS OF ENEMY AIR FORCES

FAMILY NAME: SURNAME / LAST NAME } B e n s

FIRST NAME: CHRISTIAN NAME / GIVEN NAME } M.H.

RANK: Unknown

IDENTIFICATION NUMBER: SERIAL / SERVICE 37231127 T43 O

NATIONALITY: USA

STATEMENTS MADE AT TIME OF CAPTURE:
DATE OF CAPTURE:
EXACT LOCATION OF CAPTURE:
CAPTURE EFFECTED BY:

STATEMENT MADE AT RECOVERY OF DEAD:
DATE & TIME & PLACE OF RECOVERY: 20 March 44
CONDITION OF BODY: destruction of the body

THE PRISONER WORE (*UNIFORM*)

DESCRIPTION OF IDENTIFICATION TAG:
HOW WERE PERSONAL RECORDS OF DEAD ASCERTAINED: by Identification Tag

DATE AND TIME OF BURIAL: 21 March 1944
GRAVE LOCATION: Community Cemetery of Courlandon

POSSIBLE IMPUTATION *(PLACING)* UNDER SERVICE OF THE G.F.P. OR S.D., FOR PURPOSE OF ASCERTAINING ENEMY PATRONAGE OR FAVOR:

Inventory of Personnel Property:

6 Passes (Foto)
1 Dictionary

DELIVERED TO HOSPITAL:
DATE:

DATE AND TIME OF TRANSPORTATION TO PRISONER CONCENTRATION POINT:

Deutschbein
S/Sgt. and Commander of Receiving Unit.

REMARKS:

*(ATTEMPTED ESCAPE. PECULIARITIES IN BEHAVIOR OF PRISONER, ETC.)*

INVENTORY OF SECURED, PERSONAL EFFECTS OF PRISONER OR DEAD:

INVENTORY OF PERSONAL EFFECTS AND EQUIPMENT OF PRISONER OR DEAD:

6-3334,AF(3)

FORM LKAF #1 KU 1374

STATEMENT OF CAPTURE OR RECOVERY OF MEMBERS OF ENEMY AIR FORCES

REPORT IS MADE THROUGH:

OFFICE OR STATION: Air Base Headquarters A 23/XI

LOCATION: R e i m s

DISTRIBUTION: Air District Headqu. Belgium-North France Ic, Transit Camp, Oberursel, Air Base Headquarter Rer,

OFFICE OF APPRAISAL-VALUE:

REGARDING: DOWNED / EMERGENCY LANDINGS / CRASH ) 1 P-17-F

DATE AND TIME: 20 March 1944 1300

AT: [illegible] between Courlandon and Breuil (25 kilometer west of Reims)

PERSONAL RECORD OF MEMBERS OF ENEMY AIR FORCES

FAMILY NAME: SURNAME / LAST NAME ) H o o k Jr

FIRST NAME: CHRISTIAN NAME / GIVEN NAME ) William G.

RANK: Officer

IDENTIFICATION NUMBER: SERIAL / SERVICE 0-811776 T 43 A

NATIONALITY: USA

STATEMENTS MADE AT TIME OF CAPTURE:
DATE OF CAPTURE:
EXACT LOCATION OF CAPTURE:
CAPTURE EFFECTED BY:

THE PRISONER WORE *(UNIFORM)*

STATEMENT MADE AT RECOVERY OF DEAD:
DATE & TIME & PLACE OF RECOVERY: 21 March 44
CONDITION OF BODY: destruction of the body

DESCRIPTION OF IDENTIFICATION TAG:
HOW WERE PERSONAL RECORDS OF DEAD ASCERTAINED: by identification tag

DATE AND TIME OF BURIAL: 21 March 1944
GRAVE LOCATION: Community Cemetery of Courlandon.

POSSIBLE IMPUTATION *(PLACING)* UNDER SERVICE OF THE G.F.P. OR S.D., FOR PURPOSE OF ASCERTAINING ENEMY PATRONAGE OR FAVOR:

Inventory of Personnel Property:
2 engl. Pound Bills
1 engl. Coins
1 foto sketch
1 journal leaf
1 Dictionary

DELIVERED TO HOSPITAL:
DATE:

DATE AND TIME OF TRANSPORTATION TO PRISONER CONCENTRATION POINT:

Deutschbein
S/Sgt. and Commander of Receiving Unit.

REMARKS:

*(ATTEMPTED ESCAPE. PECULIARITIES IN BEHAVIOR OF PRISONER, ETC.)*

INVENTORY OF SECURED, PERSONAL EFFECTS OF PRISONER OR DEAD:

INVENTORY OF PERSONAL EFFECTS AND EQUIPMENT OF PRISONER OR DEAD:

6-3234.AF(3)

KU 1274

TELEGRAM FORM

DISTANCE - MESSAGE -OBERURSEL-

NAME OF DISTANCE-MESSAGE WRITER: WI-Oberursel
LPOS 17

ACCEPTED:
RECEIVED:

DELIVERED:
DATE:-
TIME:
TO:

DATE: 3 April 1944
TIME: 1620
FROM: LWKO
THROUGH: Koehler

THROUGH:
ROLL:

REMARKS:

S LLVL ANST KR 101 21 March 1944 2205
TO Transit Camp Air Oberursel.
On 20 March 1944 1300/ crash of 1 Boeing B 17F at Brepil (23 kilometer west of Reims) on returning flight by fighter. Letter marks on fusilage:M-U Ustern,on side stabilizer - 238033 M yellow writng,on horizontal rudder blue S.- Crashed and burned 100%.- 2 dead: Bens M.H. Serial Nr. 37231127 T 43. Mock William G. Serial Nr. 811775 T 43 A P . 5 prisonner: Sgt.Cowley John W. Serial Nr. 34601869 .Meanwhile died at Field Hospital Reims from lung and stomach gunshot wound: Sgt. Busch WalterR. Serial Nr. 391257 T 43 . With eye and calf injuries at Field Hospital Reims: Sgt. Mastronardy J.B. Serial Nr.34613370 T 43, Officer Kane,Henry, Serial Nr. -0-690106 T 43 A / Officer Dunaway,John A. Serial Nr 0-745054. Rest of the crew probably escaped. To date search without result.

Air Base Headquartwers Ber. 11/Rom six Rom one Co F.A.

6-3224,AF(5)

-26-

FORM LEAF #1 | ZS 3274

STATEMENT ON CAPTURE OR RECOVERY OF MEMBERS OF ENEMY AIR FORCES

REPORT IS MADE THROUGH: NCO and substituted leader of operation

OFFICE OR STATION: B 231/31
Air base Headquarter Juvincourt

LOCATION: Juvincourt

DISTRIBUTION:
Air District Hdqu. Belgium-North France
Transit Camp, Oberursel
Air Base Headquarter Ber.

OFFICE OR APPRAISAL-VALUES:

---

REGARDING: DOWNED / EMERGENCY LANDINGS / CRASH ) 1 Boeing B 17 F

DATE AND TIME: 20 March 1944 1300

AT: NEAR: Breuil 20 kilometer West of Reims

PERSONAL RECORD OF MEMBERS OF ENEMY AIR FORCES

FAMILY NAME: SURNAME / LAST NAME ) H o r s t Jr

FIRST NAME: CHRISTIAN NAME / GIVEN NAME ) Harry C

RANK:

IDENTIFICATION NUMBER: SERIAL / SERVICE 36289777 T 42-43 0

NATIONALITY: USA

STATEMENTS MADE AT TIME OF CAPTURE:
DATE OF CAPTURE:
EXACT LOCATION OF CAPTURE:
CAPTURE EFFECTED BY:

THE PRISONER WORE (UNIFORM)

STATEMENT MADE AT RECOVERY OF DEAD:
DATE & TIME & PLACE OF RECOVERY: 27 March 44
CONDITION OF BODY: compound fracture of the skull

DESCRIPTION OF IDENTIFICATION TAG:
HOW WERE PERSONAL RECORDS OF DEAD ASCERTAINED? by identification tag

DATE AND TIME OF BURIAL: 30 March 1944 1600
GRAVE LOCATION: Community Cemetary Breuil

---

POSSIBLE IMPUTATION *(PLACING)* UNDER SERVICE OF THE G.F.P. OR S.D., FOR PURPOSE OF ASCERTAINING ENEMY PATRONAGE OR FAVOR:

DELIVERED TO HOSPITAL:
DATE:

DATE AND TIME OF TRANSPORTATION TO PRISONER CONCENTRATION POINT:

REMARKS:

*(ATTEMPTED ESCAPE. PECULIARITIES IN BEHAVIOR OF PRISONER, ETC.)*

INVENTORY OF SECURED, PERSONAL EFFECTS OF PRISONER OR DEAD:

INVENTORY OF PERSONAL EFFECTS AND EQUIPMENT OF PRISONER OR DEAD:

-27-

6-3324, AF(3)

**ADDENDUM #1**

What Happened to the Crew-Members of
"Man-O'-War" After Bailout 20 March 1944?

1. Lt. Jack Dunaway Pilot, with two engines lost and the wing on fire gave the signal to bailout, and put the B-17 on automatic pilot before bailing out himself. Dunaway was captured near Breuell, France, held as a POW until liberated by the American Army.

2. Lt. Henry Kane Co-Pilot, bailed out near Breuell, France, held as a POW and liberated by the American Army. He remained in the Air Force, attaining the rank of Lt. Colonel, flying the "Berlin Airlift" during the cold war of the June 1948 to September 1949, transporting food, clothing and medical supplies to the West Berliners, crashed and died in an aircraft accident.

3. Lt. William Mock Navigator, wounded, and assisted by Lt. Ted Krol to bail-out, died on ground impact as his chute "candled."

4. Lt. Ted Krol, Bombardier, bailed out near Courville, France and fractured his left foot on landing. He dragged his disabled foot south to the town of Goussancourt where he knocked on a door, seeking assistance for his pain and injuries. Luckily he happened on a door of friends of the Resistance who treated his injuries and put his foot in a cast. Ted was turned over to the French underground that secreted him in Paris, right under the Gestapo noses. He moved out of Paris to work with the Marquis wreaking havoc on German resources. Contact with American patrols of the invasion forces provided Ted with transportation back to England where his story of the fate of "Man-O-War" and crew corroborated the story of S/Sgt. John Katsaros. This had to be an eye opener for Division Intelligence.

5. T/Sgt. Harry Horst, Top-Turret Gunner killed-in-action at his station by enemy fighter 20mm cannon fire.

6. T/Sgt. Marvin Benz, Tail-Gunner, killed-in-action at his post by enemy fighter 20 mm cannon fire.

7. T/Sgt.Frank Mastronardi Radio/Gunner held in solitary confinement in this Reims, France prison (pictured below). Mastronardi was wounded and the last one to bailout. German soldiers operating an 88MM, anti-aircraft gun emplacement saw Frank's parachute and they waited, open arms to capture him. He was given a hasty physical examination and taken to a German Prison in Reims, where a German medic treated him for his combat wounds. Three flak fragments were extracted from his right side, his wounds were bandaged and he was given needle injections. He was temporarily placed in solitary confinement before transfer to Frankfurt, Germany for interrogation where again he was placed in solitary. His final prison location was Stalag #1, Barth, Germany on the Baltic Sea. The Russian Army overran the prison in the spring of 1945, saving Frank the experience of a "forced" death march by the Germans. Along with 9,000 POWs, B-17 aircraft from the German built runway nearby, to the American camp "Lucky Strike", at Le Harve, France, transported him. Several days later, he endured a three-week ship ocean crossing to Newport News, Virginia.

8. S/Sgt. Walter Rusch, Ball-Turret Gunner was trapped in his turret by spent .50 cal machine-gun shells locked in the gear track. Frank with John set Walter free, John bailed out. Walter not quite free was again assisted by Frank to extricate himself only to snag his parachute, which blossomed in the planes waist section. Frank helped Walter to gather the chute and to bail out. Walter landed on a picket fence piercing his stomach. A young garcon carried Walter in a wheelbarrow some 50 yards to a nearby woodshed where he was quickly taken into custody and transported by the Gestapo on a motorcycle sidecar to a French hospital in Reims.

Walter viewed Jack Crowley, the left waist gunner, in surgery and was later told by a Russian (prisoner) medical aid that Jack did not survive the surgery. The Luftwaffe preferred that French doctors rather than their own treat the Allies in that bomber flyers may have been responsible for the deaths of their family members. Walter remained in the Reims, France hospital for 52 days then escorted to *Stalag Luft* prison at Frankfurt Germany, to be confined and interrogated for two days, after which he was sent to Buchenwald to be exterminated. Walter was deloused, head shaven and stripped to shower when it was discovered that he was an uncircumcised man and not a Jew, as previously identified by his name. Unfortunately, the German authorities notified the USAAF that Walter was Killed in Action and Walter's father received notification from the Chief of Staff, War Department. The USAAF paid his dad the proceeds of a $10.000.00 insurance policy that all KIA families received, and a funeral was held for Walter at his hometown. There still exists a monument to Walter bearing his name in the local cemetery. Upon his return home from captivity, Walter probably was the only POW to grow up to six feet and gained so many pounds that he was not recognized by the local natives. After all he was a small boy of 17 years old at enlistment and returned a grown man. For many years thereafter, Walter had trouble proving his identity that included loss of his Social Security number. An article appeared in the Reader's Digest entitled, "A Man without a Country", explaining his dilemma. By the end of May he with other prisoners, was put into a boxcar for shipment to Stalag 17B near Krems, Austria. Walter made an attempt to escape, apprehended by a guard and received a rifle butt to the nose for his efforts. With the help of Joseph and Michael Belmonte, researches of our ill fated bombing mission to Frankfurt, Germany, newly obtained German Intelligence report on 20 March 1944; was reported that Walter was captured near Unchair, France 23 Km west of Reims and being treated by German medical staff for wounds received in combat. Unfortunately, the next German report stated "he was dead, Killed In Action". Yet, a German document dated 20 July 1944 that was recently declassified and in my possession, is a copy sent by the International Red Cross, Geneva, Switzerland to German Authorities, stating: We received a request to investigate the case of the American flier, Walter R. Rusch who was reported dead in your telegram 21 April 1944 and in your casualty report 10 June 1944. We received, however, a PW-Card from the above named dated 20 May 1944 that he was a Prisoner of War in *Stalag Luft*. Besides, we received word from France (by our delegate in Paris) on 23 May 1944, that Walter Rusch left the war-hospital in Reims. We beg you politely to check on this case and to inform us about the fate and remains of Sgt. Walter Rusch. On 7 October 1944, the German Lt. Col and Vice-Commander in charge sent a document to the International Red Cross. The above named American is stationed in Stalag V-II B at the Krems Compound of the Air Force. Rusch, Walter is in good health.

L. to R. - T/Sgt. Frank Mastronardi, Lt. Ted Krol, S/Sgt. Walter Rusch S/Sgt. John Katsaros at 401st Bomb Group Reunion, England.

According to Walter, his POW friend Ben Phelper, the author of the book *Kriege Memories* that was made into the academy award winning movie *Stalag 17* was given a signed copy, at the movie premier with the inscription; "Walt may you always be free and happy, Good Luck, Ben." Walter has one of only five books that were published. On 8 April 1945, 4,000 of the POW's at Stalag 17-B endured an 18 day forced march of 281 miles from Krems, Austria to Braunau, Austria to evade the coming Russians, to the west across Europe, in the ice and snow in bitter weather. Old German soldiers guarded the prisoners. They were liberated by the American Army, 13th Armored Division on 3 May 1945, and flown in C47's to camp "Lucky Strike" where they met General Dwight D. Eisenhower. Several days later, they boarded the ship *Marine Dragon* and left Le Harve, France for Boston. Many of the prisoners, including Walter still carried shrapnel in their bodies. 900 prisoners too ill to make the march were left behind in the hospitals. The Russians liberated these POW'S on 9 May 1945. In 1955, two years after the release of his movie "Stalag 17", Ben Phelper died. According to T/Sgt Elmer "Bud" Lincoln, also a POW at Stalag 17-B, a radio operator with the 8th Air Force 453rd BG (H) 733rd Sqdn., two Stalag 17-B POW's have writing credits of the "play"; Stalag 17 (1953), Donald Bevan and Edmund Trzcenski.

9. S/Sgt. John Katsaros, Right Waist-Gunner - Wounded, captured and twice escaped from Gestapo. His story is written in these pages.

10. S/Sgt. John Crowley, Left Waist-Gunner -Serious shrapnel wound to neck, John wrapped scarf around wound and the bleeding stopped. The bleeding quickly coagulated because of freezing temperature; helped to bailout, captured by enemy and died in surgery in a French hospital at Reims, France.

John and Mary Katsaros pictured in front of the replaced picket fence. The lady in the middle still lives in the house. She was a child in 1944 and remembers Walter's landing.

Walter remained in the Reims, France hospital.

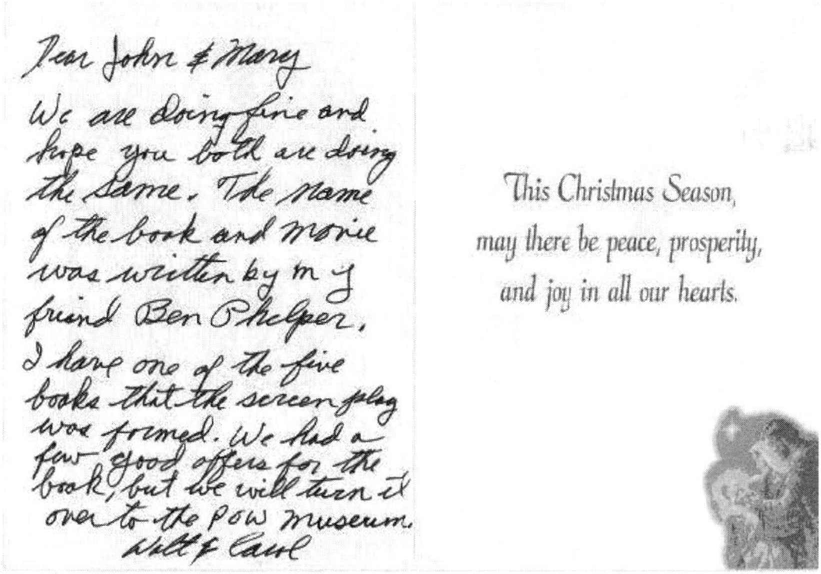
Dear John & Mary
We are doing fine and hope you both are doing the same. The name of the book and movie was written by my friend Ben Phelper.
I have one of the five books that the screen play was formed. We had a few good offers for the book, but we will turn it over to the POW museum.
Walt & Carol

This Christmas Season,
may there be peace, prosperity,
and joy in all our hearts.

According to Walter, his POW friend Ben Phelper, the author the book *Kriege Memories* that was made into the academy award winning movie *Stalag 17* was given a signed copy, at the movie premier with the inscription; “Walt may you always be free and happy, Good Luck, Ben.” Walter has one of only five books that were published.

L/R. Virginia Krol, Mary Katsaros, Walter Rusch Major/Gen. "Hal" Bowman, John Katsaros, Bertranne Auvert, Ted Krol at Savannah, Ga. 401st reunion.

Joe Lovoi, Capt. USAAF (Ret) EX-POW Radar Navigator; Monti Basbas Capt. USAAF (Ret) Former Mayor of Newton, MA with John.

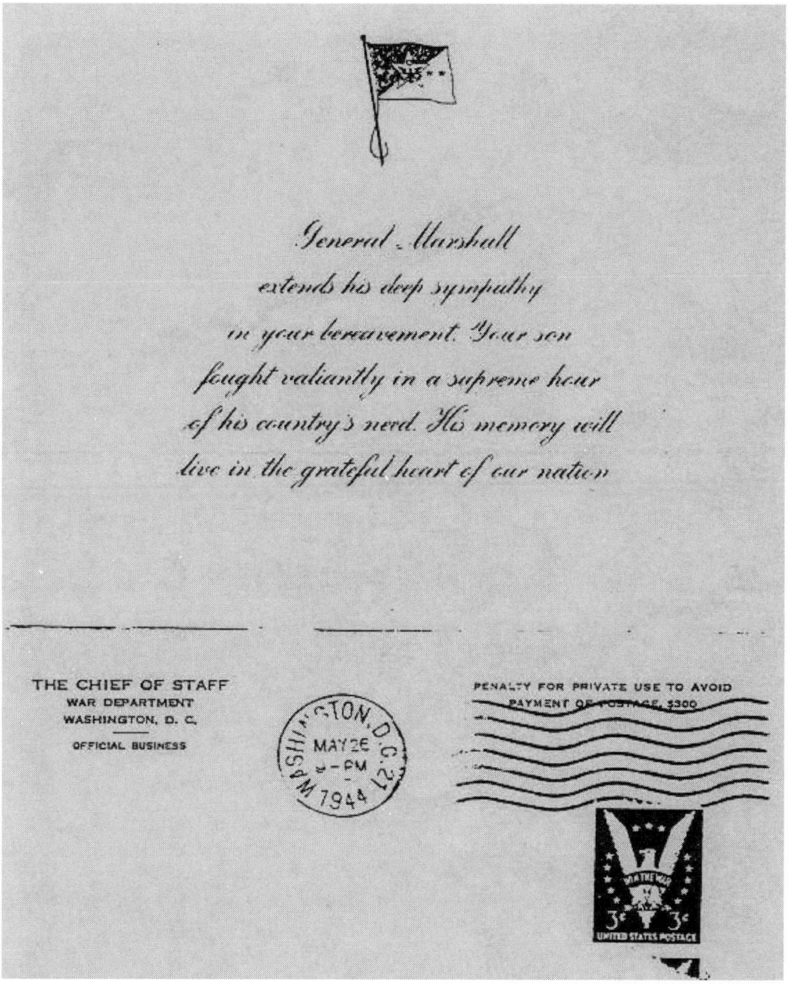

General Marshall
extends his deep sympathy
in your bereavement. Your son
fought valiantly in a supreme hour
of his country's need. His memory will
live in the grateful heart of our nation

THE CHIEF OF STAFF
WAR DEPARTMENT
WASHINGTON, D. C.

OFFICIAL BUSINESS

WASHINGTON, D.C.
MAY 26
PM
1944

PENALTY FOR PRIVATE USE TO AVOID
PAYMENT OF POSTAGE, $300

WIN THE WAR
3¢ 3¢
UNITED STATES POSTAGE

This is the copy of the original letter Walter's folks received from General Marshall, "extending his deep sympathy in their bereavement. Your son fought valiantly in a supreme hour of his county's need. His memory will live in the grateful heart of our nation". The letter was dated on May 26, 1944 while Walter was alive and a prisoner of war, in Germany.

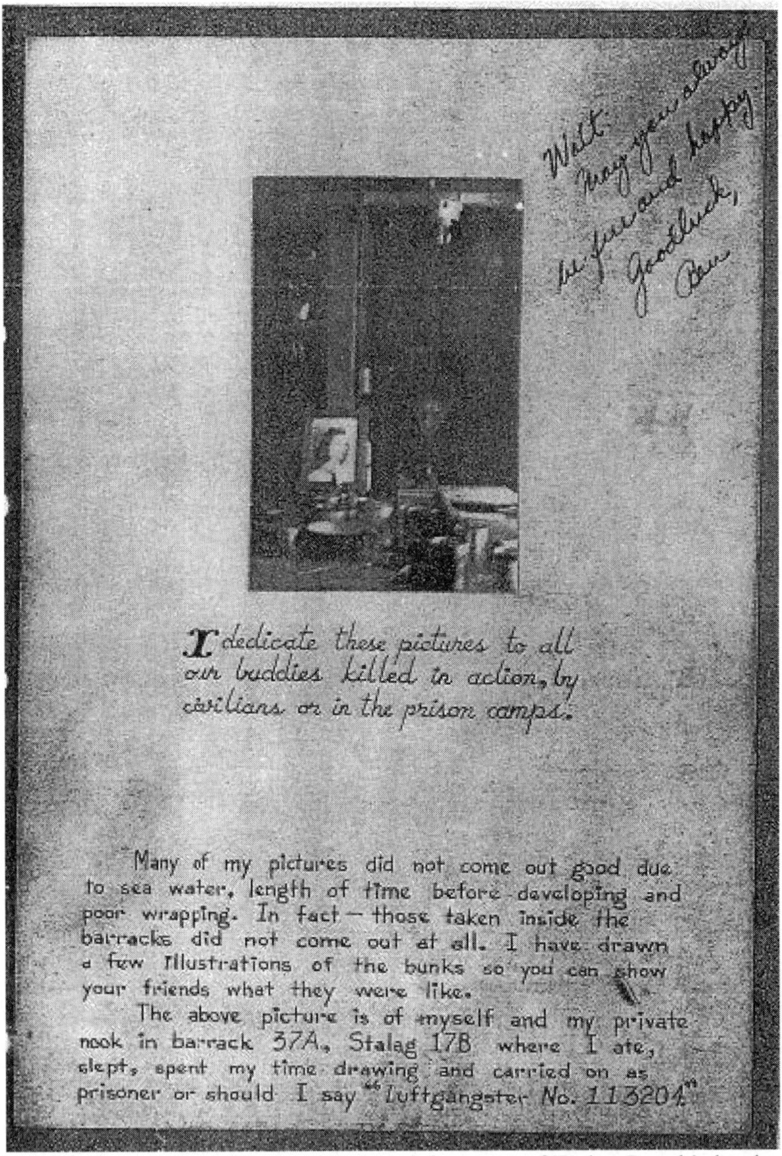

Walt:
May you always be free and happy.
Goodluck,
Ben
I dedicate these pictures to all our buddies killed in action, by civilians or in the prison camps.
"Many of my pictures did not come out good due to sea water, length of time before developing and poor wrapping. In fact — those taken inside the barracks did not come out at all. I have drawn a few illustrations of the bunks so you can show your friends what they were like.
The above picture is of myself and my private nook in barrack 37A, Stalag 17B where I ate, slept, spent my time drawing and carried on as prisoner or should I say "Luftgangster No. 113204"

Ben Phelper, author of *Stalag 17*, signed the cover of Walter Rusch's book.

**ADDENDUM #2**

Andre Molhos, a Greek by birth, was a student of medicine during WWII, as was Bertranne Auvert (Later married to Dr. Jean Auvert). Bertranne, of royal blood, was in line to be a future Queen of France, had royalty prospered. Ted Krol, with Bertranne bicycled to a "safe haven" in a forest controlled by the French Resistance, where Ted was liberated by American forces during the invasion of Europe.

Ted Krol hobbled fifteen kilometers on a broken foot, sustained on the hard parachute landing, before he was forced to seek help. By good fortune, heedless of the danger, he knocked on the friendly door of a Resistance member who gave him safe comfort, food, clothing and contacted two medical students, Bertranne and Andre, who gave the medical help needed. At this safe-house and later at a safe-house secreted in the forest, Ted was able to avoid detection by the Gestapo until his repatriation by American military forces.

Bertranne Auvert helped Ted Krol to evade - pictured with Ted's wife Virginia.

## Accomplishments of the 401st Heavy Bomb Group:

The 401st Bomb Group opened the base at Deenethorpe, England and flew its first mission on 26 November 1943. In May 1945, the 40st1 left England to return to America. The war was over. The base was shut down and officially closed on 17 June 1945. The 401st Heavy Bomb Group, in its seventeen months of operation, flew 254 missions of destruction to the Axis powers.

1. Combat Missions Flown - 254
2. Two Presidential, Distinguished Unit Citations
3. Aircraft loss on operational missions: 94
4. Tons of bombs dropped (all Targets): 17,784
5. Enemy aircraft claimed (confirmed): 193
6. Total battle casualties (KIA, MIA, wounded): 1078
7. Individual awards and decorations: 11,884
8. Total airmen entering enemy air territory: 69,910
9. Rounds of ammunition fired: 916,920
10. Aircraft returning with battle damage: 1872
11. Accredited Sorties: 7,413
12. Best bombing accuracy record among B-17 groups in the 8th Air Force
13. Second lowest loss ratio among B-17 groups in the Eight Air Force
14. First group in the ETO to complete 100 combat missions in 7 months
15. Percentage of aircraft available for each mission: 95.6%

## Lt.. Dunaway and Crew Citation

Lt. Jack Dunaway and crew, 612th Squadron, 401st Bomb Group (H), 94th Wing, 1st Air Division, 8th Air Force.

*"For outstanding performance of duty in armed combat against the enemy. During the intense campaign against the Axis resources, the Group was ordered to attack and destroy the ME-109 Aircraft Factory at Frankfurt, Germany. A successful completion of this important mission would inhibit the enemy of its offensive and defensive capabilities affecting air superiority over Europe, and allow the Allies an air-free invasion of Europe. On 20 March 1944, thirty-five Bombers heavily loaded with maximum tonnage, arose out of England, in lousy weather, to accompany a formation totaling 500 B-17 Aircraft, set on a course to their destination. The huge formation, flying in heavily overcast skies, was having difficulty with the aircraft keeping in formation. Suddenly, within minutes of the I.P., a bomb-loaded aircraft, out of control, fell from the formation above, endangering Man O' War. Pilot, Lt. Jack Dunaway, exhibiting outstanding professionalism to avert collision with the falling aircraft and other aircraft adjacent and below, put his plane in a precipitate dive and pull to the left. This maneuver put the plane in a rough turbulent downdraft and the plane dropped over a thousand feet before the pilot recovered control. The lost altitude was regained to return the ship to formation; it was nowhere to be found. Unaware of the Group recall, because of radio silence, due to bad weather conditions, the pilot decided to continue on to target, expecting to meet up with the Group. The Navigator set the course to target, where the cloud cover cleared; the Bombardier viewed the target through his Norden bomb sight, steadied the plane run and dropped the bombs for a direct hit on target. Unmindful of the heavy concentration of the anti-aircraft barrage, which inflicted severe damage to the aircraft, the courageous crew brought their aircraft through the flak for a highly successful bombing run, razing grave damage to the vital enemy aircraft factory. Turning off target, the plane was aggressively attacked by four to five enemy fighters. The gallant gunners fought off the brutal attack by the fighters who dogged the plane all the way back to Reims, France where the gunners ran out of ammunition and the fighters used them for*

*target practice. The gunners accounted for two probable and the battered aircraft had two engines knocked out with the wing on fire. The navigator and three gunners were killed in action and the crew sustaining multiple wounds, were forced to abandon Man O' War. By outstanding gallantry, airmanship and grim determination of the combat crew, the 612th Squadron, 401st Bomb Group has reflected great credit upon itself and the Armed Forces of the United States of America."*

## ACKNOWLEDGMENTS

Now, I give recognition to those individuals, groups of individuals and organizations without whose help I could not have survived the day-to- day living on my journey through France.

Level 1: Pierre Demarchez - Leader of the Resistance at Chaumuzy, France.
Julienne Demarchez – Co-Leader of the Resistance at Chaumuzy, France.
Who, when captured, survived the Gestapo's favorite means of torture, the pulling out the finger nails with a pair of pliers. A loud, noisy cement mixer was activated out front of Gestapo Headquarters to muffle the howls and screams of the torture. Julienne Demarchez is a brave woman and told them nothing. Captured at the bakery and was held prisoner at Ravensbruk for one and one half years until she was liberated by American troops at the end of WWII. Her health deteriorated in prison camp but she survived to tell her story. She never complained about the misfortunes of war or her personal tragedy, and stated that she would, if needed, for liberty, do the same thing again.

Jean and Suzanne Joly - Head of the Resistance at Reims, France.

René and Madaleine Felix - Members of the Resistance at Reims, France.

Special recognition is given to Pierre, Jean and René who, in a bold plan, stormed the farm home *La Bonne Maison* where I was held prisoner, shot the German military guards, and spirited me away to the safety of the French Underground.

At an honors ceremony, after the war, accompanied by English Prime Minister, Winston Churchill, General Dwight David Eisenhower, and General Charles De Gaulle honored Pierre and Julienne Demarchez, leaders of the Resistance during the war with France's *Ceux De La Resistance* (1941-1945) and *Le Croix de Guerre*, France's highest "award for bravery in action on their heroic work for France and the Allies."

Prime Minister Churchill, paid tribute to the honorees with a Certificate of Commendation, from the English Parliament and the King of England, in gratitude and appreciation of the English people for gallant services in assisting the escape of Allied soldiers from the enemy

General Eisenhower praised the honorees with a written commendation from the President of the United States, expressing the gratitude and appreciation of the American people for gallant services in assisting the escape of Allied soldiers from the enemy.

Doctor Levy and his wife – A French nurse. The surgeon, a French Jew, in hiding from the Gestapo, assisted by his wife, performed three surgeries on my arm to save it and my life.

Chief of Police, Reims, France - Engineered my second escape from the hands of the Gestapo, while in transit during station transfer by overcoming the guards without firing a shot. A very clever plan!

Level 2: Mr. And Mrs. Erhard Govin, (alias Gerhart) - Owner of Café de Bourgogne where I stayed a couple of days. My dog tag is still affixed to the mirror back of the bar. He sacrificed his life to free the French and France.

Gendarme Marcellin and Marie Villemont - Safe-housed two days with them in Paris and accompanied him wearing one of his gendarme uniforms; was often stopped by German soldiers asking for directions to the pissoire or a light for a cigarette.

Jewish Photographer - Recommended by Paris Chief of Police, Jean Moulars; she provided me a new photograph and ID. Her information about the Holocaust was passed on to Allied Intelligence on my return to England.

Mademoiselle Ferands Moulis (Madame Francoise) - gave me a night's shelter at Toulouse, France on my travels to the Pyrenees.

Jean Moulars - Paris Chief of Gendarmes and head of the Paris Resistance, who arranged for proper photograph identification and guide escort.

Geneviève Camus Soulié - 260 Boulevard Voltaire, 75011 Paris, France. Resistance Cell Leader. English-speaking guide who took me to the home of Gendarme Marcellin and Marie Villemont in Paris.

Basque guide - He quickly and skillfully guided my escape group of seventeen individuals from the foothills and over the Pyrenees Mountains from France to Spain, avoiding detection from enemy hunting parties and air search planes.

Henri - Farm worker who witnessed my parachute landing at *La Bonne Maison*, and secreted me in the farmhouse.

Jean and Yvonne Chauvin and daughter, owner of the farm, *La Bonne Maison*; scene of my first capture and shoot-out to rescue and escape.

Madame Ramoge - The teacher/English translator who muzzled my loud groaning at the home of Mr. and Mrs. Felix. Overnighted at her home where she gave me a warm water bath.

Mother of Julienne Demarchez -Captured by the Gestapo along with Julienne and me. After interrogation she was released.

Polo - The driver of the horse and buggy taxi, provided transportation to the medical clinic at Reims, France; to Ste. Jean Le Baptiste on Easter Sunday morning, 9 April 1944 to receive Communion; and to the "safe -house" of Rene and Madaleine Felix.

Robert Billion and female friend - Lifted me out of the gutter at the Reims clinic to take me to safe hiding at "The Circus".

Mr. And Mrs. Bronis Korach and son - The owners of the farm where Jack Hoad and I were secreted from the Gestapo by hiding in a dry well.

Guides – All members of the French Resistance. The many dedicated men and women who placed their lives in peril to direct us through Reims, Epernay, Paris, Montauban, Toulouse and the little town of St. Girons at the Pyrenees Mountains foothills.

Gaby - Guide directed Jack Hoad and me to the Jewess' photographer studio in Paris, then escorted us to the Electric building.

Level 3: Jack Hoad - British Lancaster bombardier. We met at the Korach farm and journeyed together through France, over the Pyrenees, to Gibraltar and back to England.

The old Gendarme (Mr. Dumas) - Guarded me at "The Circus" where my identity was questioned.

Old Woman - She, daily, brought me a sparse meal and water while at "The Circus".

Le Butcher (Petitbon) - Provided my hosts, and me, with small portions of welcomed meat provisions.

"The Wrestler" - A body guard who accompanied me to church on Easter Sunday and later to dinner at the Felix house.

ME-110 Luftwaffe Colonel - Good stories and drinks at "Café de Bourgogne".

Owner of the Champagne factory at Reims - Toured the factory while the marshaling yards were under air raid by the 8th Air Force.

Georges Broussine - 40 Rue Vansau, 75007 Paris, France. Head of the Resistance Cell, Bourgogne, France. On March 25, 2007 Elizabeth McDade of Rochester, NY contacted me. She met Drue Tartiere 25 years ago living in Valencia, Spain a member of the French Underground and the Burgundy Network who aided flyers shot down during WWII. She is the author of the book "A House Near Paris", that mentions the name of two-dozen airmen she helped. Ms. McDade, in her research, learned that Georges Broussine authored a book named, *L'evade de la France Libre: Le réseau* Bourgogne that mentions a flyer with my last name, was assisted by the Burgundy network. At Elizabeth McDade's recommendation to read Mr. Broussine's book *L'evade de la France Libre*, he indeed mentions six USAAF Pyrenees climbers and me, that he helped, along with the Burgundy Network and Genèvieve Soulié Camus, Marcellin, Marie Villemont and Drue Tartiere, to escape and evade from the enemy in France over the Pyrenees mountains into Spain.

Martin Caidin - Great insight into the airman's life in combat and the great B-17 flying machine in his book *Flying Forts*.

Allan Noyes - USAAF friend. (Retired as a Brig. General, and Asst. Adj. General for Air, Vermont National Guard. Presently he is Executive Director of Vermont Association of Broadcasters. Allan's son is now the Deputy Adj. Gen. for Air, Vermont National Guard.

Jean Sirot - a French citizen from Reims, who independently researched the flight and ill-fated crash of our B-17 and recorded the parachute landing of Lts. Dunaway, Kane, Mock and Krol and Sergeants Crowley, Mastronardi, Rusch and Katsaros.

Joseph Lovoi, Capt. USAF (Ret.) - Author, *Listen My Children*, encouraged me to write my story for posterity; and for the children of today's and future generations to have some insight as to what happened in the European Theater of Operation during World War Two. Also what a group of American Army Air Force, Bomber Crew-Members, had to struggle and endure to keep our Freedom.

Atty. Alfred J. Cirome – Capt. U.S. Army Reserve (Ret.) Legal Advisor, Researcher/ Friend.

Henri Ronald Albert – French Language Interpreter.

Salah Hamani – French and German Language Translator

Frank Consentino - U.S. Navy Radar man SN (Ret.), Author

401st Bomb Group (H) 612th Squadron (H), 8th Air Force - For photos and research

Haverhill Gazette and Eagle Tribune, Newspapers –Bernard "Barney" Gallagher, William "Bill" Cantwell and Tom Vartabedian.

Book, *Bombers of WWII over Germany*

EX-POW Boston Group and their VA representatives.

Credit is given to those individuals who assisted in accumulation of data and materials in preparation of the manuscript.

Coldwell Banker Real Estate Erminio 'Erm' Grasso, Manager Rick Daneau, Betty Ann McCarthy, Charles Coco, Michael Rivera and Kim Chilpjian, of the Haverhill, Massachusetts Office

The Boston, Haverhill, Merrimac, Massachusetts Public Libraries, Boynton Beach Florida City Library, Tina Follansbee, Patrick Kelly, Yuri Konnikov, Michael Bennett, Rohit Singh, Patricia Mooar, Joe Green, and Craig Clark

Electra Bilmazes Gerber

Meg Heckman – Staff Writer, *The Concord Monitor* Concord, N.H.

Christian and Lynne K. Miller, my daughter and son-in law for the final image editing and book cover design..

Laurie Katsaros, for her many hours of computer help

Mike Pride, Editor In Chief, *The Concord Monitor* newspaper, Concord, N.H.

Penny Bowman, President Boston Chapter EAA-106 (Experimental Aircraft Association). For helping to install my Power Point Book Presentation, and her husband Ray.

Kumar Persad and Tri-State Litho, Kingston, NY 12401, for exceptional service in the 1st through 4th printing of my book, *Code Burgundy-The Long Escape*.

William "Bill" Bond, introduced me to Kumar Persad and Tri-State Litho and encouraged me to complete my book and go on a successful speaking tour, making presentations of *Code Burgundy-The Long Escape*.

Dr. Leonard Popowitz, Captain US Army (Ret) - Photography Edit, friend

Michael and Joseph Belmonte brothers, for their research and obtaining the declassified secret German and American intelligence documents from the US government on "What happened to the *Man O' War* crew after bailout", and for presenting me with an exact model they built of a two foot wing span B-17 *Man O' War* we were shot down in on 20 March 1944.

Atty. Jay Cleary, host of the Haverhill, MA. Cable TV (HCTV) who has an interest in WWII, interviewed me on several occasions regarding my book, *Code Burgundy-The Long Escape*, and produced the programs on CD's for viewing. Jay's father Atty. James Cleary, was a classmate of mine at Haverhill High School.

Bonnie Coltin, Chairperson of the Haverhill High School French Department, (Ret); Interpreter of names, places, assistance and my honoring of over 200 French Resistance Helpers, who provided the resources to nurse me back to health, saved my life and assisted in my long escapes; for her translation of *Code Burgundy-The Long Escape* from English to French, for the WWII Liberation Museum of France.

Colonel Richard 'Rick' Martell, Commander of 157 ARW Wing Pease Air National Guard Base Portsmouth, NH; KC135 Boom Operators, M/Sgt John E. Lennon; for arranging presentations with the Operations Group and Air Refueling Wing and assistance from M/Sgt Elaina M. D'Orto

American Hellenic Educational Progressive Association (AHEPA), Haverhill, MA President James Tzitzon, VP Dimitri Miras,Treasurer,James Antonopoulos, Past President Dr. Byron Chopas, Governor Alex Geourantas, Lt. Governor John Tationos, International President, Nicholas Karacostas, International Vice President, Dr. John Grossomanides and Executive Director, Basil N. Mossaidis; for their encouragement and interest to leave a legacy of WWII stories that provided us with "Freedom".

Harvey and his wife, Lee Sawyer for the flights, on their twin engine, six passenger AZTEC airplane, based at the Silver Ranch Park Airport at Jaffrey, NH., from the Lawrence Municipal Airport, MA., for my wife Mary and me, helpers Atty. Alfred J. Cirome, Charles Coco and equipment to give my talks and video presentations in New Hampshire's distant cities, and a return back to our home in Haverhill, MA

Level 4: Those that who contributed to the presentations of *Code Burgundy - The Long Escape*.

Lt General Duncan J. McNabb Commander United States Transportation Command, Scott Field AFB, IL. An honored friend of (AFEES) Air Forces Escape and Evasion Society.

Brig. General Albin F. Irzyk, USA (Ret.) Author of *He Rode Up Front For General Patton*, WWII Fourth Armored Division.

Colonel Steve MacIssac USAF (Ret.) For his help and contributions to the (AFEES) Air Forces Escape and Evasion Society and the retired Air Force Pilot's, the Daedalian Group.

Major Peter J. Vergados, USAF (Ret.) Viet Nam combat Pilot, 2500 hours; B-52, F-100, C-97. L-19, F-84F; for book presentations and promotions with the help of his wife Angelica

Homer Helter, owner of "Antique and Military Mall", Naples, Florida - his dedication and support of all Veterans and arranging my presentation and book signings with the Naples, FL Museum, and his Military Mall.

Kenneth O. Killilea, WWII Marine, 4th Division Machine Gunner, Squad Leader , Five Pacific Island Invasions, wounded in Iwo Jima; for arranging my many book presentations, with the help of his wife Marilyn, my Haverhill High School , classmate.

Albert Grant, Producer of the Veterans Program, *Call to Serve* for The Library of Congress and (MCTV) Methuen, MA Community TV and staff.

Corinne La Charitie, Co-Producer of the Veterans Program, *Call to Serve* for The Library of Congress and (MCTV) Methuen, MA Community TV and staff.

Katheleen Corey Rhame, Interviewer of the Veterans Program, *Call to Serve* for The Library of Congress and (MCTV)Methuen, MA Community TV

Dave Hartnett, Assistant Coordinator, Headquarters Veterans Administration, Boston

Charles J. Walsh, EX-POW Coordinator, Veterans Administration, Boston, MA

Robert Daniels, EX-POW Coordinator, Veterans Administration, Lowell, MA

Michael Larson, Medical Director and staff, Veterans Administration Boston, MA Healthcare System

Experimental Aircraft Association (EAA), B-17 Flying Fortress and crew, Oshkosh, WI and Lawrence, MA Municipal Airport

Collings Foundation (Robert Collings) Stow, MA. Restore and fly WWII Combat Airplanes B-17 Flying Fortress, B-24 Liberator Bombers, P-51 Mustang Fighters and many others.

Liberty Bell, B-17 Flying Fortress and crew

Robert Worden, owner of Pinnacle Therapy, Plaistow, NH; for help in book promotion

Charles Coco and Betty Ann McCarthy; for their patience in providing me with computer help

Robert Roche; for the countless of pertinent information and photos included in my 2nd edition of *Code Burgundy-The Long Escape*

Claudine Thibault Phillipe Barriere, Claude Phillipe Barriere, residence of Paris, France and son Narayan Sengupta of the USA; my English/French connection with WWII Resistance Helpers in the Paris, France region.

Thank you to my wife Mary, daughters Laurie and Lynne for your help and understanding amidst all the distractions while writing my story. I regret having kept you in the dark all these years of my "Long Escape."

*Ambassade de France*
*aux États-Unis*

*L'Ambassadeur*

N°2447

Washington, October 12, 2010

Dear Mr.Katsaros:

I am pleased to inform you that by a decree signed by the President of the French Republic on September 28, 2010 you have been named a "Chevalier" of the Legion of Honor.

This award testifies to the President of the French Republic's high esteem for your merits and accomplishments. In particular, it is a sign of France's true and unforgettable gratitude and appreciation for your personal, precious contribution to the United States' decisive role in the liberation of our country during World War II.

The Legion of Honor was created by Napoléon in 1802 to acknowledge services rendered to France by persons of great merit. The French people will never forget your courage and your devotion to the great cause of freedom.

It is a personal pleasure for me to convey to you my sincere and warm congratulations.

Sincerely,

P. V

Pierre Vimont

On 6 September 2011 the French Consulate General of Boston, Mr. Christopher Guilhou, arrived at Haverhill, MA. to decorate John with the "Chevalier" of the Legion of Honor. He said, "It is such a commemorative event that unites France with the United States.

## MY GRATITUDE TO THE FRENCH RESISTANCE

I will forever be grateful to the French Resistance for my first escape and evasion from the Gestapo. Once taken under the wings of Pierre Demarchez, Jean Joly and René Felix, their families and members of the "Underground" cell, I felt great confidence in their ability to provide safe harbor for me. My sense of security was shattered when the Gestapo, informed by unknown betrayers, hungry for a $10,000.00 reward, stormed the bakery where I was hidden to take me prisoner again, along with Julienne Demarchez. The rule, a fugitive airman is to be secreted at a safe-house for a day or two, at the most; my prolong stay for several weeks at the bakery broke the rules, placing me and my host in severe danger of being exposed. That same day of my recapture I was scheduled for relocation; bad timing was injurious to the cause; the Resistance Cell was found out by the Gestapo and dissolved.

My faith in the French Resistance was not shaken, however, because I believe in their courage, their bravery and their daring; I looked up to them as my leaders.

The French Resistance was at war with the enemy; they fought in their way, disrupting troop movements, derailing train cars, blowing up bridges; everything to wreak havoc on the enemy. This same people created a net work of Resistance Cells throughout France to organize their activities with leadership and purpose – for France. They selected their targets with thoughtful planning and execution, rescuing downed airmen, to secret them throughout networks of safe-houses, to feed, clothe and nurse them and pass them on their way to eventually be returned to England through the Pyrenees Mountains, by boat and aircraft. The Chief of Police, head of the Resistance at Reims, planned and executed my second escape from the convoy. Not a shot was fired; the Gestapo was taken by surprise and was left dumbfounded as we sped away.

There were also Resistance cells in Belgium, Holland, Denmark, Norway, Italy, Greece, China and Czechoslovakia.

I, John Katsaros, Staff Sergeant USAAF am proud to be an adopted citizen of France. My adopted family and friends de Resistance gave me hope without them there would be no life for me.

# REIMS

## Ceux de la résistance : disparition de Jean Joly

*Jean Joly, résistant émérite.*

«*C'était un homme parfait. Il s'est toujours beaucoup dépensé pour les autres*». Jean Joly vient de disparaître à l'age de 89 ans. Il était président de l'association «Ceux de la résistance», fonction qu'il occupait depuis la mort du colonel Bouchez en 1982. Rémois de souche, M.Joly fonda son entreprise de pneumatiques en 1942. Il en fut le PDG jusqu'au jour de sa retraite, qu'il prit à l'âge de 75 ans.

Mais c'est surtout pour son action de résistant que Jean Joly se distingua. En 1943, il fut nommé chef d'Etat-major FFI pour l'arrondissement de Reims, où il mit en place l'ensemble des actions de la Résistance. Recherché par la Gestapo, il vécut dans la clandestinité avec sa famille. Devenu capitaine FFI, il fut incorporé à la Libération au 4ème Cuirassier jusqu'à la fin des hostilités.

Pour l'ensemble de ses actions, Jean Joly a reçu la médaille de la Résistance; la Croix de guerre 39/45; la croix de Combattant volontaire de la Résistance. Il était également chevalier de la Légion d'honneur.

A Suzanne Joly son épouse, et à ses enfants André et Jacqueline, **l'union** présente ses condoléances les plus sincères.

Reims, April 16th

Dear Friends,

This short letter to le
you know about M. Joly's death
on April 11th.
A lot of thanks for th
pictures you sent to me: I thin
that, at last. I'll write soon

Best regards

Madame Jean JOLY, son épouse ;
Monsieur et Madame Daniel MARQUET,
Monsieur André JOLY,
ses enfants ;
Eric et Laure, Florence et Laurent,
Christophe, Philippe,
ses petits-enfants ;
Aymeric, Natacha, Océane,
ses arrière-petits-enfants ;
Madame Marthe BILLARD, sa sœur
Et toute la famille
ont la douleur de vous faire part du décès de

**Monsieur Jean JOLY**

**Président honoraire de « Ceux de la Résistance »**
**Chevalier de la Légion d'honneur**
**Médaille de la Résistance**
**Croix de guerre 1939-1945**
**Croix du combattant volontaire de la Résistance**

survenu le lundi 11 avril 1994.

Selon la volonté du défunt, l'inhumation a eu lieu dans la plus stricte intimité.

REIMS. – 15, boulevard du Général-Leclerc.

THOSE OF THE RESISTANCE DEPARTED
JEAN JOLY
Jean Joly Honored Resistance.
This was a perfect gentleman who always gave a great deal for others.
Jean Jolt died at the age of 89. He was President of the resistance organization.
A position he occupied since the death of Colonel Bouche in 1982.
Joly founded Pneumatics in 1942; he was a PDG to the day of retirement
At 75 years old. But it is above all for his action in the resistance that he is
Distinguished.
In 1943 he was named officer of the FFI for the surrounding area of Reims, France,
Where he created the framework of the resistance in Riems and sought out by the
German Gestapo.
He lived a clandestine life with his family. He became Captain of the FFI and
Was incorporated with the liberation 4th Paratroopers right up to the end of the
Hostilities. As a result of his actions:
He received the Medal Of Resistance, Croix De Guere 1939/45; also the
Croix De Combatant for voluntary service for the Resistance during WW11.
He was also a Knight Of The Legion Of Honor.
Suzzane Joly, his wife and his children Andre and Jacqueline, the union presents its
sincere condolences.

PLEASE NOTE: Jean Joly, Pierre DerMarchez and Rene Felix, were the three leaders of the Reims Resistance that rescued John Katsaros of Haverhill, Ma. From the Gestapo two times. They saved his life by arranging three operations on the critically combat Wounded Katsaros and arranged for his escape and evasion over the Pyrenees Mountains To Spain where he was once again held Prisoner Of War and released a few days after D-Day.

## Jean Joly's Obituary and Awards

Jean Joly in 1943, was named as an officer of the FFI, Reims, France where he had created the framework of the resistance. He rose to Captain of the FFI, and he became a member of the liberation 4th Paratroopers to the end of hostilities. For his gallant services to France and his bravery in rescue of Allied Airmen, Jean Joly was awarded the *Medal de Resistance, Croix de Guerre 1939/45, The Croix de Combatant WWII* and The Knight of the Legion of Honor.

In my research, I was not able to determine the honors bestowed upon Suzanne Joly, René and Madaleine Felix, Marcellin and Marie Villemont, or others of the resistance.

**Julienne Demarchez Memoirs**

Julienne Dermarchez wrote the following memoirs while awaiting execution for harboring me at her home. Because of me and a collaborator who was paid $10,000.00 for my 2nd capture, she was also taken prisoner and tortured. These words she wrote were translated from French to English and sent to me by her son Didier. Because of me she had to endure the thought of death, hunger, humiliation, etc., but she never held this against me or the other downed airmen she and her husband helped. In fact she told me when Mary and I paid our visits to their home a few years ago, that she would have again done the same in similar circumstances. Eventually, the Germans realized her worth as a baker of bread, deserts and office/clerical help, that helped her survive. She wrote this book in prison and if caught would have been executed.

*"A new supervisor ( a fat woman) who looked like a devil to all of us, arrived ...with anger showing me the supervisor.*

*Next day, the Komando 453 was all briefed at the Sprafkolone. We were replaced by Jewish women from Hungary who were evacuated from Auschwitz via Nuremberg who doubled production. Soon the factory was bombarded and the train of ammunition that was waiting for a month for its departure exploded - breaking all the windows and destroying most of the ceiling.*

*We arrived May 5th. We did not have time to enjoy the countryside. When in the month of June, we were informed that the following Sunday the arrival of a convoy of French women - we were overcome with anxiety because of the death of the flowers in the beautiful forest. We wanted badly to offer our friends the beauty and the comfort of the nature to offset the despair which was inevitable working for the German war.*

*Little by little we learned always to overcome abuse and humiliation that were inflicted on us.*

*We were always taking into consideration what was happening to our friends at the concentration camp - we were waiting for the allied victory and the end of Germany. We have to save our integrity and our morality, and reiterate the fight for our cause and the little importance to our personality.*

*Despite the fatigue and the threat a few of us sang at night before going to bed. Others compose or learn poetry during their twelve hours of work. On Sunday we debate books that we read and countries we dream of.*

*The crazy behavior of the Nazis became so intolerable that we cannot have any dialogue between us or being to pay attention to anything. We became very incoherent -the little strength left is to fight against the cold, the exhaustion, and the hunger.*

*At that moment, the only conversation we have is about the distribution of bread and soup. We try to avoid the humiliation and degradation of the feeling of hunger that invades us at dinnertime. It is possible to overcome one's suffering by being altruistic.*

*At this moment where the struggle to live became very harsh - the selfishness with shame - yes at this time of suffering of everyone is incremented in comparison to others - we did not pretend to be better than others or being heroes.*

*We know very much more that those people who did not know the camps - that we are ordinary people. But we have learned something that will remain with us forever. During hard moments, it seems impossible for us to hold our tears and face our destiny."*

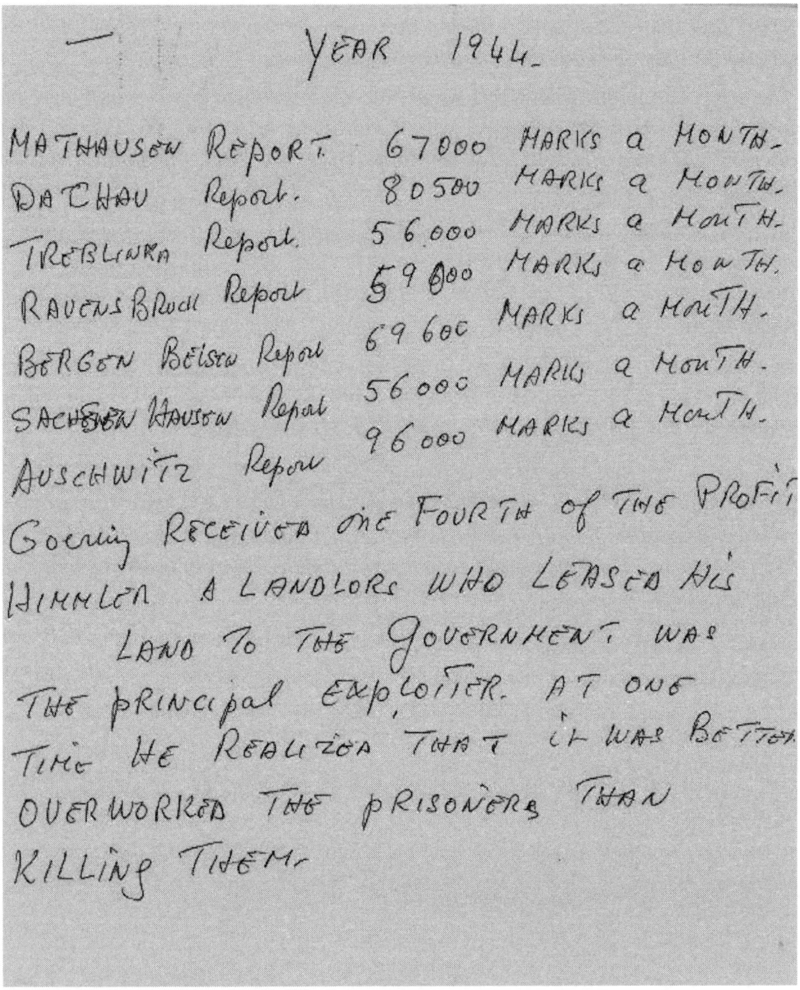

YEAR 1944.

MATHAUSEN REPORT. 67000 MARKS a MONTH.
DATCHAU Report. 80500 MARKS a MONTH.
TREBLINKA Report. 56.000 MARKS a MONTH.
RAVENSBRUCK Report 59000 MARKS a MONTH.
69600 MARKS a MONTH.
BERGEN BELSEN Report
56000 MARKS a MONTH.
SACHSEN HAUSEN Report
96000 MARKS a MONTH.
AUSCHWITZ Report

Goering RECEIVED ONE FOURTH of THE PROFIT
HIMMLER A LANDLORD WHO LEASED HIS LAND TO THE GOVERNMENT WAS THE principal EXPLOITER. AT ONE TIME HE REALIZED THAT IT WAS BETTER OVERWORKED THE PRISONERS THAN KILLING THEM.

Julienne Demarchez found records of Himmler's remunerations as land owner, in the year 1944 of seven German concentration camps . Goering received 25% of the profits.

**S/Sgt. John Katsaros 401st Heavy Bomb Group, 612th Heavy Bomb Sqdn. 94th Wing, 1st Air Division, 8th Air Force, Combat Missions. (Including two flown as a replacement crew-member).**

1. 11 FEBRUARY 1944 – FRANKFURT, GERMANY
2. 20 FEBRUARY 1944 – LEIPZIG, GERMANY (PART OF BIG WEEK 20-25 FEBRUARY, 1944)
3. 21 FEBRUARY 1944 – LIPPSTADT, GERMANY
4. 2 MARCH 1944 – FRANKFURT, GERMANY
5. 3 MARCH 1944 – WILHELMSHAVEN, GERMANY
6. 4 MARCH 1944 – COLOGNE, GERMANY
7. 6 MARCH 1944 – BERLIN, GERMANY. (GROUP'S 1ST MISSION TO BERLIN)
8. 9 MARCH 1944- BERLIN/ERKNER, GERMANY
9. 16 MARCH 1944 – AUGSBURG, GERMANY
10. 18 MARCH 1944 – LANDSBURG AM LECH, GERMANY
11. 20 MARCH 1944 – FRANKFURT, GERMANY (LAST AND FATAL MISSION)

## Café de Bourgogne: Connection

In the spring of 2006, Beth Evers of Charlotte, North Carolina and her Husband Jerry, a flight attendant for US Air, traveled to France to search out the exact location where her maternal uncle, Jack McCollum, a B-24 Liberator radio operator, assigned to the 93rd Bomb Group 8th Air Force, was shot down 1 April 1944 over Bourgogne, France. His crew was flying on a bombing mission over Ludwigshavan, Germany. He did not survive his injuries on their hunting expedition. They ran into Linette Deletang, the daughter of Erhard Govin of Café de Bourgogne, an 8 year old back in April 1944. She and her husband Lucien live in the area and provided Jerry Evers enough information about me, and my flying background to cause Jerry to call me from N.C. to learn if I had any association with Beth's uncle.

Strange how we all continue to relive those years over and over again in ways unimaginable.

Linette's father, the real Erhard Govin, was previously reported as having been executed by the Gestapo after being caught cutting telephone cables. She passed the information that her dad was shot escaping from the act of sabotage and went into hiding. He died of his wounds later, on 23 August 1944. The Mr. and Mrs. Evers were shown the plaque of names and their pictures dedicated of all the British Royal Air Force who were supported by Govin.

According to Jack McCollum, Linette told him that, John Katsaros was the only American that her father helped.

Linette Govin Deletang's letter

Bourgogne le 6-01-07

John, Mary,

Your card surprised me pleasantly. I thank you for your best wishes I send good wishes to you and your wife for a very happy and healthy New Year.

Mam didn't speak to us about a Luftwaffe pilote to fly allied soldiers back to England. Can you tell me mote?

You could cross France and over the Pyrenees mountains into Spain, it is an extraordinary story. Certainly, it was difficult and dangerous. I would like you told me your adventure.

I know my parents had harboured 48 parachuted allied soldiers during the war. I only was 8 years old. I remember Jack, an English pilot. He came back and visited Mam with his wife, Betti, several times. He also received Mam twice or three times. I also saw a Canadian, Vic. He went at Bourgogne with his wife and his daughter several times. Mam went to his home, in Canada, where she was received by government with Mr and Mrs BILLON, Dad's friends who, also, harboured parachuted allied soldiers.

I remember an American Soldier who called John. He was wounded. His arm was plastered. Dad cut the plaster with a pruning shears, it was very difficult! I was a little girl and for me, John was a tall young man. I beleive his hair was frizzled.

I don't know Mr. and Mrs EVERS. Had they given you my name and my address? Was he harboured by Dad?

When Dad was killed by German soldiers, Mam was pregnant. My little sister, Claudine, is born on december 1944. She died on 2000. My brothers, Claude and Janick, also died. Three all were married and each of them had 2 daughters. My 3e brother, Dany, is married and has 2 sons. He lives near Toulouse. I am married with Lucien who was agriculturist at Bourgogne. I was a teacher at Bourgogne until 1988. Then I was the mayor for 12 years. Now, we are retired. We have 4 daughters and 1 son. It's a beautiful family. All the children are married and we have 11 grand-children. On 2007, there will be 2 big events: in april, we shall celebrate our gold-wedding and in june, we shall be great-grand-parents.

I wrote to Linette Govin Deletang, at her home and on 28 February 2007. Linette responded with an interesting letter and three photos, depicting her father's funeral procession, a copy of la Café de Bourgogne and the third one a picture taken of her mother, two year old brother Danny, Jack Hoad, Bronis Korach, a Canadian Victor McCreight and several friends and me. Also many relatives.

Below is a copy of Linette Govin Deletang's letter. Linette is a retired school teacher who has a wonderful command of the English language, and in her own words, I have typed her letter exactly as she has written it. Linette retired after serving 12 years as Mayor of Bourgogne, France.

*Orbey le 28-02-2007*

*John,*

*What a joy when I received your long letter with pictures. Now, we stay in the Vosges, (mountains in the east of France) with two grandchildren, Coralie (she is nineteen on next month) and Thomas (he is 15). It snowed when we arrived so we can ski. But this year, it's not very good.*

*The story of your mission in Deutschland is very interesting and sharp, it was a difficult and extremely dangerous mission on account of the clouds, the excessive loading of the B-17 and also the great number of planes. A formation of 500 B-17's, certainly that was very impressive. The Allies had put the most for destroying this airplane factory in Germany. What place did you hold in your crew? It's incredible that you could survive all your wounds, escape the Gestapo several times, bear fatigue of a so long travel and climb the Pyrenees when you were so weak. You have shown proof of much determination, bearing and courage.*

*I remember Dr. Levy who was reputed in Reims. Sometimes, Mom spoke about Jean Joly or René Felix but never about Pierre Demarchez, I think she didn't know him. I phoned to the Mayor of Chaumuzy to take indications about Pierre Dermarchez and, perhaps, to meet him. But he doesn't live in Chaumuzy. After the war, he bought a baker's shop at Reims and another at Boulogne.*

*You speak about Bronis Korach. I knew him very well because he was Dad's friend. After the war, he lived at Bourgogne until he dies on, (the date is at home). He 'lended' to me the photo that Lucien, my husband, made for you.*

*After the war Mr. and Mrs. Korach had a son, they called him Erhard in remembrance of my father. On the photo, I know, from left to right, Vic (Canadian), Mrs. Job, (a neighbor), my mother, a client, and behind him my brother Danny (3 years old), you John and Simone (my parent's servant), Jack Hoad, and Bronis Korach. When you were hidden in the forest, near Bronis's house, it was in a buried Blockhouse, which was built during the First World War.*

*The Canadian was called Victor McCreight, we said Vic. He often came to visit Mom and her friends, also members of the French Resistance, (Mr. and Mrs. Robert Billion). Do you meet them? When they went to Canada, Vic had sent a message on TV for trying to meet again other persons who were harbored by my parents or Mr. Billion. Vic had explained that, during the war, for security, the harbored allies only knew and called their surname and Vic remembered Sam, William, Bond, Albert, and John.*

*Jack Hoad wrote to Mom until she died, on 1980. My sister, Claudine, who lived with Mom, wrote to him once or twice then she stopped. Jack and his wife, Betty, lived at Solihull. There is their address.*

*Mr. and Mrs. Jack Hoad*
*The White Cottage*
*Ullenhall Solihull*
*Warwicks (England)*

*I don't know if they are always alive. The story with the German Colonel didn't surprise me very much because Mom told that Dad looked to play tricks, to enjoy one's self with his friends, to make the feast. She liked to tell that, once, Dad had opened a champagne bottle at the bar, so called for his birthday, but it was an Allied parachutist and a German officer drink together. Then he laughed when he told it to his friends. In the village, people didn't understand why Dad offered champagne to German officer? (He's my father-in-law who told me). To travel in train dressed as a Gendarme in order to be unseen, it's extraordinary. It's true, the German soldiers couldn't imagine your nationality, and the risk was really enormous for you and your accompanist.*

*The postal card shows the café-bar where you had been harbored but the front has changed. In 1944, there are little glasses and iron shutters as you can see in the enclosed pictures.*

*When Dad was denounced to the Gestapo, we had time enough for leaving off Bourgogne and we have been received by Mr. and Mrs. Paul Camelin that Dad knew. (After Dad's death, they always were very sure and very faithful friends for our family and my brother, Claude, married her daughter).*

*When we were harbored at Reims Mom wished that Dad stops his activities in the resistance during some time but Dad wished to displace very quickly the Allies harbored by his cell, for security. Then he continued. By night, he has cut phone wires to stop communications 'Commandantur', but he has been called upon by a German patrol. Dad chose to escape but a soldier shot with grapeshot and Dad has been wounded. In spite of his wounds (36 perforations in the intestines), he went to a friend's house who conducted him at the clinic with a false name because the Gestapo always sought him. Dad has been operated but the dog-days heat caused an infection and Dad died on August 23, 1944, (he was 33).The American Army liberated Reims on August 30, just a week between these 2 dates.*

*When the Gestapo arrived at the bar, in Bourgogne, they met my maternal grandmother. She lived in Bourgogne but in another house. She had refused to set off with us. The Gestapo has taken her away to the 'Commandantur' to question her. She has answered that she didn't know where Dad stayed "because she was displeased with him". The German soldiers had beaten her but she always answered the same one. They had taken all the money in the cash-drawer of the bar and the grocery. Before my grandmother, they put this money in an envelope and wrote on it [Mr. Erhard Govin]. The officer said to my grandmother: "We only wish and question your son-in-law. When he will have answered to us, we shall give back this money to him". My grandmother asked to the officer, "A little money for paying a ticket and going back to Bourgogne by train?" The officer answered, "Seek very well, madam, certainly you will find an American taxicab which will go back with you to your home".*

*Until the liberation, we did not walk out very much in the streets of Reims because the Gestapo had taken my brother and mine's pictures which were set on the furniture, in the kitchen.*

*Dad was buried a first time in Reims, with a false name, then a second time at Bourgogne, after the liberation. On that day, they were very much people: the Prefect, soldiers, Resistance, policemen, all the inhabitants of Bourgogne and children. Six soldiers bore his coffin. All the persons have done homage to him. In Bourgogne, a street bears his name.*

*We are proud about him. John, you give thanks to France and to Resistance because they help you. But it's to me and to all the French people to say thank you. You went and had delivered us against the German occupation. We didn't know how to defend us and the French government had capitulated. Thank you, John, for your participation to our fight.*

*I regret very much that Mr. Joly and Mr. Felix didn't accompanied you to Bourgogne; I had liked to see you again. When did you come in France? Friendships to Mary and to you. Linette*

Linette, Claude and Danny, pictured with their father, Gerhard Govin - April 1944

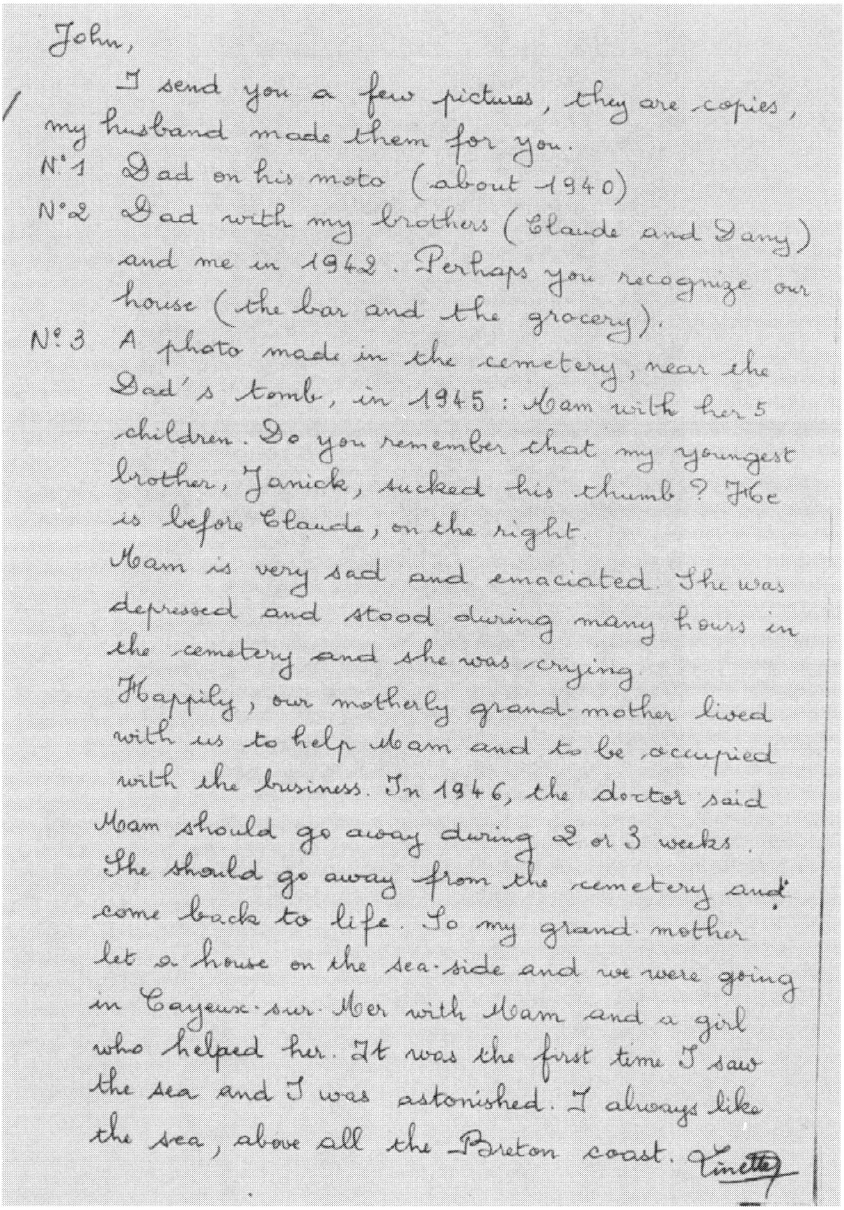

John,

I send you a few pictures, they are copies, my husband made them for you.

N°1 Dad on his moto (about 1940)

N°2 Dad with my brothers (Claude and Dany) and me in 1942. Perhaps you recognize our house (the bar and the grocery).

N°3 A photo made in the cemetery, near the Dad's tomb, in 1945: Mam with her 5 children. Do you remember that my youngest brother, Janick, sucked his thumb? He is before Claude, on the right.

Mam is very sad and emaciated. She was depressed and stood during many hours in the cemetery and she was crying.

Happily, our motherly grand-mother lived with us to help Mam and to be occupied with the business. In 1946, the doctor said Mam should go away during 2 or 3 weeks. She should go away from the cemetery and come back to life. So my grand-mother let a house on the sea-side and we were going in Cayeux-sur-Mer with Mam and a girl who helped her. It was the first time I saw the sea and I was astonished. I always like the sea, above all the Breton coast. Linette

Linette Govin's letter to John

Gerhard Govin, my Cafe de Bourgogne helper. Mr. Govin was shot and killed by the Germans a few weeks after I left his safe-house.

1945 photo of Mrs. Govin, the sad wife of Gerhard, visiting his grave at the local cemetery and five children

Linette (daughter of Gerhard Govin) and her husband, Lucien Deletang

Victor McCreigh a Canadian MIA, Govin Family, John. Jack Hoad and Bronis Korach at the Café Bourgogne safe-house, April 1944.

Gerhard Govin's funeral passing by his home and Café Bourgogne.

March 13, 2007

Linnette,

It certainly was a pleasure to receive your letter and pictures. Also, to bring me up to date on the many questions I have had over these many years.
I take it that the picture of the procession was taken at your father's second funeral.
Also, I was very pleased to receive the picture with your mother, brother, Jack Hoad, Bronos, myself, etc. I will try to include them in my book. Were the pictures taken in front of your parents' home? I would like to include pictures your mother and father and you, if you have copies could you mail copies to me? Please excuse my typing, as I am learning to write this letter as well as my book on a computer.

It is interesting to learn that your family skis. I recently stopped skiing after 75 years, and my Two daughters Lynne 45 years old Laurie 43 years old, granddaughter Caroline 16, grandson's Craig 15, Cameron 13, Corey 11, along with my wife Mary all skied.

Thanks for Jack Hoad's address. Unfortunately, It was not given to me in 1944, apparently for security reasons. Jack wrote me years ago but did not include his address. I will write him at that address and hope he still lives their.

You asked what my position was on our airplane; I was a right waist gunner, assistant engineer, Photographer.

I shall forever feel grateful to all the members of the French Resistance in the Reims, Bourgogne, Chaumuzy, Bonne Maison Erpany, Paris, Toulouse, etc. areas. It took such dedicated people to save the lives of the allied airmen and to help liberate France. Without their sacrifice I would not be alive today. It was interesting to note that you knew Dr. and Mrs Levy, M/M Bronos Korach, M/M Jean Joly (she still lives in Reims), M/M Rene Felix (she lives in Bordeaux). Were M/M Robert Billon the two Resistance members who picked me out of the gutter after I was forced to leave the Reims Clinic, because a collaborater ~~was~~ had been placed in the clinic, by the Nazi's? A young girl and man by the name of Robert brought me to the safe house, referred to by the name "The Circus", (I believe it was a WWI Calvary Training Center).

I do not recall Victor McCreight, Sam, William,Bod or Albert. I probably was the John you mention.

M/M Pierre Dermarchez, both are deceased. Their son Didier and grandson Frederic continue to operate the bakery in Boulonge Ser Mer .

Your father introduced me to a German officer, the Colonel, and we drank Champagne in the bar.Your father-in-law was correct.

I visited Reims three times. Once around 15 years ago, with my three living crew members, Ted Krol, bombardier, who evaded with the Resistance in Gausancourt, was liberated by the US Army in June 1944, Frank Mastronardi, radio and Walter Rusch, ball turret gunner, both captured by the Germans and became prisoners of war. They were liberated by US Army and the Russians in the Spring of 1945. The Reims Vice- Mayor honored us at the City Hall. I requested information about your folks, but told they were deceased. I am sorry that you were not advised by Jean Joly.

My wife Mary and I made two trips to France and Reims, 10 years ago and 5 years ago. I would have loved to have met so many of my helpers but they did not appear.

I plan to have my book published within the next 3 months, if possible.

Thank you for your letter and pictures. I am forever grateful for the so many French people that helped me fed, cloths and made my escape possible, and I am saddened that so many suffered, to help us. I feel sorry that you lost your father at the age of 33. It must have been a great loss to your mother as well as you and your brothers.

Best regards to you, your husband and all your family.

Your friends in the U.S.A. Mary and John

John

Photo of Mary and John Katsaros

March 15, 2007

Jack and Betty Hoad,

The White Cottage, Ullenhall

Solihull, Warwicks (England)

I am John Katsaros, the American airman that was shot down near Reims, France on March 20, 1944. After a long search, I finally was able to get your address from linette Deletang the daughter of Mr. and Mrs Erhard Govin. (I believe that is his name) She lives at 5 av.de la Gare, 51110 Bourgogne, France.

Jack, I was never given your address. You wrote to me many years ago and were disappointed that I had not written. I am dearly sorry. Jack, when I received your letter, you did not include your mailing address. Nor was I able to obtain it from any military sources. That is the reason you have not heard fro me in 63 long years, until now.

Hopefully, you and your family are in good health, and able to respond to this letter.

Not a day has gone by, without thoughts of you and our helpers that helped us to escape and evade the enemy. I would be very thankful to receive a letter from either of you, saying that all is well, along with any change of address you may have.

Regards from my wife Mary and, John Katsaros 109 Crosby St. Ext.

Haverhill, Ma. 01830. Phone 978-374-7357. We will be at my winter home in Florida until May 15.

Apt. 305 6530 North Ocean Blvd., Ocean Ridge, Florida 33435 Home Tel. 1-561-737-8341

I am sending three pictures sent to me by Linette, with you, me and others as depicted on the picture. Mr. Govin's funeral procession, and picture of the bar of Govin's safe house.

John

JOHN

Unhappily, this letter to Jack Hoad was returned to me undelivered.

Genèvieve Soulié Camus and husband, Jean Camus

M. Mme Jean CAMUS
260 boulevard Voltaire
75011 PARIS

21st. June 2009

Dear Elizabeth

I am awfully sorry to be so late to thank you for your kind letter and John Katsaros' book. In fact I did write a letter but never sent it because I started reading the book and was fascinated and couldn't stop! It is so very truthful and precise after all these years! He must have kept a "memory diary"! A wonderful story!

Yes I am the Genevieve he mentions on page 160+162 (thank you for the mark). I was the only Genevieve in the group and the only one bilingual, being half British on my mother's side. Georges Broussine found that very useful for questioning the airmen and also to visit them at the lodgers if they needed something or ask them to be patient if they found the waiting too long and thought they could try the evasion on their own! J.K. mentions the fact

The only mistake is that I wasn't a "brunette" but as fair as could be! I probably wore a hat or beret – In those days you didn't go out bareheaded!

Genèvieve Soulié Camus' letter to Elizabeth McDade with copy to me. Ms. McDade, a director of AFEES (Air Force Escape and Evasion Society, provided me with my April 1944 Paris guide, Genèvieve's, address.

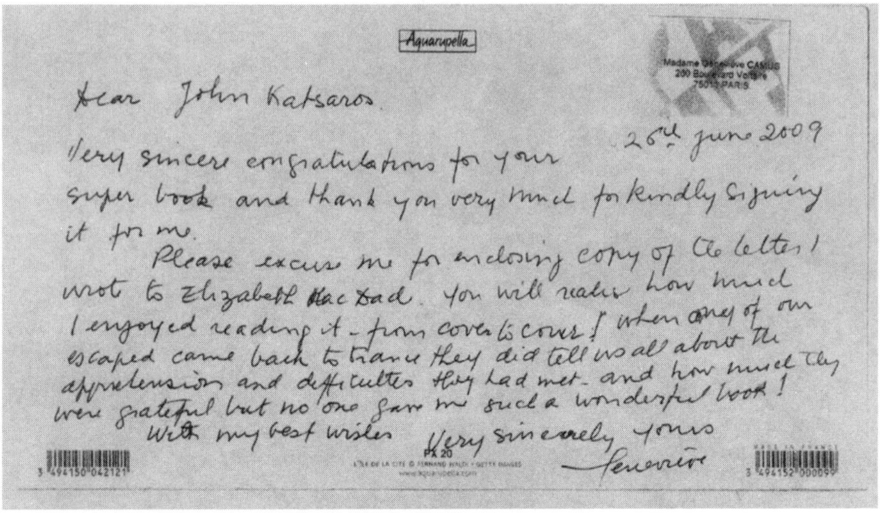
Aquarupella

Madame Geneviève CAMUS
200 Boulevard Voltaire
75011 PARIS

Dear John Katsaros.

26th june 2009

Very sincere congratulations for your super book and thank you very much for kindly signing it for me.

Please excuse me for enclosing copy of the letter I wrote to Elizabeth MacDad. You will realise how much I enjoyed reading it - from cover to cover! When any of our escaped came back to France they did tell us all about the apprehension and difficulties they had met - and how much they were grateful but no one gave me such a wonderful book!

With my best wishes

Very sincerely yours

Geneviève

A card that Genèvieve Soulié Camus sent me from Paris, France

Jean et Geneviève CAMUS
260, boulevard Voltaire
75011 PARIS
☎ 01 43 71 71 90 ou 01 64 04 28 09

Faremoutiers, 10th August 2009

Dear John, and Mary

I postponed my jam making to have a chat with you.

First of all, thank you ever so much for your kind and interesting letter and the photos. I hope you have kept this lovely smile of yours! Congratulations also for all the work you do in Schools, museums & veterans' groups. Yes I have done my share in schools and we are faithful veterans and members of several vet. associations. My husband Jean (John) is President of the veterans association in our village. I am a member of R.A.F.A. and also receive the AFEES bulletin. The last one had a very good article about your wonderful book. Would you like me to ~~give~~ a copy of ~~book~~ the "Code Burgundy – the Long Escape" to the Royal – Air Force in Paris or have you done so? And perhaps, if you can spare one, I could put it in the library of the Free French Club.. the members who can read English would certainly appreciate it. Of course not compulsory!

I will write again – very soon I hope –; Something interesting is to take place in a village, a few miles away from where we have our country cottage.

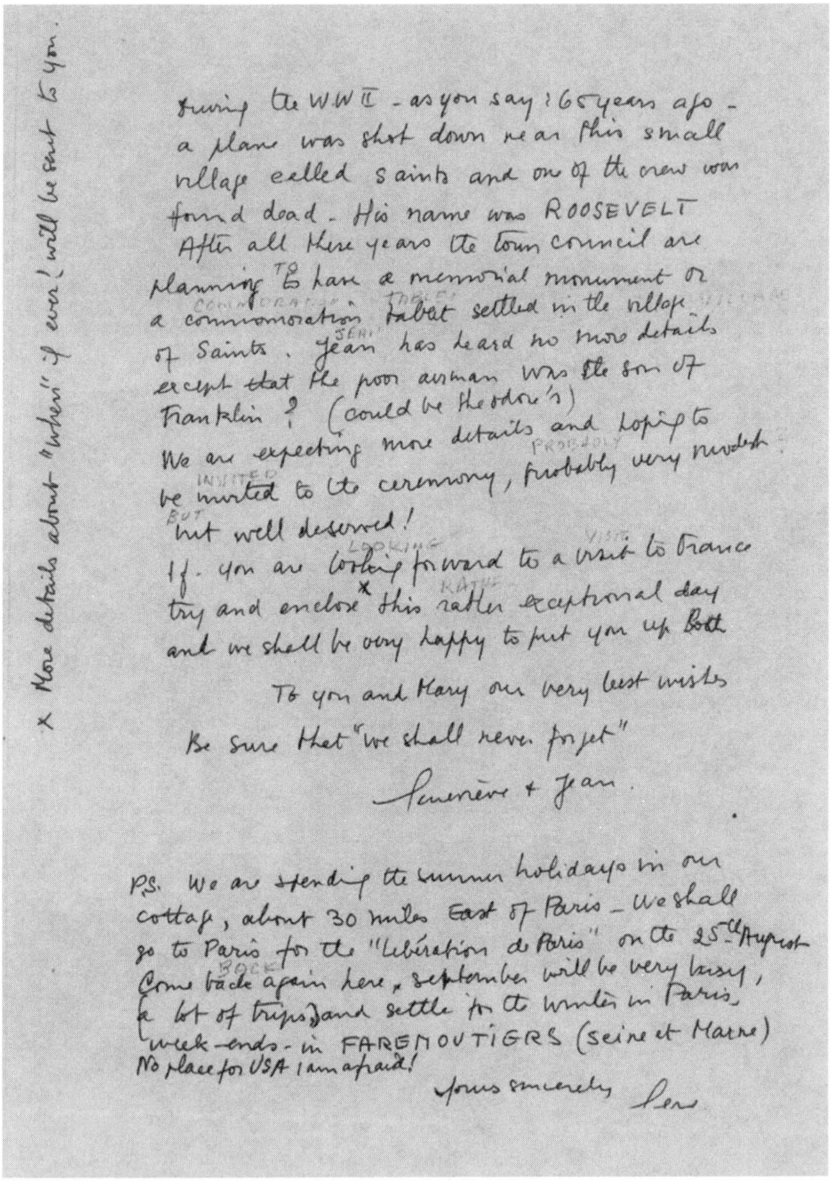

during the WW II - as you say: 65 years ago - a plane was shot down near this small village called Saints and one of the crew was found dead. His name was ROOSEVELT

After all these years the town council are planning to have a memorial monument or a commemoration tablet settled in the village of Saints. Jean has heard no more details except that the poor airman was the son of Franklin? (could be Theodore's)

We are expecting more details and hoping to be invited to the ceremony, probably very modest but well deserved!

If you are looking forward to a visit to France try and enclose* this rather exceptional day and we shall be very happy to put you up both

To you and Mary our very best wishes

Be sure that "we shall never forget"

Geneviève + Jean.

P.S. We are spending the summer holidays in our cottage, about 30 miles East of Paris - We shall go to Paris for the "Libération de Paris" on the 25th August Come back again here, september will be very busy, a lot of trips, and settle for the winter in Paris, week-ends - in FAREMOUTIERS (Seine et Marne) No place for USA I am afraid!

Yours sincerely Gen

x More details about "when" if ever! will be sent to you.

Faremoutiers
24th August 2009

Dear John,

Thank you so much for your letter and the two copies of "Cod. Burgundy – The long escape". They arrived safely. How very kind of you!
I shall meet RAFA members on 15th September "Remembrance Day of the Battle of Britain" and I shall give them their dedicated one. Thank you again. The Free French Club will reopen in September. I will then put their one in the library.

I will try to get on the phone the Winchester group in St Germain-en-Laye. It sounds interesting.

What you mention about Col. Elliot Roosevelt's death sounds more plausible. but !...

As soon as we get more details, I shall write again. Jean was interested by your statement and will meet the Mayor when he comes back from holiday: August = no work!

Very sincerely yours

Geneviève.

Front left to right: Bertranne, a Greek resistance helper I believe to be Dr. Moulis, directly behind Bertranne is my bombardier, Ted Krol, and two other evaders at her Paris apartment. Circa 1944

## Freedom

I learned from the POW's imprisoned in Stalags that they felt fortunate to be with their military comrades to share despondent moments. Yes, they were imprisoned, but they found comfort in companionship and never felt like lost souls.

The POW's envied the G.I. on the run for his freedom from the barbed wire fences, traveling at night to avoid capture by the Gestapo, and the challenge to survive as a fugitive. Yet, they felt disconsolate for the fugitive being alone, hunted like an animal and being without friend or country.

In many cases of the fugitive, this may be true, however, I was fortunate to be picked up by the French Resistance who dressed my wounds, provided surgery to save my arm and my life, put their own lives on the line in two daring rescues and escapes from the Gestapo; and gave me food, warmth, comfort and the love of family. I became family and never thought of loneliness. How could I? I learned to imitate their thoughts and their thinking - to plan, to avoid, to escape and evade - that was my life on the run, moving discreetly from safe-house to safe-house, but that also was the clandestine life of the French Resistance. This was not just my war; it was our war and we fought it together, side by side as best we could, until it was my time to depart. That was their self-appointed duty, to protect and preserve me and to send me on my way.

I cherish all the French Resistance, the French people including those who gave of themselves but could not afford to be exposed for the sake of the lives of their families; and especially to my heroes, my rescuers Pierre Demarchez, Jean Joly and René Felix who in my first escape rescued me in a firefight with the Gestapo in a well executed plan; and the Reims Chief of Police in my second escape, who set a clever ambush of the German convoy, in my transfer, and it came off so well not a shot was fired. The Nazi military was trumped and was left dumb-founded as we rapidly sped away.

I experienced freedom while on the run, and it tasted great in every close call. On the ground as a fugitive a taste of that freedom came often, just like the feel of freedom on the bomb run.

John Katsaros

*Cherish Your Freedom*

**To order your new translated French book,**
**'Code Burgundy-La Longue E'vasion',**
**contact me at 978-869-3035 or jkatsaros3@comcast.net.**
**$25.00 add $3:00 for S&H (USA)**

Thanks to the below named Translators, Editors and French Consulate Generals:

Solange Batisse Bouge and her three daughters, Camille, Cecile, and Cornelie of St. Cloud, France for their translation of, Code Burgundy-The Long Escape, from English to French.

Joel Paubert, St. Cloud, France, who unfortunately passed away after editing the translation of the first half of the book.

Mr. Edouard Reniere of Brussels, Belgium WWII Helper and a member of the US Air Forces Escape and Evasion Society, for encouraging me to print the book in French.

Christophe Guilhou former French Consulate General Boston, MA., in November 2013 was promoted to, 'Directeur Organisation Internationale Paris, France Embassy' and Gael de Maissonneuve, French Consulate General of Miami, FL. for their interest and assistance to distribute, donated, translated and edited French books to my WWII French Resistance Helpers, Families, libraries, military museums and organizations and the Embassies of the French Republic.

The End